# Discrimination in Housing

AUSTRALIA
The Law Book Company
Brisbane • Sydney • Melbourne • Perth

CANADA
Ottawa • Toronto • Calgary • Montreal • Vancouver

Agents:
Steimatzky's Agency Ltd., Tel Aviv;
N.M. Tripathi (Private) Ltd., Bombay;
Eastern Law House (Private) Ltd., Calcutta;
M.P.P. House, Bangalore;
Universal Book Traders, Delhi;
Aditya Books, Delhi;
MacMillan Shuppan KK, Tokyo;
Pakistan Law House, Karachi, Lahore

# Discrimination in Housing

by

Christopher Handy

*LL.M., M.I.H., M.B.I.M.,*
*Chief Executive, Accord Housing Group*

London
Sweet & Maxwell
1993

Published in 1993 by
Sweet & Maxwell Ltd. of
South Quay Plaza, 183 Marsh Wall,
London, E14 9FT
Computerset by P.B. Computer Typesetting,
Pickering, N. Yorks
Printed and Bound in Great Britain by Butler and
Tanner Ltd., Frome and London

British Library Cataloguing Data

A catalogue record for this book is available from the British Libary

ISBN: 0421–390–204

The index was prepared by Patricia Baker.



No natural forests were destroyed to make this product. Farmed timber was used and replanted.

To my wife Patricia and children
Sarah and Rebecca.

# Preface

Little attention has previously been given to discrimination law in the housing field. Law books on the subject have concentrated on employment or else have been general. There is though considerable literature on housing discrimination in the wider social sense. This book has therefore been written to provide a concise, simple and comprehensive account of race and sex discrimination law in the housing field. It is intended to be useful for lawyers and non-lawyers, particularly housing professionals.

The Equal Opportunities Commission and the Commission for Racial Equality in particular find evidence of sex and race discrimination seemingly wherever they look. Even though the main Acts (Sex Discrimination Act 1975 and Race Relations Act 1976) have been in operation for almost two decades, discrimination is still widespread. The Commission for Racial Equality has recently, in its second Review of the Race Relations Act 1976 (1992), asked for an overhaul of the legislation which Anthony Lester Q.C. says has been drafted with "grotesque and unnecessary complexity and obscurity . . . " Not only is the law inadequate in addressing race and sex discrimination (for example there are no provisions which effectively protect against sexual and racial harassment), it fails entirely to address other forms of unfair discrimination, for example on the grounds of age, disability, sexuality, religion or politics. Even the powers and resources of the Commissions are woefully inadequate to properly equip them for their respective tasks. The Commissions' power to issue codes of practice should be greatly extended. These devices suggest good practices and positive action to assist in overcoming discrimination. They help to positively generate a mood change within organisations.

This text firstly addresses general aspects of discrimination, direct and indirect discrimination and the relevant exceptions to the law. It moves on then to consider discrimination in the public, quasi-public and private housing sectors and closes by examining administration and individual enforcement aspects of the legislation.

Many thanks for help offered by Professor J. Alder of Keele University, Ken Gulliver of Focus Housing Association for advice on sociological sources and references, Peter Oteng of the Commission for Racial Equality, Paul Munion of the Equal Opportunities Commission, Jaz Sidhu and Barbara Dennis for informal advice on some aspects of discrimination. Thanks also to the law library staff of

Wolverhampton University for help and advice and Doreen Turner for typing part of the manuscript.

The law is stated as at July 1, 1993.

# Table of Contents

# Table of Cases

# Table of Statutes

# Chapter one

# Introduction: The Nature, Background and Development of Discrimination Law

## INTRODUCTION

At common law the disadvantaged have only very limited rights.[1] Thus, Parliament has seen it necessary to introduce legislation to protect the rights of individuals belonging to defined disadvantaged groups. As such, "anti-discrimination law" can be seen as a rare example in this country of codified civil rights legislation for the benefit of particular interest groups, rather than government's traditional reliance on the so called "flexibility" of civil rights protection provided under the unwritten constitution.

Why then is such anti-discrimination law necessary? In a reasonable world there should be no need for any law to protect the rights of individuals against unfair treatment, but we do not live in such a world, and people are, in many ways, treated unfairly. As a result, society needs laws which protect people and ensure individuals have equal freedoms under those laws and in doing so attempt to eliminate what "incomplete freedoms" exist. Thus, anti-discrimination law is concerned with the rights of individuals who belong to legally defined disadvantaged groups to ensure equality of treatment.

Allegations of unfair discrimination are most frequently made on the basis of sex or race or colour.[2] This is not to say that allegations of unfair discrimination do not arise in relation to other issues; there is increasing concern that discrimination takes place due to disablement,

[1] See *Schlegel* v. *Corcoran* [1942] I.R. 19; *Adler* v. *Upper Grosvenor Street Investments* [1957] 1 W.L.R. 227.
[2] See discussion by Professor H. Street, *Freedom, The Individual and The Law*, p. 297.

criminal record, age, sexuality, mental illness or handicap, religion, way of life, and more recently because of infections and diseases.[3] The needs, to a limited extent, of the disabled and the elderly are recognised within the context of the "renovation grant" system under the Local Government and Housing Act 1989.[4] In the field of employment law some protection is offered to the disabled (Disabled Person Act 1967) and ex-offenders (Rehabilitation of Offenders Act 1974). In Northern Ireland, again in the employment field, religious groups have been given some protection.[5] The increasing impact of European law may, particularly in the employment field, yield protection to the interests of individuals amongst a much wider range of disadvantaged groups.[6]

An increasing number of public, private and quasi-public housing agencies have introduced anti-discriminatory policies and procedures which address these wider issues. These policy statements and procedures provide groups not covered by legislative protection some apparent safeguards against unfair treatment.[7] The safeguards are though modest, and there are doubts as to whether, at least in the case of private housing agencies, failures to adhere to the policies and procedures are actionable through the courts. What certainly is of benefit is that such policies and procedures provide a strong indication that a climate of non-discrimination operates, or is intended to operate, within the particular housing agency. There are often accompanying complaints or grievance procedures which can be followed by people who feel they have been unfairly treated. These procedures though are often limited to internal appeals and rarely provide for external independent arbitration.

Section 106(2) of the Housing Act 1985 requires landlord authorities (local housing authorities, registered housing associations other than co-operative housing associations, housing trusts which are charities, development corporations, urban development corporations and The Development Board for Rural Wales; s.114 *ibid.*) to maintain a set of rules and procedures for housing allocation. Many public or quasi-public housing agencies include within such rules and procedures non-discrimination provisions which cover a wide range of disadvantage groups well beyond the statutory protection afforded due to race or sex. There is a direct statutory obligation to comply with this requirement. This ought clearly to be a matter of public

[3] See for example London Housing Unit, *Just Homes*, (1988) pp. 21–32; E.O.C., *Discrimination in Age Employment: A Survey*, E.O.R. May/June 1989.
[4] See ss. 114 and 131.
[5] *e.g.*, Northern Ireland Fair Employment Act 1976.
[6] See European Communities Act 1972, s. 2(1) for supremacy of Community Law in the United Kingdom and for example the Equal Treatment Directive 76/207 in relation to "family status".
[7] See Appendix A for an example of a policy statement.

law and therefore enforceable by means of an application for judicial review in the High Court. It is unlikely that any private right of action for damages is conferred by this statutory obligation thus denying access to the local county court.[8] An applicant for housing accommodation would be within the range of beneficiaries of the statute and thus have sufficient *locus standi* to pursue an action for judicial review.[9]

Nonetheless it is unclear to what extent rights may be enforced in this way. That housing agencies operate within a statutory context and with the support of public money does not bring a substantive power, for example the allocation of tenancies, into the public law arena.[10] This approach has been criticised as too formalistic.[11] Arguably an applicant placed on a waiting list may well have a "legitimate expectation" of being offered housing accommodation. Thus conferring at least the right of a fair hearing in accordance with the rules of natural justice. The notions of natural justice and legitimate expectation are not confined to the realms of public law.[12]

Beyond the judicial review process there would seem to be little legal protection for aggrieved individuals. The position is equally as complicated in the provision of housing management and maintenance services once accommodation is let, since again, although there exists statutory rights, the issues which arise from the landlord and tenant relationship have been seen as issues of private law. With private landlords the position is even more uncertain. Decisions taken by contractual bodies such as trade unions and professional institutions have long been seen to be open to challenge on the grounds that a power has not been exercised "fairly."[13] Why should the notion of "fairness" not apply in the exercise of powers by private agencies? Otherwise there is very little protection afforded under these anti-discrimination policies and procedures. There would seem to be no contractual relationship between a prospective applicant and the housing agencies concerned and thus no right to enforce the policies or procedures through the courts. Whether a collateral contractual relationship is in existence in such circumstances is highly tenuous.

Where policies and procedures or anti-discriminatory conditions are incorporated into the tenancy agreement then rights do arise by virtue of the landlord and tenant relationship and aggrieved individuals can enforce such rights through the county courts and claim damages. Thus if committed, housing agencies can bind themselves and tenants

[8] See *Cocks* v. *Thanet District Council* [1983] A.C. 286 and Supreme Court Act 1981, s.31.

[9] See *I.R.C.* v. *National Federation of Self-Employed and Small Businesses Limited* [1982] A.C. 617.

[10] See *Peabody Housing Association* v. *Green* (1978) 38 P. & C.R. 644.

[11] See *Alder and Handy op. cit.* p. 365.

[12] See *McInnes* v. *Onslow-Fane* [1978] 1 W.L.R. 1520.

[13] *Law* v. *National Greyhound Racing Club* [1983] 1 W.L.R. 1302, and *McInnes* v. *Onslow-Fane* [1978] 1 W.L.R. 1520.

to anti-discriminatory obligations much wider than afforded under statute. Such an approach, except for action against racial harassment, has not been widely adopted.

With public sector landlords, aggrieved individuals do have recourse to make a complaint to the Parliamentary Commissioner for Local Government. The Housing Corporation has introduced a similar right to customers of registered housing associations.[14]

Nonetheless, to date, anti-discrimination law in Britain has been largely confined to matters of sex and race. The Sex Discrimination Act 1975 (S.D.A.) protects the rights of women and men from unfair, essentially defined as unlawful, discrimination on the basis of their sex or marital status. Similarly the Race Relations Act 1976 (R.R.A.) protects the rights of people from unfair treatment on the basis of their colour, race, nationality or ethnic or national origins. Hence a framework of legal protections has been established to ensure that people regardless of their sex or race have equal rights under the law. This work is concerned with an exploration of those rights within the context of housing.

## DEVELOPMENT OF ANTI-DISCRIMINATION LAW

The two principal Acts, which will be discussed in detail in Chapter 2, can be seen largely as legislative responses to growing social unease about the unequal rights experienced within our society by women and ethnic minorities. Historically the low status within society of both these groups has been particularly noticeable in socio-economic terms. This is also true of their position with respect to rights and standing under the law. At the beginning of this century women were still regarded as "non-persons" under the common law and husbands had the right to beat them with a "stick no thicker than a man's thumb" and ethnic minorities were bought and sold as slaves.[15]

The S.D.A. and the R.R.A. can be seen as the culmination of increasing rights being granted to women and ethnic minorities. The Acts exist to provide a degree of protection against the effects of the possible discriminatory practices which exist in society. Certain provisions of the Acts go a step further and attempt to strike at the practices which indirectly discriminate against women and ethnic

[14] See H.C., *Resolving Housing Association Tenant Complaints: The Way Forward* (1993).

[15] See discussion by Sachs, A. and Wilson, J. H., *Sexism and The Law*, (1978) Chapter 1, Pannick, D., *Sex Discrimination* (1980) Chapter 1 and Lester, A. and Bindman, G., *Race and Law* (1972) Chapter 1.

minorities.[16] In this respect the statutes attempt to deal with institutional racism and sexism and the two Commissions set up by the Acts, the Commission for Racial Equality and the Equal Opportunities Commission, have specific powers to assist in the process.[17]

## Development of sex discrimination law

At the time the Sex Discrimination Act came into force on December 29, 1975, it was described as the "most comprehensive and far reaching legislation of its kind in the world."[18] It could be seen as the culmination of a slow and cumbersome process which has step by step extended basic rights to women by giving them full rights of citizenship and the capacity to sign contracts and own property,[19] the right to vote[20] and the right to hold public office and carry on a profession or vocation.[21] Before World War I, women had very few rights and in essence, in law, were treated similarly to children: they were therefore "non-persons". Women were "inherently incapacitated on the grounds of gender alone".[22] More recently such new rights have included the recognition of a deserted wife's legal interest in the matrimonial home,[23] her right to a share in the matrimonial property upon divorce,[24] her rights to choose a different home or domicile to her husband[25] and a women's right to protection from abuse by her partner.[26] The Sex Discrimination Act 1975 provided protection on a wider basis from the more generalised discrimination evident in society; but even so, the protection can still be seen as inadequate as the White Paper, *Equality for Women* stated, the "... status of women in relation to social security, taxation, nationality and matrimonial and family law is governed by separate legislation and will be dealt with in the future."[27] In the main, measures to deal with these aspects of the law are still awaited.

According to Pannick[28] prior "to 1975 women suffered from an undeniable pattern and practice of sex discrimination in areas of crucial importance to their welfare". The Sex Discrimination Act 1975,

[16] For example the provisions relating to discriminatory practices, Parts IV of the S.D.A. and R.R.A.
[17] Outlined in Chapter 13.
[18] Lord Harris of Greenwich 362 H.L. 96 quoted by Pannick *op. cit.*
[19] Married Women's Property Acts 1870 and 1882.
[20] Representation of the People (Equal Franchise) Act 1922.
[21] Sex Disqualification (Removal) Act 1919.
[22] A. Sachs and J. Hoff-Wilson, *op. cit.* p. 5.
[23] Matrimonial Homes Act 1967.
[24] Matrimonial Causes Act 1973.
[25] Domicile and Matrimonial Proceedings Act 1973.
[26] Domestic Violence and Matrimonial Proceedings Act 1976.
[27] Cmnd. 5724 (1974) Para. 77.
[28] *op. cit.* p. 14.

along with the Equal Pay Act 1970, was introduced in an attempt to encourage greater equality of opportunity between the sexes. Hence the White Paper justifying the Government's interest, said:

> "The issue ... is not a question of private relationships. In general the Government does not and should not seek to intervene in the private relationships of citizens. The status of women in society, the disabilities and disadvantages imposed on women, and their consequences, are social quesitons. They are legitimate subjects of the public interest and are appropriate matters for Government action."[29]

Indeed, a number of bills had been introduced in the Commons and the Lords during the early 1970's. During this period the Government set up a Select Committee which undertook a thorough investigation into the need for legislation to encourage equal opportunity for women. As a result the White Paper was published and the Sex Discrimination Bill was introduced. Its provisions were heavily influenced by evidence gained from the United States and the operation of the earlier Race Relations Act of 1968. For example the recognition of indirect discrimination was drawn from the experience of the effects of "passive" discrimination encourtered under American law.[30] As a result the Act attempted to straddle and tackle both "individual instances of prejudiced behaviour" and the "structural causes of inequality faced by women."[31] For the first time, once the Act had become law, "to treat a woman diffirently from a man just because she was a woman or because she was married" was unlawful.[32]

# DEVELOPMENT OF RACE RELATIONS LAW

Before the Race Relations Act 1965 and later legislation, under the common law "people could discriminate against others on the ground of colour, etc., to their hearts' content."[33] According to Simon L.J. this

> "...unbridled capacity to discriminate was the mischief and defect for which common law did not provide. The remedy Parliament resolved and appointed, was to make certain acts of

[29] *Ibid.* para. 3.
[30] See for example *Griggs* v. *Duke Power*, U.S. (1971).
[31] See S. Atkins and B. Hoggett, *Women and the Law* (1984) p. 22.
[32] *op. cit.* p. 23.
[33] *Per* Simon L.J. in *Applin* v. *Race Relations Board* [1975] A.C. 259 at p. 286; see also comments of Diplock L.J. in *Race Relations Board* v. *Dockers Club* [1979] A.C. 286 at pp. 295–296; also *Schlegel* v. *Corcoran* [1942] I.R. 19 and *Adler* v. *Upper Grosvenor Street Investments* [1957] 1 W.L.R. 227.

> discrimination unlawful. The reason for the remedy must have been that discrimination was thought to be socially devisive ... and derogatory to human dignity."[34]

Clearly, where common law provided no protection and society wished to provide protection, then Parliament should legislate accordingly. Attempts had been made to introduce racial discrimination bills during the 1950's, for example the Colour Bar Bill of 1950 and the Racial Discrimination Bill of 1956. Both bills were concerned with making discrimination on the basis of race in public spaces criminal offences. The 1956 Bill had been introduced to Parliament by Fenner Brockway M.P. and during the next eight years he introduced a further eight bills, only one of which achieved a second reading. By that time, following the Notting Hill disturbances, the Labour Party had committed itself to making racial discrimination illegal. The intention to introduce legislation was part of its winning election manifesto of 1964.

North American evidence suggested "... that anti-discrimination laws were more likely to be effectively enforced by administrative machinery than by proceedings in the criminal courts."[35] However, after a stormy reception the 1965 Race Relations Act was introduced and covered aspects of race discrimination in public places—"places of public resort"—treating discriminatory acts as criminal offences, effectively creating an extension to public order law. In addition the act outlawed discriminatory practices in relation to the disposal of tenancies.[36] Pressure continued to mount for the very limited scope of the Act to be extended and for its provisions to provide civil remedies rather than criminal offence remedies. In particular

> "... to cover racial and religious discrimination in employment, housing, the granting of credit facilities and mortgages, and in insurance."[37]

Eventually after a further stormy reception the Race Relations Act 1968 became law, making racial discrimination in the wider sense unlawful and dealing with discriminatory acts through administrative action rather than by criminal sanctions. The act strengthened the powers of the Race Relations Board set up under the 1965 Act and created the Community Relations Commission with the task of promoting "harmonious community relations." As a result a network of local community relations councils were established, many of which still operate today on a local authority basis.

[34] *Race Relations Board* v. *Applin op. cit.* at p. 286.
[35] A. Lester and G. Bindman, *op. cit.* p. 111 and generally Chapter 3 gives an excellent account on the background to race relations law.
[36] R.R.A. 1965, s. 5.
[37] *Ibid.* p. 123; for the extent of racial disadvantages of the time, including the housing field see the P.E.P. Report of 1967, W. Daniels, *Racial Discrimination in England.*

During the 1970's there grew an awareness of racial discrimination and disadvantage. The 1976 Race Relations Act became law as a result of problems with the operation of the 1968 Act and the need to make three main changes to the law. These were:

(a) to introduce new provisions relating to discrimination on racial grounds;
(b) to bring race relations law into line with sex discrimination law, and
(c) to establish a new enforcement process by creating the Commission for Racial Equality and abolishing the Race Relations Board.

# DISCRIMINATION

To eliminate all forms of discrimination would be both undesirable and impractical. This view is supported by D. J. Walker:[38]

> "In every choice between two or more individuals, in every offer of goods, facilities, services or premises, in every promotion or relegation, there is, and must be, some element of discrimination, even if it is only on a "first come first served" basis, and the Act [Sex Discrimination Act 1975] does not seek to outlaw or restrict discrimination as such, but only certain narrowly defined instances of it."

These words equally apply to issued of race. Malone, in his *Practical Guide to Discrimination Law* (1980) says, "Discrimination can be normal, legitimate and even necessary ... When a council house becomes vacant, the council has to discriminate in favour of one family on its waiting list against all others."

Clearly some terms of discriminatory behaviour are unacceptable. People can be treated unfairly simply because they belong to a particular group. Every day we use connective characteristics to identify particular groups. At the heart of unacceptable discrimination is the generalised belief that all people with particular characteristics behave in exactly the same way and therefore possess the same traits. This labelling or stereotyping leads us to attribute properties or characteristics to people which are not actually there. Upon closer examination it would be extremely difficult when applying such generalisations to show any factual connection between these attributed connective characteristics. The connections do not in reality exist. An example might be the "mean Scot." We protect our system of

[38] See *Sex Discrimination* (1975).

beliefs by ensuring that proof is built into the definition, "Scots cannot fail to be mean. A person who is not mean cannot be a true Scot." Denial of disproof is central to stereotyping. We must cling to our generalisation or we do not know where we stand. If we act on such attributed characteristics and treat people accordingly it would clearly lead to unfairness. The discriminator fails to treat people as individuals but treats them according to damaging stereotypes. Thus in *Hurley* v. *Mustoe*[39] an employer wrongly saw all women with children to be unreliable. In *Alexander* v. *Home Office*[40] a West Indian prisoner was refused a request to work in the kitchens since his induction report stated he displayed "the anti-authoritarian arrogance that seems to be common in most coloured inmates." Thus he was treated not as an individual but on the basis of a damaging stereotype. People can easily assume that husbands are the breadwinners in a family.[41] Indeed, within the housing context building societies have refused to consider a woman's salary as the main salary even where evidence shows she earns more.[42] Decisions should be based upon the particular relevant characteristics in an individual case rather than generalised assumptions.[43]

## Discrimination: its legal nature

Consequently, anti-discrimination law[44] has developed to provide protection against undesirable forms of discrimination; it does not, though, address discriminatory influences in their wider everyday context. Both principal statutes[45] recognise a similar approach in defining discrimination. Necessarily, the specifics of discrimination relating to sex will be different from those relating to race. The definitions in these different contexts are accordingly different. However, certain characteristics are present in both definitions and in their application and are therefore at the heart of the legal nature of discrimination:

(a) a recognition of direct discrimination;
(b) a recognition of indirect discrimination and the use of similar principles to test whether indirect discrimination has arisen;

39 [1981] I.C.R. 490.
40 [1988] I.R.L.R. 190 C.A.
41 *Coleman* v. *Skytrail Oceanic*, *The Times*, July 28, 1981, C.A.
42 See E.O.C., *It's not your business, It's how the Society Works* (1978).
43 See also *Perera* v. *Civil Service Commission & Department of Customs & Excise* [1983] I.R.L.R. 166, C.A., and *Coyne* v. *Export Credits Guarantee Department* [1981] I.R.L.R. 51.
44 For the application of this term see A. Arden and M. Partington, *Housing Law* (1985), Chapter 17.
45 S.D.A. and R.R.A.

(c) a recognition of victimisation as a form of discrimination;
(d) the use of "less favourable treatment" and "detriment" as measures of discrimination,
(e) the restriction that discrimination must arise in circumstances relevant for purposes defined in the provisions of the Acts,
(f) the use of similar wording in the sections of the statutes defining discrimination,
(g) the use of the "comparitor" and "relevant circumstances" concepts in measuring whether a person has been unfairly treated relative to other people, and
(h) the use of similar legal remedies.

## Direct and indirect discrimination

Both Acts recognise that there may be direct discrimination or indirect discrimination. Although we shall deal with direct and indirect discrimination in detail later, we need to briefly introduce the concepts at this stage since they are "the foundation garments" of the whole of the legislation.

### *Direct discrimination*

Direct discrimination takes place when a person is treated less favourably on the grounds of race or sex or marital status than another person is treated or would be treated.[46] An example would be where a person was not allowed to apply for accommodation because of their colour; or where a woman was asked for a guarantee when entering into a lease, whereas a man would not be so asked. Thus these provisions deal with questions of overt discrimination.

### *Indirect discrimination*

Indirect discrimination takes place when a requirement or condition is applied which although having equal application to all people, cannot be met as easily by persons of a particular sex or racial group.[47] Thus apparently neutral "rules" can have a discriminatory effect when applied to some individuals or groups. But we can see from a close examination of the relevant subsections of the Acts, "tests" to determine whether unlawful discrimination has taken place

[46] S.D.A., s. 1(1)(*a*), and R.R.A.
[47] S.D.A. s. 1(1)(*b*), and R.R.A., see below on who comprises a "racial group".

are more detailed. Discrimination arises only where the tests of "compliance", "justifiability" and "detriment" are satisfied.[48]

## Discrimination: a single act

Unlike previous anti-discrimination legislation[49] under which it was necessary to determine a "course of action" which amounted to discrimination, under the two principal Acts it is only necessary to show a single act or incident of discrimination which is prohibited under the provisions of the Acts for discrimination to be unlawful. For example, the Commission for Racial Equality can issue a non-discrimination notice[50] on the basis of a single act of discrimination.[51]

## Discrimination by association

Under the Sex Discrimination Act 1975 a person can, in the main, only claim unlawful discrimination because of unfavourable treatment on the basis of his or her own sex or marital status. Whereas under the Race Relations Act 1976 discrimination can arise on "racial grounds,"[52] consequently providing a much wider concept of protection. Accordingly, a person can be discriminated against on racial grounds due to the colour, race, nationality or national origins of a partner, friend, colleague or some other person because of this concept of "discrimination by association". Conceivably, a housing agency may suffer unlawful discrimination because of the colour of its tenants or staff.

## Sex discrimination

The basic legislative provisions relating to sex discrimination are contained within section 1–5 of the S.D.A. We shall consider two aspects of sex discrimination at this point—sex discrimination against women and against men. In addition we shall touch upon the non-application in the housing field of discrimination against married persons. Because discrimination by way of victimisation has equal application to both matters of sex and race we shall consider it later.

[48] These tests are considered in more detail in Chapter 4.
[49] See Race Relations Act 1965.
[50] See Chapter 13.
[51] R.R.A. s. 58, but see *Race Relations Board* v. *Daniel Thwaites*, Report of the Race Relations Board (R.R.B.) for 1975–1976 at p. 53 for the attitude of judiciary on single act complaints.
[52] See later section of this chapter for more detail.

## *Grounds for sex discrimination*

The S.D.A. identifies a number of grounds under which sex discrimination can arise. These grounds fall under four headings:

(a) *treating a woman less favourably* than a man on the basis of sex (s. 1);
(b) *treating a man less favourably* than a woman on the basis of sex (s. 2);
(c) treating someone who is married less favourably than someone who is not on the grounds of marriage (this provision applies only to matters of employment, see s. 3); and
(d) *victimisation* of a person who has invoked the provisions of the Act (s. 4, but see Chapter 2).

As already indicated, unlike the provisions of the R.R.A. an individual must suffer discrimination themselves on the grounds of sex or marital status.

## (a) *Sex discrimination against women*

Under section 1 of the S.D.A. it is unlawful for a person to discriminate against a woman if:

"(a) on the ground of her sex he treats her less favourably than he treats or would treat a man, or
(b) he applies to her a requirement or condition which he applies or would apply equally to a man but—
  (i) which is such that the proportion of women who can comply with it is considerably smaller than the proportion of men who can comply with it, and
  (ii) which he cannot show to be justifiable irrespective of the sex of the person to whom it is applied, and
  (iii) which is to her detriment because she cannot comply with it."

Thus it can be seen that there exists protection against "direct" discrimination,[53] and indirect discrimination,[54] under the S.D.A.

## (b) *Sex discrimination against men*

The provisions against unlawful discrimination which apply to women are to be read "as applying equally to the treatment of men." For this

[53] s. 1(*a*).
[54] s. 1(*b*).

purpose, section 2 states that section 1 and Parts I and II of the S.D.A. shall have equal application to men "with such modifications as are requisite." An exception is the special treatment afforded to a woman with respect to childbirth and pregnancy; since such matters cannot apply directly to a man, no discrimination can arise.

### (c) *Non-application of discrimination against married persons*

Although the S.D.A. recognises that discrimination against married persons takes place, the provisions have application only in the "employment field." Section 3 dealing with this aspect of discrimination was introduced purely with the intention of dealing with the "marriage bar" to getting a job.

### (d) *Victimisation*

In order that individuals can freely bring actions or give evidence in instances of sex or race discrimination both Acts protect them for being victimised for doing so.[55]

## Racial discrimination

The basic provisions relating to racial discrimination are set out in sections 1 to 3 of the R.R.A. Here we will briefly consider the basic definition of racial discrimination and its related concepts.

### *Racial discrimination: a basic definition*

Under section 1 of the R.R.A. a person discriminates against another if:

"(a) on racial grounds he treats the other less favourably than he treats or would treat other persons; or

(b) he applies to that other a requirement or condition which he applies or would apply equally to persons not of the same racial group as that other but—

(i) which is such that the proportion of persons of the same racial group as that other who can comply with it is considerably smaller than the proportion of persons not of that racial group who can comply with it; and

[55] See fuller discussion in Chapter 3.

(ii) which he cannot show to be justifiable irrespective of the colour, race, nationality or ethnic or national origins of the person to whom it applied; and
(iii) which is to the detriment of that other because he cannot comply with it."

The provisions thus have a similarity to the Sex Discrimination Act 1975 in recognising "direct" discrimination[56] and "indirect" discrimination.[57]

## *A note on segregation*

In addition, section 1(2) states that segregation of "a person from other persons on racial grounds" amounts strictly to less favourable treatment and therefore unlawful racial discrimination within the purposes of the R.R.A. Segregation, therefore, rules out any notion that "separate treatment is equal treatment."[58]

According to the *Shorter Oxford English Dictionary* "segregate" means, "to separate a person (or a body or class of persons) from the general body, or from some particular class; to set apart, isolate, seclude."

For segregation to occur in law there must be some definite act, on racial grounds, on the part of the discriminator in separating people, rather than segregation arising impassively or naturally due to the desires of people themselves. Arguably, though, where a practice results in the segregation of people then that result may still amount to direct discrimination. Where, say, a local housing authority has a practice when allocating accommodation of only housing ethnic minorities in specific areas or within certain parts of a housing scheme then discrimination by segregation may arise. On the other hand where ethnic minorities are concentrated in one area as a result of the local authority meeting expressed desires as to area, perhaps because of family ties, location of local churches or mosques, local community groups or associations and schools and other educational facilities, it is highly unlikely that unlawful discrimination would arise.

Since a matter which amounts to segregation is regarded as an act of direct discrimination, a landlord, or any other discriminator, cannot argue that the policy was a justifiable one. "Justification" as an issue which arises only in instances of indirect discrimination.[59]

An interesting development in recent years has been the production of housing schemes specifically for ethnic minorities, brought about by

[56] s. 1(*a*).
[57] s. 1(*b*).
[58] See Macdonald, *Race Relations—The New Law* (1977) at pp. 10–11.
[59] See Chapter 4.

inadequate provision of accommodation for such groups; for example, elderly Asians, because of the needs which have arisen within this group due to the gradual breakdown of the extended family within some Asian communities. Although positive acts of discrimination are permitted under the terms of the R.R.A.[60] these relate only to Parts II and IV of the Act and not to section 1(2) in a more general sense. At any rate, the schemes are not intended to segregate people on racial grounds, they are intended to meet the housing needs of a distinct group of people. Technically speaking, therefore, these housing developments may not be seen as schemes which segregate: it is the purpose of providing for unmet needs which must be examined rather than the final result.

## *Racial grounds and racial groups*

"Racial Grounds" are described by section 3(1) to mean any of the following grounds,

> "colour, race, nationality or ethnic or national origins."

And "racial group" is defined by the same section to mean,

> "a group of persons defined by reference to colour, race, nationality or ethnic origins, and reference to a person's racial group refer to any racial group into which he falls."

Indeed, the fact that a racial group comprises two or more distinct racial groups does not prevent it from constituting a particular racial group.[61]

A group is identifiable in terms of its "ethnic origins" if it is "a segment of the population distinguished from others by a sufficient combination of shared customs, beliefs, traditions and characteristics derived from a common or presumed common past, even if not drawn from what in biological terms is a common racial stock, "in that it is such a combination which gives them an historically determined social identity . . ."[62]

It is wrong to hold that a group can be defined by reference to its "ethnic origins" only where that group can be distinguished by virtue of having "common descent characteristics pertaining or peculiar to race." Thus Sikhs, who form a distinct religious group but who do not necessarily have "common descent characteristics", can still be regarded as a distinct ethnic group for the purposes of the R.R.A.

[60] s. 35.
[61] s. 3(2) and see *Gwynedd County Council* v. *Jones* [1986] I.C.R. 833 (E.A.T.).
[62] As *per* Richardson, J. in *King-Ansell* v. *Police* [1979] 2 N.Z.L.R. 531.

"Ethnic" is a term to be used in a sense much wider than strict adherence to its biological or racial meaning.[63]

For a group to constitute an ethnic group in the sense of the R.R.A., it must regard itself, and be regarded by others, as a distinct community by virtue of certain characteristics. Some of these characteristics are essential, others are not essential but one or more of them will commonly be found and will help to distinguish the group from the surrounding community. The essential conditions according to Fraser L.J. are:

"(1) a long shared history, of which the group is conscious as distinguishing it from other groups, and the memory of which it keeps alive;
(2) a cultural tradition of its own, including family and social customs and manners, often but not necessarily associated with religious observance."

In addition, Lord Fraser identified further characteristics which are relevant and help distinguish a group from the surrounding community, but which are not essential characteristics:

"(3) either a common geographical origin, or descent from a small number of common ancestors;
(4) a common language, not necessarily peculiar to that group;
(5) a common literature peculiar to that group;
(6) a common religion different from that of neighbouring groups or from the general community surrounding it;
(7) being a minority or being an oppressed or a dominant group within a larger community."[64]

Reliance cannot be placed purely on these relevant factors. Thus a "racial group" cannot be defined by a "language factor" alone.[65]

Indeed the "real test is whether individual members of the group or the group itself regard themselves and are regarded by others in the community as having a particular historical identity in terms of their colour or their racial, national or ethnic origins."[66] This view was confirmed and extended by the House of Lords in *Mandla* v. *Lee*,[67] where Lord Fraser argued that provided a "person who joins the group feels himself or herself to be a member of it, and is accepted by other members, then he is for the purposes of the Act, a member."

This view is consistent with section 3(1) of the R.R.A. which says that, "reference to a person's racial group refers to any racial group

[63] *Mandla* v. *Lee* [1983] 2 A.C. 548; [1983] Q.B. 1.
[64] *Mandla* v. *Lee* [1983] 2 W.L.R. 625.
[65] *Gwynedd County Council* v. *Jones* [1986] I.C.R. 833 (E.A.T.).
[66] *Per* Richardson, J. in *King-Ansell* v. *Police* [1979] 2 N.Z.L.R. 531.
[67] *Supra.*

into which he falls." A person may "treat another relatively unfavourably 'on racial grounds' because he regards that other person as being of a particular racial group, even if his belief is, from a scientific point of view, completely erroneous."[68]

The approach adopted in *Mandla* was followed by the Court of Appeal,[69] when considering whether gypsies could be considered an ethnic or racial group, Nicholls L.J. stated "despite their long presence in England, gypsies have not merged wholly with the population, as have the Saxons and the Danes, and altogether lost their separate identity. They, or many of them, have retained a separateness, a self-awareness of still being gypsies." He saw gypsies as having a long-shared history, a common geographical origin and other shared characteristics, such as customs, folktales and language. Perversely, though, Rastafarians are not an ethnic group because they lack a long-shared history.

## *National origins*

Although the term "ethnic origins" is interpreted fairly widely the term "national origins" refers to race in a much more restricted way and does not apply to matters of citizenship or residence.[70] Thus, even though a person who "comes from abroad" may be treated differently from other people and therefore discriminated against, any such discrimination is not unlawful.

The distinction which the House of Lords raised under the Race Relations Act 1968 between the terms "national origins" and "nationality" in *Ealing London Borough Council* v. *Race Relations Board*[71] which excluded "nationality" from the definition of "national origins" has now effectively been removed by the inclusion in the R.R.A of "nationality" as a racial ground and an aspect when determining a racial group. The Act confirms the view taken in the *Tejani* case, that "nationality" includes citizenship.[72]

## *Religious discrimination*

No references are made in the R.R.A. about religious discrimination and therefore strictly speaking discrimination on the basis of religion is not unlawful. This is somewhat surprising bearing in mind that acts of

[68] See remarks by Fraser, L.J. in *Mandla* v. *Lee* [1983] 2 W.L.R. p. 625.
[69] *Commission for Racial Equality* v. *Dutton* [1989] I.R.L.R. 8, C.A.; *c/f Dawkins* v. *Dept. of Environment* [1993] I.R.L.R. 284.
[70] See *Tejani* v. *Superintendent Registrar for the District of Peterborough* [1986] I.R.L.R. 502, C.A. and *Ealing London Borough Council* v. *Race Relations Board* [1972] A.C. 342.
[71] [1972] A.C. 342.
[72] R.R.A., s. 77(1) but also see Article 9 of Regulation 1612/68 under E.C. Law.

racial discrimination are often directed towards religious beliefs.[73] Indeed very often racial matters and religion are difficult to separate as issues. Some protection at least is allowed where discrimination shows itself through religious expression but which is essentially racial in nature. The concept of indirect discrimination now supposedly offers a great deal of protection to those discriminated against due to their religioius observance.[74] Surely, however, a better approach would be that adopted by the Fair Employment (Northern Ireland) Act 1976 which attempts to provide equality of opportunity between persons of different religious beliefs.

Under English law, where a particular racial group, for example Sikhs, are the subject of discrimination, it is irrelevant that the discrimination is directed towards the group due to religion or race. This approach can be applied to many racial groups where religion and race are for all practical purposes indivisible. The effect of such discrimination essentially is still to discriminate against a "racial group" and on racial grounds, these being indistinguishable from the particular religion. As we have already seen, Fraser L.J. saw religion as a "common descent characteristic."[75]

## Application

Fundamental to the R.R.A. and S.D.A. is the approach that unless a particular instance of discrimination falls within one of the categories or types of discrimination specifically identified, then as such, it is not unlawful.[76] Therefore, for discrimination to be unlawful it must arise "in any circumstances relevant to the purposes of any provision in this Act."[77]

By the application of a two-part test we can determine whether in a particular instance discrimination has arisen and whether if so the act, omission or requirement is unlawful. First, has there been sex or racial discrimination as defined by the Acts? And secondly, does that discrimination fall within the specific prohibitions set out in the Acts?[78]

In cases of direct discrimination the application of this two-fold test is straightforward in that if less favourable treatment has taken place, as long as that treatment is in relation to a subject covered by the provisions of the Acts then unlawful discrimination has arisen. On the other hand in instances of indirect discrimination, the application of the

[73] See Hansard H.C. Standing Committee A, May 29, 1976, col. 84.
[74] See Race Relations Act 1965, Select Committee, col. 102.
[75] See the *Mandla* case, [1983] 2 W.L.R. p. 625.
[76] *Ealing London Borough Council* v. *Race Relations Board* [1972] A.C. 342 and *Tejani* v. *Superintendent Registrar for the District of Peterborough* [1986] I.R.L.R. 502, C.A.
[77] S.D.A., s. 1(1) and R.R.A., s. 1(1).
[78] See *Encyclopedia of Housing Law and Practice*, para. 2–2588/4.

two-fold test is rather more complex in that there are a number of subsidiary tests which must be applied before it can be determined whether discrimination has taken place. These subsidiary tests are explored fully in Chapter 4.

# EFFECT OF ANTI-DISCRIMINATION LAW

## Does the law prevent discrimination?

In practice it appears that the law is not enough. There still exists a significant "gap" between what the law provides for and what protection in practice exists from day to day. This latter point is dependent upon the attitudes of individuals who make up society as a whole. Street raises the question[79]: "To say that the law does not discriminate is one thing, but does the law compel persons not to discriminate, or otherwise protect those who are liable to be discriminated against?" He goes on to answer this point in the racial context saying: "Nobody should believe that law alone can create racial harmony; yet without legal sanctions, the prospects are much worse. This Act [Race Relations Act 1976] creates the legislative framework for better race relations in all those areas of potential conflict.[80]

So at best, the legislation provides a framework of protection relating to aspects of discrimination which potentially create conflict. The law can positively support the purpose of the legislation in the way the courts interpret the provisions of the Acts. In this respect it can adopt a purposive rather than a restrictive approach, when interpreting statutory provisions. In addition, it can tell those people who come to it for help because they are at the receiving end of unfair treatment, that they have done the right thing, and that the law exists to protect them. It can do this, if their cases are justified, by finding in their favour and awarding the appropriate remedies and in doing so, it can help close the "gap" which exists between the standards set by the law and the standards each of us applies from day to day. In doing this, it can therefore try and influence attitudes and thus assist in making unfair discrimination morally unacceptable, and influence unacceptable behaviour. It can do much in this respect by influencing and guiding institutions and encouraging them away from discriminatory practices and procedures. In fact, the administrative agencies of the law, the Equal Opportunities Commission (E.O.C.) and Commission for Racial Equality (C.R.E.), are given specific powers of enforcement in this

[79] *op. cit.* p. 301.
[80] *op. cit.* at p. 306.

respect along with the respective duties of promoting good relations between the sexes and between persons of different racial groups.

It is arguable whether the law itself can change society; certainly, there is doubt whether it can influence deep-seated prejudices. All it can do is to provide penalties for the physical manifestation of those prejudices where such acts are seen to be unacceptable. Instead, perhaps, the best legislators can hope for is that the law can influence behaviour and perhaps by doing so, in turn, influence middle ground opinion by its moral weight.

Legislation is even less likely to succeed if it is half-hearted or if within it there exist gaps or loopholes or if it is entirely defensive in nature. Anti-discrimination law in Britain, unlike America, is primarily defensive, it penalises people who act in contravention of its provisions rather than encouraging positive action. There are gaps in the present law, in particular in respect of racial and sexual harassment, in costly and cumbersome enforcement provisions and the limited powers of the Commissions. Problems of disadvantage remain within the "fragile peace" of many inner city areas. Michael Day, the chairman of the Commission for Racial Equality has commented that the "structural disadvantage which affects those in deprived areas of our country amongst whom there is often an over-representation of minority ethnic communities has not been addressed with sufficient urgency." He called for the R.R.A. to be overhauled asking for it to be clearer, less cumbersome in application and wider in scope.[81]

## Achieving equality: negative to positive

It has been suggested by P. Niner and V. Karn, that the introduction of protective law in this area tends to breed negative thinking and defensiveness.[82] They assert that a more positive approach in line with the spirit of the legislation is needed, rather than an approach involving doing just as much to comply with the legislation and no more. No legal duties exist for people or organisations to perform positive acts. However, surely the promotion of equality of opportunity necessitates a move to the positive. Otherwise the inequalities which exist will continue. (See Chapter 6 on the position of positive action, which offers advice on lawful action). Inevitably such an approach involves keeping accurate records of sex and ethnic origin and monitoring these records to identify any problem areas and to allow analysis of results to ascertain reasons for any apparent discrimination. Additionally, adopting fair housing programmes relating to sex and race which incorporate clear statements of equal opportunities coupled with

[81] See *The Times*, June 13, 1991, p. 5.
[82] *Housing Association Allocations—Achieving Racial Equality* (1985), at pp. 149–150.

effective training of staff, go a long way in avoiding discrimination positively and systematically.

## Housing discrimination

There is evidence of widespread discrimination on the basis of race in the housing field. Ethnic minorities tend to have to wait longer to be housed, are given poorer and older accommodation and are housed in areas of multiple stress and deprivation.[83]

There is less evidence of discrimination in the housing field on the basis of sex. During 1984 the E.O.C. received 35 complaints concerning accommodation and 20 concerning mortgage facilities. These figures had reduced to 26 and 13 respectively in 1985 and increased slightly to 34 and 16 respectively in 1986. But this does not say there is no housing discrimination on the basis of sex.

The E.O.C. have highlighted a range of issues which include:

(a) the provision of mortgage facilities;
(b) voting rights with building society mortgage accounts;
(c) home improvement company refusals to give quotations unless husbands are present;
(d) allocation of retirement housing and use of age differentials;[84]
(e) female property rights;[85]
(f) potentially discriminatory aspects of the Right to Buy Scheme;
(g) women's inequality in taking over service accommodation and caravan accommodation.[86]

Discrimination in the housing field, then, does take place. It is rarely direct in the way that it applies. Rather, indirect practices and procedures which unintentionally discriminate seem to be more likely.[87]

### *Paucity of case law*

There is very little case law of housing discrimination. Because of this, it has been necessary to draw upon the case law in other discrimination law fields, in particularly the employment field. The S.D.A. and the R.R.A. are to be interpreted identically unless the context demands otherwise. Indeed, sections within the statute are written in similar terms to generally aid interpretation. Because of this

[83] See the Campaign for Racial Equality *Report of Formal Investigations*, but in particular *Housing and Ethnic Minorities: Statistical Information* (1988), see also National Federation of Housing Associations, *Race and Housing*, series of reports.
[84] *A. Capon* v. *Liverpool City Council* (1988) unreported, case details from E.O.C.
[85] *Williams and Glyn's Bank* v. *Boland* (1980) unreported, case details from E.O.C.
[86] *Taylor* v. *Burnett and Hilltree park Limited* (1983) E.O.C. Annual Report (at p. 8).
[87] Generally see C.R.E., *Report of Formal Investigations.*

we are able to draw upon the decisions of the courts relating to the Acts and apply the principles more widely, mindful of changing contexts. The principles which underlie whether indirect discrimination is justifiable in the objective sense do not change whether the context is employment or housing, it is simply the context which is different.

Thus, there has been heavy reliance on the principles which have been used in construing wording relating to employment cases. This is a useful and enlightening process but we must be aware of its limitations. Until the application of such principles is considered by the courts in the housing context we cannot be entirely sure of the outcome.

Perhaps one of the reasons for the paucity of case law in the housing field is that there does not exist an expedited procedure through the use of tribunals as in the employment field. This must result in fewer cases being taken to court, albeit legal aid, assistance and advice is available.

## *Paucity of administrative action*

There is little evidence that the E.O.C. has actively pursued housing discrimination as an issue, much of its work being concentrated in the employment field where sex discrimination is at its greatest. It has actively and successfully campaigned for building societies to change their lending practices when women are the main earners of a household. But perhaps the biggest difficulty is the Commission's lack of resources, a problem which was made more stark since the late 1980's. On the other hand the C.R.E. has made use of its formal investigation and non-discrimination notice powers in the housing field, particularly in relation to local authority housing. See its reports *re* Walsall, Hackney, Tower Hamlets as examples. However, in undertaking formal investigations it has been severely hampered by court decisions.[88] Both Commissions have asked for more straight-forward statutory procedures when undertaking formal investigations, in particular in attempting to alleviate the burden placed on the commissions by the Court of Appeal following the judgment in the *Hillingdon* case.[89]

[88] See the *Hillingdon*, *Amari Plastics* and *Prestige* cases.
[89] See for example C.R.E. *Second Review of The Race Relations Act 1976* (1992).

# Chapter two

# Present Legislative and Administrative Framework

## INTRODUCTION

Anti-discrimination law with respect to housing, as already indicated, is contained primarily in two statutes: the S.D.A. and the R.R.A. In addition there are provisions in other statutes which are important in the context of housing. In this chapter we shall briefly consider the present legal framework contained in the statutes, including key interpretative issues, and we shall go on to consider the administrative framework through codes of practice, enforcement, and the two quasi-judicial enforcement agencies: The Commission for Racial Equality and the Equal Opportunities Commission.[1]

### The main acts

The S.D.A. and the R.R.A. are structured almost identically. This was the intention of Parliament. Part I of each Act sets out the legal nature of unlawful discrimination. Discrimination defined in Part I is only unlawful if it occurs within one of the fields set out by the Acts.[2] Parts II and III of the Acts set out the fields to which the Acts apply. Parts II of both Acts are concerned with the employment field. This was the main field of application and special arrangements have been created in order that cases of unlawful discrimination can be heard quickly and effectively through Industrial Tribunals and Employment Appeal Tribunals. Such speedy processes do not apply to the other fields set out in the Acts. It is not surprising that much of the case law on race and sex discrimination is in the employment field rather than to the

[1] Although see Chapter 13.
[2] *R.* v. *Immigration Appeal Tribunal, ex. parte Kassam* [1980] 1 W.L.R. 1037 (C.A.) and *R.* v. *Entry Clearance Officer: Bombay, ex parte Amin* [1983] 2 A.C. 818 (H.L.).

other fields to which the Acts apply. This is due to two main reasons: firstly, that the effects of discrimination in employment tend to be immediately felt and because of this are more obvious than in other fields; and secondly, as commented already, the tribunal process provides easier and quicker redress for victims than that provided through court proceedings.

Parts III of the Acts set out the other fields to which the Acts apply: education, the provision of goods, facilities and services and the disposal and management of premises. It is with Part III of the Acts that we are mainly concerned.

Parts IV of the Acts go on to deal with other discriminatory acts and practices including discriminatory advertisements, giving instructions to discriminate, exerting pressure to discriminate, aiding unlawful acts and the liability of employers and principals. For any such discriminatory acts or practices to be unlawful it must apply to a field set out in Part III of the Acts.

There are exceptions to the provisions of the Acts which render discrimination lawful. These "general exceptions" are set out in Part IV of each Act. Additionally, there are specific exceptions from the discrimination provisions relating to the disposal and management of premises. These are to be found in Part III of each Act.[3]

The remaining parts of the Acts deal with the constitutions of the two commissions — the Equal Opportunities Commission and the Commission for Racial Equality — and cover the general enforcement arrangements.

## INTERPRETATION

The two Acts are written in almost identical terms with the intention of avoiding differences in their judicial interpretation. The clear intention being

> "to harmonise the powers and procedures for dealing with sex and race discrimination so as to secure genuine equality of opportunity in both fields ... except for good reason, the two statutes and the procedures for their administration and enforcement will be framed in similar terms".[4]

The courts have in practice tended to follow this course in interpreting the statutes. For example Popplewell J. pointed out that the "provisions of section 1(1)(*b*)(ii) of the Sex Discrimination Act 1975 and section

[3] See Chapter 5 for a detailed examination of these exceptions.
[4] See White Paper, *Racial Discrimination* (1975) Cmnd. 6234, paras. 48, 50 and 680.

1(1)(*b*)(ii) of the Race Relations Act 1976 are identical in their phraseology and are therefore to be construed in like manner".[5]

However, where wording in the statues differs, the same approach cannot necessarily be adopted. Even though the S.D.A. "is to be read as one with the Equal Pay Act 1970"[6] the standard for justifying indirect discrimination under the Equal Pay Act 1970 is different. For example "justification" in the context of the Equal Pay Act 1970 is considered to mean both "necessary" and "real" need. This interpretation does not automatically extend to the S.D.A. nor consequently to the R.R.A., because the wording of the Acts is different.[7] Thus the decisions relating to equal pay considered by the European Court and the House of Lords do not necessarily apply to other aspects of race and sex discrimination and the "sound and tolerable reasons" test in determining whether indirect discrimination is justifiable, laid down by the Court of Appeal in *Ojutiku* remains. Such interpretations require "objective balance" between the discriminatory effect of a requirement and the reasonable needs of the person who applies it. According to Balcombe L.J. "it is obviously desirable that the tests of justifiability applied in these closely related fields should be consistent with each other".[8] Even though in this example wording differs there is no significant difference in the standard for justifying indirect discrimination under the three Acts.[9]

Where statutory language is the same, the interpretation adopted under one Act can be applied to the similar provisions of the other Act. This may even apply to sections within a different part of one Act which are written in the same or similar language. For example, the words "by dismissing him or subjecting him to any other detriment" under section 4(2)(*c*) of the R.R.A. under its employment provision are similar to the words "by evicting him or subjecting him to any other detriment" which apply in the housing provisions of the S.D.A.[10] There is no reason to believe these words should be construed differently since they are founded on the same principles and simply apply to different fields of protection offered by the R.R.A. Because of this similarity in construction, it is immaterial whether judicial interpretation of wording arises under one Act or the other or different sections of the Acts.[11]

[5] *Hampson* v. *Department of Education* [1988] I.C.R. 278 at p. 292.
[6] *Ibid.*, p. 292.
[7] *Ibid.*, pp. 292–295.
[8] *Hampson* v. *Department of Education and Science* [1989] I.R.L.R. 69 (C.A.) at p. 76.
[9] *Ibid*; see also *Bilka-Kaufthaus GmbH* v. *Weber van Hartz* [1987] I.C.R. 100; *Rainey* v. *Greater Glasgow Health Board* [1987] A.C. 224 H.L. and *Ojutiku and Oburoni* v. *Manpower Services Commission* [1982] I.C.R. 661 C.A. and further discussion in Chapter 4.
[10] s. 2(2)(*b*).
[11] See preface to M. Rubenstein, *Discrimination: A Guide to the Relevant Case Law on Race and Sex Discrimination and Equal Pay*, p. 1.

# PURPOSIVE VIEW TO INTERPRETATION

Since legislation was introduced to prevent unlawful sex and race discrimination the courts have tended to consider the relevant law as an infringement on the freedom of the individual and therefore have, certainly with early case law, taken the view that the statutes required restrictive interpretation. However, more recently the courts have adopted, in the employment field, a much more purposive approach, looking at the intention of the statutes rather than treating them as an incursion into a person's liberty. Michael Rubenstein believes that this shift in emphasis gives "cause to be optimistic about equal opportunities law" and may create a "virtuous circle" because

> "successful cases engender more complaints as potential applicants come to believe that using the law can provide an effective remedy. The more cases there are, the better educated the judges become and the more the law is likely to be interpreted in accordance with its underlying objectives. Therefore, the more complaints that are brought, the more likely it is that complaints will succeed".[12]

# CODES OF PRACTICE

Both Commissions (the Commission for Racial Equality and the Equal Opportunities Commission) have produced codes of practice in the employment field these being the Race Relations Code of Practice Order 1983 and the Sex Discrimination Code Practice Order 1985.[13] The Housing Act 1988[14] and the Local Government and Housing Act 1989[15] provide a power for the Commission of Racial Equality to introduce codes of practice in the field of housing and rented housing. Both the provisions amend section 47(1) of the Race Relations Act 1976 which is concerned with the introduction of Codes of Practice by adding the following paragraphs,

"(c) the elimination of discrimination in the field of housing

[12] See M. Rubenstein, *Creating a Virtuous Circle: The New Case Law and Its Implications* [1988] E.O.R. No. 20 p. 48; *West Midlands Passenger Transport Executive* v. *Singh* [1988] 1 W.L.R. 730; *Noone* v. *North West Thames Regional Health Authority* [1988] I.C.R. 813; Alexanders v. *Home Office* [1988] 1 W.L.R. 968; but also see a recent restrictive interpretation in *Barclays Bank plc* v. *Kapur and Others* [1989] I.R.L.R. 57 E.A.T.

[13] For the statutory power to introduce these codes see s. 56A S.D.A., and R.R.A., s. 47.

[14] s. 137.

[15] s. 180.

(d) the promotion of equality of opportunity in the field of housing between persons of different racial groups."

When the Commission is in the course of preparing any such draft code of practice, it shall consult with such organisations or bodies as the Commission consider appropriate bearing in mind the content of the draft.[16] The Codes of Practice do not have the full force of law. Failure to observe a Code of Practice does not render a person "liable to any proceedings." But in any proceedings under the R.R.A. before a court, any Codes of Practice which have been issued under section 47 are admissible as evidence.[17] If any provision of such a Code appears to the court to be relevant to any questions arising in the proceedings it shall be taken into account in determining that question.[18] Whether failure to adhere to the provisions of a Code of Practice amounts to a presumption of unlawful discrimination is arguable, but the wording of section 47(10) suggests that such a presumption may arise where the provisions of a Code of Practice are directly relevant to the circumstances of a particular case. If so, then the burden of proof may well be shifted, in such circumstances, to the defendant to show that he did not unlawfully discriminate. Failure to adhere to the Codes may, then raise the presumption of discrimination. No such power exists for the Equal Opportunities Commission to introduce Codes of Practice with respect to sex discrimination in the field of housing.[19]

# TORTIOUS NATURE OF DISCRIMINATION LAW

Unlawful discrimination on the basis of sex or race is not a criminal offence. Instead the law provides in cases of unlawful discrimination a range of civil remedies for victims. This means that discrimination law is essentially tortious in nature. Early thinking, particularly in the race relations field, went along with a criminal law approach to discrimination. Following evidence based on American experience, reliance on criminal law as an effective approach was dropped by Parliament.[20] Certain discriminatory acts, though, are made criminal offences, where they amount to racial abuse. These acts in the main are covered under the Public Order Act 1986. Additionally, racial and sexual harassment where accompanied by insulting, threatening, or abusive behaviour or

[16] s. 137(3) Housing Act 1988 amending s. 47 of the R.R.A. by adding s. 47(3A) and amended by s. 180 of the Local Government and Housing Act 1989.
[17] R.R.A., s. 47(10).
[18] R.R.A., s. 47(10).
[19] Copies of the two Codes of Practice issued in the housing field are printed in Appendices 2 and 3.
[20] See discussion by Lister and Bindman, *Race and the Law* pp. 110–116.

violence may also amount to a criminal offence under the Public Order Act.[21]

## ADMINISTRATIVE ACTION

Although discrimination law is essentially tortious in nature and provides individual civil remedies for certain discriminatory acts only the Commission for Racial Equality or the Equal Opportunities Commission in their respective fields can take enforcement action. These acts in the main relate to discriminatory practices[22] and discriminatory advertisements.[23] The Commissions exist primarily to combat institutional discrimination and have investigatory and enforcement powers as part of their armoury. They can also assist individual claimants, thus "making up for their inexperience as litigants, as well as their lack of financial resources".[24] Where the relevant Commission fails to act to aid a victim the only remedy available to the individual would seem to be to make an application for judicial review of the Commission's actions.[25]

Additionally, local authorities and the Housing Corporation[26] have a duty

> "to make appropriate arrangements with a view to securing that their various functions are carried out with due regard to the need:
> (a) to eliminate unlawful racial discrimination; and
> (b) to promote equality of opportunity, and good relations, between persons of different racial groups."

Consequently, local authorities and the Housing Corporation are brought into the administrative framework and can assume the necessary administrative powers to carry out their duties.[27]

## LIMITS OF THE LAW: THE NEED FOR CHANGE

It has been argued by Lustgarten that little can be achieved to eliminate discrimination against minorities through legal means. Instead

[21] See Chapter 12.
[22] S.D.A., s. 37(3) and R.R.A., s. 28(3).
[23] S.D.A., ss. 38, 67, 71 and 72 and R.R.A., ss. 29, 58–61 and 63.
[24] See C. Bourn and J. Whitmore, *Discrimination and Equal Pay* p. 3.
[25] The full range of powers and the nature of the Commissions is considered in Chapter 13.
[26] R.R.A., s. 71 and Housing Act 1988, s. 56.
[27] See Chapters 10 and 11.

there should be a shift to the adoption of wider scale administrative measures, such as contract compliance.[28] To achieve this there needs to be a move towards a more "positive action" framework.[29] A major step forward would be for "Codes of Practice", which tend to be positive in nature, to have full legal force and be more widely employed.

The law as it stands has done little to alter discrimination. Relatively few people make use of the legislation, particularly for non-employment issues.[30] One reason for this may be that the courts, in the main, rather than generate the "virtuous circle" argued for by Rubenstein[31] have adopted a narrow approach certainly until recently when interpreting the legislation and have failed to catch up with the modern approach adopted by the European Court, particularly in relation to the E.C. Treaty and the European Convention on Human Rights.[32]

The effectiveness of the law is also severely limited by other *lacunae*. The Commissions have been seen as paper tigers because they face too many administrative difficulties[33] and are under funded.[34] The law itself is "grotesquely complicated and obsure"[35] and is in need of greater simplicity both legislatively and administratively.[36] The possibility that the "resourceful" can employ delaying tactics should be removed.[37] Such delays and legal complexities which have in particular bedevilled formal investigations by the Commissions should be reduced.[38]

[28] Racial Equality and The Limits of The Law M.L.R. vol. 49 No. 1 p. 68.
[29] See C. McCrudden, Rethinking Positive Action, I.L.J. 15 December 4, 1989 pp. 219–244 and V. Karn and P. Niner, *Housing Association Allocations: Achieving Racial Equality* (1986).
[30] See R. Dutta and G. Taylor, *Housing Equality* (1989) p. 2.
[31] *op. cit.* p. 48.
[32] See A. Lister, Foreward to C. Palmer and K. Poulton, *Sex and Race Discrimination in Employment* (1987) and R. Dutta and G. Taylor, *op. cit.* pp. 2–3.
[33] See First Report of The House Affairs Select Committee 1981/82 and The Scarman Report Cmnd 8427 1981 p. 11.
[34] A. Lester *op. cit.*
[35] *Ibid.*
[36] See Equal Opportunities Commission, *Legislating for Change*, (1988).
[37] C. Bourn and J. Whitmore, *op. cit.* p. 203.
[38] See *Commission Seeks Tougher Laws on Discrimination*, *The Times*, June 13, 1991 p. 5.

# Chapter three

# Direct Discrimination

## INTRODUCTION

In Chapter one we briefly examined the nature of discrimination and saw that there were primarily, within the statutory framework, two forms of discrimination: direct and indirect. The distinction is important since in practice the protection offered to an individual may well differ depending on the form of discrimination in question. A finding of unlawful direct discrimination will usually lead to an award of damages. Such a result in a case of indirect discrimintation is far less likely, a discriminator having a much better chance of escaping such liability.

In this chapter we will examine direct discrimination in greater depth and we will go on to consider a further form of direct discrimination, victimisation.

## THE NATURE OF DIRECT DISCRIMINATION

Direct discrimination has three essential elements:

1. there must be less favourable treatment;
2. on specified racial or sex grounds under the provisions of the Acts, and
3. the relevant circumstances of comparison of one case to another should be the same, or not materially different.

### Less favourable treatment

The relevant statutory provisions state that for direct discrimination to arise a person must be less favourably treated on racial ground or on the grounds of her or his sex.[1]

Mere prejudice is not unlawful. The law does not prevent the free expression of opinions.[2] A person must have suffered "less favourable

[1] S.D.A., s. 1(1)(*a*), and R.R.A., s. 1(1)(*a*).
[2] Except for recognising the crime of enticement to racial hatred under the Public Order Act, 1986 considered in Chapter 9.

treatment" as a result of the practical application of prejudice. But the words a person uses may very well assist in determining whether there was a "racial" or "sex" motive, *i.e.*, a "discriminatory motive", if an instance of less favourable treatment has arisen.

Moreover "words of discouragement" on racial grounds and on the basis of sex can, in appropriate circumstances, in respect of the person discouraged, amount to "less favourable treatment" than that given to other persons. Simply asking a question about a person's religious faith, however, particularly if the same question is asked of all persons in similar circumstances, may not conclusively determine that there was any discouragement intended.[3]

But is it important to look at the treatment of a person rather than the consequences of that treatment to see whether a victim is treated less favourable on the basis of his or her sex or racial origins.[4] This approach was also adopted in *Din* v. *Carrington Viyella*[5]

> "What has to be inquired into is the reason why a particular course was adopted: the question is 'Was it on racial grounds?' "

If a decision involved drawing a distinction on say the basis of sex or on racial grounds, then it will be discriminatory even though the motive behind it did not necessarily involve a prejudice of a racial or sexual kind. The reason for drawing the distinction is still on the basis of sex or race. It is the reason for raising that distinction rather than the general purpose of the distinction which is important. Therefore even though treatment may be "no less unpleasant" it was the "specific nature of the unpleasantness" which is the important issue. If part of the treatment was "meted out because a person is a woman" then there is less favourable treatment.[6]

"Less favourable treatment" can also arise where the racial or sex factor is not the sole factor but where it is a factor of some significance.[7]

Less favourable treatment can broadly be seen as a deprivation of choice or narrowing of opportunities, as Brightman L.J. suggests:[8]

> "I do not say that the mere deprivation of choice for one sex, or some differentiation in their treatment, is necessarily unlawful discrimination. The deprivation of choice, or differentiation, must be associated with a detriment. It is possible to imagine a case where one sex has a choice but the other does not, yet there is

[3] *Simon* v. *Brinham Associates* [1987] I.C.R. 596 (C.A.).
[4] See *Balgobin and Francis* v. *London Borough of Tower Hamlets* [1987] I.R.L.R. 401 (E.A.T.).
[5] [1982] I.C.R. 256 E.A.T.
[6] See Lord Grieve's comments in *Porcelli* v. *Strathclyde Council (C.S.)* [1986] I.C.R. 569 at p. 573.
[7] *Owen & Briggs* v. *James* [1982] I.C.R. 618.
[8] *Jeremiah* v. *Ministry of Defence* [1979] I.R.L.R. 436, C.A. at 440.

> nevertheless no detriment to the latter sex and therefore no unlawful discrimination."

Thus there must be a loss of choice or a loss of something of value[9] in order for there to exist "less favourable treatment". It is enough that the individual concerned is deprived of a choice which is of value to them, even though it may not be of value to others. The choice which is lost, though, must be a choice which is of value, on reasonable grounds, to "many others" even though it may not be "better."[10]

Intention or motive to discriminate is not a necessary condition to show less favourable treatment.[11] It is the treatment which is at the heart of direct discrimination not the "motive or objective" of the person responsible for it.[12] Otherwise a directly discriminatory act done with good or worthy motives which treated people unfairly because of their sex or race would be lawful.[13] Therefore, it is necessary to only look at the reason why the defendant treated the plaintiff less favourably, not the "causative link" between the defendant's behaviour and the less favourable treatment meted out. There can be a "clear distinction" between the reason why a person acts and his intentions. Therefore, the "legally determinant matter" is the true reason for the discriminatory behaviour rather than a person's intention or motive.[14]

Where though, a racial consideration or a consideration of sex was an important factor in a decision, for example by a landlord, then that is sufficient to show that direct discrimination took place.[15] However, it is not sufficient merely to show that an individual is of a particular racial group. This may not be part of the background or the *causa sine qua non* of what happened.[16] Malone in *A Practice Guide to Discriminative Law*, commenting on "discriminatory motive" says that it

> "relates to the mental attitude of the person handing out the unfavourable treatment. If the person receiving such treatment cannot show one of the forbidden grounds for the treatment, there has been no discrimination . . ."[17]

The first ingredient is directly linked to the second we identified, that the unfavourable treatment must be within the context of the provision of the Acts. Consequently if a person is treated unfairly but not under

[9] *R.* v. *Birmingham City Council ex p., E.O.C.* [1988] 3 W.L.R. 837.
[10] *R.* v. *Birmingham City Council ex p., E.O.C.* [1989] I.R.L.R. 173 H.L.
[11] *R.* v. *Birmingham City Council* [1989] I.R.L.R. 173 H.L. and *Din* v. *Carrington Viyella* [1982] I.C.R. 256 E.A.T.
[12] *Strathclyde Regional Council* v. *Porcelli* [1986] I.R.L.R. 134 C.S.
[13] *Grieg* v. *Community Industry* [1979] I.R.L.R. 158 (E.A.T.) and *R.* v. *Commission for Racial Equality ex p., Westminster City Council* [1984] I.R.L.R. 230 H.C.
[14] *James* v. *Eastleigh Borough Council* [1989] I.R.L.R. 318 (C.A.).
[15] *Owen Briggs* v. *James* [1982] I.R.L.R. 502 (C.A.).
[16] *Seide* v. *Gillette Industries Ltd* [1980] I.R.L.R. 427 (E.A.T.).
[17] *op. cit.* pp. 4–5.

the racial or sex grounds set out in the Acts then no unlawful discrimination occurs. It is always for the complainant to make out his or her case and to show that discrimination under the Acts has taken place. If there is a finding of discrimination and of difference in race, followed by an inadequate or unsatisfactory non-racial or non-sex explanation offered by the alleged discriminator, then the legitimate inference would usually be "that the discrimination has been on the grounds of race" or sex.[18]

In determining whether a non-racial or non-sex explanation offered by an alleged discriminator is satisfactory there is still a need to prove the "necessary element of causation" between the act and the alleged less favourable treatment. For example where action is taken on the basis of "a breach of trust" less favourable treatment on racial grounds cannot necessarily be inferred.[19] But in racial discrimination cases there are certain common features:

(i) if the victim shows that he or she has been treated less favourably than others consistent with the treatment being based on racial grounds, it can be inferred that such treatment was on racial grounds unless it could be shown to the contrary;
(ii) the evidence advanced in a discrimination case need not decisively prove that the discriminator acts on racial grounds so long as it tended to prove the case;
(iii) statistical evidence might establish a discernible pattern in the treatment of a particular group, giving rise to an inference of discrimination against the group;
(iv) if a practice is being operated against a group, it is reasonable to infer, in the absence of a satisfactory explanation in a particular case, that the complainant, as a member of that group, is himself being treated less favourably on the grounds of race.[20]

To assist in this process of establishing inference from primary facts it has been held that a victim may have access to such statistical evidence as is available.[21] This decision has important implications for people on housing waiting lists as well as job hunters where the "statistics were logically probative as evidence from which an inference might be drawn that" a racially discriminatory policy has been adopted "which manifested itself on other occasions and that the discriminatory policy has been manifested in the present case".[22]

[18] *Noone* v. *North West Thames Regional Health Authority* [1988] I.C.R. 813.
[19] *Aziz* v. *Trinity Street Taxis* [1988] 3 W.L.R. 79 (C.A.).
[20] *West Midlands Passenger Transport* v. *Singh* [1988] 1 W.L.R. 730 (C.A.).
[21] *Ibid.*
[22] *Ibid.*

Turning to "associated discrimination", the Court of Appeal held in *Race Relations Board* v. *Applin*[23] that less favourable treatment can arise as a result of someone else's colour. Thus for example where a housing association refused to take ethnic minority families on to their waiting list nominated by a local authority, they would not only discriminate against the families but also against the local authority. Hence the words "on racial grounds" are perfectly capable in their ordinary sense of covering any reason for an action based on race, whether it be the race of the person affected by the action or of others.[24] Such provisions as we have already explored do not apply to cases of discrimination on the basis of sex, associated discrimination is not covered by the statute.

## Racial or sex grounds under the acts

Of the second element identified, racial or sex grounds within the housing context under the provisions of the Acts, we will consider these and the exceptions in detail in Chapters 6 to 8.

However, it is worth commenting here on "stereotyped assumptions" since these have been an important consideration of the courts in establishing whether discrimination has taken place on the basis of sex or race. As Bourn and Whitmore comment[25] it is "characteristic of discriminatory behaviour to treat all members of a group as possessing some ascribed characteristic and then to act on the basis of that characteristic." Consequently the words "on the grounds of" sex or race encompass instances where discrimination occurred because of the application of generalised assumptions about people of a particular sex or racial group. Treating people stereotypically "on the grounds of sex or race" amounts to direct discrimination.[26]

## Similar relevant circumstances

Section 5(3) of the Sex Discrimination Act 1975 says:

> "A comparison of the cases of persons of different sex or marital status under section 1(1) or 3(1) must be such that the relevant circumstances in the one case are the same, or not materially different, in the other."

[23] [1975] A.C. 259.

[24] As *per* Browne-Williamson J. in *Showboat Entertainment Centre* v. *Owen* [1984] 1 W.L.R. 384, see also *Zarczynska* v. *Levy* [1979] I.C.R. 184 and *Race Relations Board* v. *Charter* [1973] A.C. 868.

[25] *op. cit.* p. 27.

[26] See *Horsey* v. *Dyfed County Council* [1982] I.R.L.R. 395 (E.A.T.); *Alexander* v. *Home Office* [1988] I.R.L.R. 190 (C.A.); *Hurley* v. *Mustoe* [1981] I.C.R. 490 and *Coleman* v. *Skyrail Oceanic Ltd* [1981] I.R.L.R. 398 (C.A.).

Similarly section 3(4) of the Race Relations Act 1976 says —

> "A comparison of the case of a person of a particular racial group with that of a person not of that group under section 1(1) must be such that the relevant circumstances in the one case are the same, or not materially different, in the other."

Proving direct discrimination therefore necessitates a comparison exercise between people of different racial groups or sex or marital status. The "relevant circumstances" of the comparison must be identical or not materially different. The comparison is between the treatment meted out and the treatment which would have been afforded to the relevant comparator, by excluding matters of sex or race.[27] The relevant circumstances are those which actually applied rather than some hypothetical circumstances involving different people. Thus, the comparison must be concerned with facts.[28]

Difficulty can arise where it is problematical to make a comparison because of the very nature of a case, for example in the case of a pregnant woman. It is also argued by Bourn and Whitmore[29] that the comparison method is faulted because it "presupposes that equality is to be achieved through a process of assimilation, rather than through the acceptance of differences."

# SEGREGATION

Segregating "a person from other persons on racial grounds is treating him less favourably than they are treated:" R.R.A. section 1(2). Thus segregation amounts to direct discrimination. However, "congregating", allowing people to create their own groups, does not amount to segregation.[30]

# VICTIMISATION

## Introduction

Before leaving the subject of direct discrimination we need to consider one final aspect. Direct discrimination can also take the form of "victimisation". For example "sex discrimination has two meanings in all the substantive sections of the Act, discrimination and victimisation".[31] Victimisation in this context, under section 4(1) of the S.D.A.

[27] *Showboat Entertainment Centre Ltd* v. *Owens* [1984] I.R.L.R. 7 (E.A.T.).
[28] *Grieg* v. *Community Industry* [1979] I.R.L.R. 158 (E.A.T.).
[29] *op. cit.* p. 16.
[30] *P.E.L. Ltd.* v. *Modgill* [1980] I.R.L.R. 142 (E.A.T.).
[31] *Cornelius* v. *University College of Swansea* (1987) 131 S.J. 359 (C.A.).

1975 and section 2(1) of the R.R.A. 1976, means the "less favourable treatment" of the person victimised where that person has:

"(a) brought proceedings against the "discriminator" or any other person under the Acts; or
(b) given evidence or information in connection with proceedings brought by any person against the discriminator or any other person under the Acts; or
(c) otherwise done anything under or by reference to the Acts in relation to the discriminator or any other person; or
(d) alleged that the discriminator or any other person has committed an act which (whether or not the allegation so states) would amount to a contravention of the Acts; or
(e) by reason that the discriminator knows the person victimised intends to do any of the above mentioned things, or suspects the person victimised has done, or intends to do, any of them."

These are what Slade L.J. calls "protected acts" in *Aziz* v. *Trinity Street Taxis*[32] and what Walker and Redman in *Racial Discrimination* refer to as "actual or apprehended acts". An act includes a "deliberate omission".[33]

## The scope of the provisions

In theory, the scope of the provisions is particularly wide offering protection not only where the Acts have been invoked but also where there is an intention to invoke them. Protection is also afforded against the acts of third parties. For example if a landlord will not house a person because that person's present landlord has suggested the prospective tenant is a troublemaker because of complaints of racial discrimination, protection is available.

## Similarity and affinity with the law of contempt

The law on victimisation has been likened to the law relating to contempt of court.[34] Indeed the law of contempt offers further protection for the victim of discrimination by way of victimisation not only where a matter has been to court[35], but also where a person is

[32] [1988] 3 W.L.R. 79 pp. 86–90.
[33] See R.R.A., s. 78(1) and S.D.A., s. 82(1).
[34] See comments of Slade L.J. in *Aziz* v. *Trinity Street Taxis* [1988] 3 W.L.R. 79 at p. 91 and those of Bingham L.J. in *Cornelius* v. *University College of Swansea* [1987] I.R.L.R. 141 at p. 145.
[35] *Littler* v. *Thompson* (1839) 2 Beav. 129.

victimised for activities which fall short of actual participation before a court.[36]

## Purpose of the provisions: elimination of fear

A significant problem with cases of discrimination is the reluctance of victims and witnesses to come forward and make complaints. The main reason for this is the fear of being victimised for doing so, not only by the "discriminator" but also by third parties. Third parties may victimise on behalf of the discriminator or simply because they regard the victims or witnesses as troublemakers or "whistleblowers". Consequently, the provisions in both Acts concerning "discrimination by way of victimisation" give protection to such victims and other people who may give evidence or other kinds of support in a case. Further to this basic protection, the provisions preclude the type of collusion we have described in cases of victimisation, since they apply equally to other persons along with the discriminator.[37]

Victimisation can take a number of forms, from creating basic inconveniences for victims through to major racial attacks and instances of sexual harassment and intimidation. Typical discriminatory landlord practices may involve the interruption of services, threatened eviction and actual eviction. Indeed victimisation can be quite subtle, particularly where the landlord gains help from third parties.

In order to reduce these problems, as MacDonald says in *Race Relations — The New Law*[38], the aim of the legislation in this respect is "to eliminate the fear and reluctance of victims of discrimination to come forward". Victims and others who wish to eliminate discrimination can easily be regarded as whistleblowers or troublemakers and therefore may not come and complain. Developing a positive atmosphere through the establishment of anti-discrimination policies and procedures. Such an approach endorsed by effective training and an encouragement to eliminate discrimination will help ensure victimisation is minimised.[39] Without the legal processes to protect people from victimisation there would possibly be far fewer cases surfacing.

### *Effectiveness of measures in eliminating fear*

Whether or not these measures of protection are effective is a very different matter. There exist a number of difficulties in practice. Firstly,

[36] *Roebuck* v. *N.U.M. (Yorkshire Area)* [1977] I.C.R. 573 and the discussion by Lustgarten in *Legal Control of Racial Discrimination*, pp. 91–2.
[37] See S.D.A., s. 4(1) and R.R.A., s. 2(1).
[38] *op. cit.*
[39] See Malone *Sex Discrimination.*

victimisation has to be proved by the victim, and as MacDonald says "there are many covert ways in which discriminators can victimise without having the finger put on them"[40]; secondly, if a third person is involved the victim has to prove a chain of causation. Indeed, a victim may have to surmount this "hurdle of causation" even where no third person is involved and where there are other possible explanations for the victimisation in question.[41] And third, where an allegation is false and made in bad faith, the alleged discriminator is free to victimise.[42]

Certainly there is little evidence to show that the victimisation measures are regularly invoked in relation to housing cases. This could be ascribed to the availability of other remedies for victims. This seems unlikely however, since there is similarly little evidence to draw upon to show the measures under landlord and tenant law, relating to illegal eviction and harassment. Such measures are not effectively geared towards protection for the instances of victimisation currently under discussion.

When the relationship between a landlord and tenant or between a tenant and his neighbours goes wrong, a quite natural reaction is for the tenant in question to want to leave and find somewhere else to live. Many local housing authorities and housing associations in cases of racial harassment, which are not necessarily instances of victimisation within the context of the present discussion, acknowledge this basic need, and help with rehousing (often, though, a painfully slow process). This process however, has the effect of cutting through the need to deal with the discriminator, whether or not that person is the landlord or a neighbour. An approach which offers help to the victim can often mean the discriminator has succeeded in his efforts of victimisation. The problem may well remain dormant only to re-appear with a future tenant. Thus no real solution is found with such an approach. Independent action against alleged discriminators might offer one answer, but this is rarely done primarily due to the "tortious" nature of discrimination law.

## *False and not in good faith*

The provisions offering protection in cases of victimisation do not apply to treatment of a person by reason of any allegation made by him where the allegation was "false and not made in good faith".[43] Consequently, if an allegation is false, a landlord or other discriminator is free to victimise as long as that victimisation does not amount to

[40] *op. cit.* p. 21.
[41] See *post* p. 30.
[42] See *post* p. 30.
[43] *Kirby* v. *Manpower Services Commission* [1980] I.C.R. 420 (E.A.T.), S.D.A., s. 4(2) and R.R.A., s. 2(2).

harassment under the Protection From Eviction Act 1977, or is unlawful or criminal in any other respect.

Whether an allegation is false and made not in good faith seems to rest upon the provisions of the Acts. If an allegation is made which is outside the scope of protection that the Acts offered, then it could render that allegation technically false under these provisions. There would still be a need to determine whether the allegation was made not in good faith. In defence though, there may be difficulties of proof, particularly since this may well rely on both the circumstances of the complaint and the mental attitude of the complainant.

This surely cannot assist the elimination of fear. Individuals are not always cognisant of legal provisions when they make a complaint, their hope is that the complaint will be heard and hopeful the problem will be rectified. For as MacDonald[44] puts it "Who is to tell when they make a complaint,

(1) that they will be able to substantiate it, or
(2) that they will not be victimised, and
(3) if they are that they will not be accused of bad faith."

It is unlikely these issues will be at the forefront of a person's mind when they initially make a complaint. Certainly these provisions may cause people to think again before making false allegations in order simply to cause trouble. Could this, though, be better achieved by awarding costs against the complainant as in industrial relations cases where there is a frivolous use of the court's or tribunal's time, or where it is clear that the complaint has been made falsely, simply in order to cause trouble?

More importantly, the provisions about allegations made falsely and not in good faith could take away the valuable protection of a victim who cannot sufficiently prove his case. Arguably, the victim will have made his allegation in "good faith", but as already pointed out, an inadequate case may well result in a contrary finding, even though the onus of proof will rest with the alleged discriminator. Even being accused of making allegations "not in good faith" may be sufficient to disincline a victim from making a complaint at all.

## *The hurdle of causation*

The provisions relating to discrimination by victimisation are concerned with the motive which caused the alleged discriminator to treat the complainant less favourably than other persons. Therefore to show unlawful discrimination has taken place, in this context, a

[44] *op. cit.* p. 21.

complainant must establish a "causal link" showing that a particular act was done consciously with the intention of treating the complainant less favourably than other persons because he had invoked or intended to invoke the provisions of the Acts. Hence in *Aziz* v. *Trinity Street Taxis*[45], it was held that a complainant must "surmount the hurdle of causation" and show that the alleged discriminator's treatment of him was done by reference to the race relations legislation. Moreover, it has to be shown that the motive for the victimisation was consciously connected with the legislation.[46]

Clearly then this necessary "mental element" must be present and the burden of proof lies with the complainant.[47] It is only necessary to surmount the hurdle of causation when the "complainant *cannot* show that the relevant protected act" was done under the legislation and then influenced the alleged discriminator's treatment of him[48]. Clearly where this can be shown, the connection is simply a question of fact, but as we will go on to see in the next section this may be especially difficult to establish because of the way the courts and tribunals have restrictively interpreted the legislative provisions relating to victimisation.

## *Restrictive interpretation*

A victim must not only show that he was victimised because he brought proceedings against his alleged discriminator, but he must also show that the basis for the victimisation was that those proceedings were brought under the Acts.[49] Not only that, but he may also be open to the allegation of complaining falsely or not in good faith.

Thus the standard of proof is very substantial, the courts and various tribunals restrictively interpreting the provisions with regard to victimisation in both race relations cases and sexual discrimination cases. Seemingly the alleged act or omission needs to be unequivocally one of victimisation recognised under the legislation, for a victim to have a chance of judicial success. If it can be construed that an alternative motive might be the causal link rather than a motive which flows from the fact that the race relations or sex discrimination legislation had been invoked, then unlawful discrimination will not have taken place; even though the victim may well have suffered due to the

[45] [1988] 3 W.L.R. 79 (C.A.).

[46] See *Equal Opportunities Review* No. 19 pp. 37–39.

[47] See also *Hampson* v. *Department of Education and Science* [1988] I.C.R. 278 (E.A.T.) and *c.f. Birmingham City Council* v. *Equal Opportunities Commission* [1988] 3 W.L.R. 837.

[48] See *Aziz* v. *Trinity Street Taxis* [1988] 3 W.L.R. 79, *ibid.*

[49] See comments of Bingham L.J. in *Cornelius* v. *University College of Swansea* [1987] I.R.L.R. 145.

unfavourable treatment meted out. And in addition, may well face the accusation that his complaint was made in bad faith.

Equivocality of motive suggests that no protection under the legislation is available. As the commentary in the Industrial Cases Law Report points out,[50]:

> "such reasoning appears to turn the proposition that the general included the particular on its head. If someone falls squarely within the language of the statute [Sex Discrimination Act 1975] by being victimised, in fact, because they brought proceedings under the Sex Discrimination Act, they do not become 'unvictimised' because they would have been victimised if they had brought proceedings at common law."

This whole approach surely does not take a "purposive" view of the particular provisions in the legislation and protection is therefore lost whenever, it would seem according to the view of the courts and tribunals, that it cannot be shown that the specific reason for the victimisation was that the mind of the alleged discriminator was influenced by the race relations or sex discrimination legislation and for no other reason, *ie.* "by reason that" the complainant had used or intended to use the provisions of the S.D.A. or the R.R.A. So long as an alternative motive can be attributed to the alleged discriminator, which surely can quite easily be shown, then protection is lost.

Bingham L.J. in *Cornelius* v. *University College of Swansea*[51] stated:

> "If the protection simply stopped at making discrimination unlawful it would be very defective because those seeking to enforce the Act [Sex Discrimination Act 1975] by the machinery provided or to promote the operation of the Act by word or deed could be subjected to penalties (or less favourable treatment) by persons who could say with some plausibility that they were not discriminating on grounds of sex by simply penalising trouble-makers. If therefore, the objects of the Act were to be achieved, there had to be protection for those who sought to rely on it or to promote its operation. That is the purpose of section 4 .."

## *Harassment, illegal eviction and racial and sexual harassment*

Perhaps the most obvious manifestation of victimisation in the housing context is harassment and, at its worst, illegal eviction. Clearly for harassment to amount to victimisation it must be meted out

[50] At p. 118 [1987] (I.R.L.R.).
[51] At p. 145.

because a victim has invoked or intended to invoke the S.D.A. or the R.R.A.

For example where a female tenant complains to the Equal Opportunities Commission about her landlord treating her less favourably, when undertaking or failing to undertake repairs to her flat, than he treats male tenants in the same block of flats, and as a result of her complaint the landlord uses insulting behaviour towards her clearly with the intention of encouraging her to leave, then this behaviour may mount to victimisation as well as harassment. Of course, for victimisation to be proved, it would be necessary to show that the landlord's behaviour was consciously influenced "by reason that" she had invoked the provisions of the Sex Discrimination Act.

In Chapter 8 we shall examine racial and sexual harassment. There is though a close connection between such harassment and victimisation which is worth brief mention here. Neither sexual nor racial harassment are specifically recognised as unlawful by the statutes. Admittedly, sexual harassment is implicitly identified from the term which offers protection to a person in being subjected "to any other detriment" under the indirect discrimination provisions.[52] However, racial harassment was the subject of a Bill which failed to reach the statute book. Accordingly, racial harassment is not in itself unlawful but may be rendered so if it is against a clause in a tenancy agreement or amounts to criminal assault. Moreover, there are difficulties in showing that harassment of any nature has taken place. To attempt to attribute motive due to the invocation of the Acts also, adds yet a further layer of difficulty. Indeed, that the perpetrator may have an alternative motive will, under the restrictive interpretations considered, almost certainly mean that the harassment does not amount to victimisation.

## *Victimisation through non-action*

An act of victimisation is an act of discrimination. And since an act of discrimination according to its definition includes a "deliberate omission,"[53] if a landlord fails to take action upon a complaint of discrimination then victimisation can arise. However, the failure must be deliberate. And here again we are faced with motive. Deliberate in this context means deliberate in the sense of the Act, because of a person's sex or race.

In theory this provision should ensure that a landlord cannot wriggle out of an obligation to uphold the requirements of the Acts through passivity. For example, victimisation through non-action may arise

[52] See *Wileman* v. *Minilec Engineering* [1988] I.C.R. 318 (E.A.T.).
[53] See R.R.A., s. 78(1) and S.D.A., s. 82(1).

where a landlord does not take action against a particular tenant in accordance with a breach of the terms of a tenancy agreement, which attempted to prevent acts of racial harassment against other tenants, because he feels doing so would upset the majority of tenants or because he gave in to pressure from other tenants.

## *A conclusion: paucity of protection*

Restrictively interpreting the victimisation provisions of the legislation creates a hiatus of protection for victims. The fear of being victimised, as we have already seen, is the principal reason why people do not come forward more frequently to expose their discriminators and gain the protection the law recognises, in theory at least, as their right. Where people cannot be sure that the law will protect them if they come forward to complain, the law is no longer effective.

The paucity of protection now afforded to people in instances of victimisation is surely a long way from the intentions of Parliament, and thus leaves some very large question marks over the law and in particular its interpretation by the courts, as it stands at the moment. The biggest danger, of course, being that fewer victims will come forward to complain.

# Chapter four

# Indirect Discrimination

## INTRODUCTION

The most forward looking of the provisions in the Acts were those intending to prevent indirect discrimination. Following American legal principles, developed to make covert discrimination unlawful, from the *Griggs* case[1], the direct discrimination provisions were aimed at limiting the effect of practices and procedures which perpetuated discrimination against disadvantaged groups. Recognising that much discrimination flows from the practice of institutions, predominantly run by middle class white men, the provisions were aimed at breaking down barriers which prevented the progress of disadvantaged groups.

Such discriminatory practices which existed were seen as not intentional discrimination but which, because of their effect or impact, operated adversely towards minority and disadvantaged groups, so called "colour blindness" for example. But broader principles may be at work including those which Kimberley Cranshaw, commenting on race relations and the American free market, calls "race consciousness"[2]

> "White race consciousness, which included the modern belief in cultural inferiority, acts to further Black subordination by justifying all the forms of unofficial racial discrimination, injury, and neglect that flourish in a society that is only formally dedicated to equality. In more subtle ways, moreover, white race consciousness reinforces and is reinforced by the myth of equal opportunity that explains and justifies broader class hierarchies."

Born out of such a meritocratic society functioning on historical or traditional values is a reinforcement of the fairness of the system and view that "those who should logically be on the bottom are on the

[1] *Griggs* v. *Duke Power Company* [1971] 401 U.S. 424 3 F.E.D. 75.

[2] *Race, Reform and Retirement—Transformation and Legitimation in Anti-discrimination Law H.R.L.* (1988) Vol. 101 No. 7, pp. 1331–87.

bottom".[3] Thus for example the 1975 White Paper, *Racial Discrimination* states

> "The law ... should also prohibit practices which are fair in a formal sense but discriminatory in their operation and effect ... Such barriers are against the public interest irrespective of motive and whether or not they operate against an identifiable individual victim."

In a correcting sense, the notion of indirect discrimination offers a "social-philosophical concept", which, if it operates effectively, may influence the way society functions by establishing a set of legal relationships which direct the way we live. However, gaps do exist, society's reaction can lag behind legislation. There may be insufficient rights offered as part of the law or the courts themselves interpret provisions restrictively.[4]

Nonetheless, even with the presence of such difficulties there is a need to use legal methods to attack social inequality directly.[5] The concept of indirect discrimination is just such a method. Although there have been barren years since both Acts came into force with regard to the judicial interpretation of provisions, more recently the courts have as we have discussed tended to adopt more of a "purposive" view.

# THE PROVISIONS

Indirect discrimination is concerned with practices and procedures, their impact and their discriminatory effect. The provisions in the two principal statutes are almost identical. Let us examine the two relevant sections. First, under section (1)(*b*) of the R.R.A., a person discriminates against another in any relevant circumstances for the purposes of the Act if:

> "he applies to that other a requirement or condition which he applies or would apply equally to persons not of the same racial group as that other but:
> (i) which is such that the proportion of persons of the same racial group as that other who can comply with it is considerably smaller than the proportion of persons not of that racial group who can comply with it; and

[3] See discussion by C. McCrudden (1977) 6 I.L.I. 241 and *Steel* v. *Union of Post Office Workers* [1978] I.C.R. 181 (E.A.T.).
[4] For a discussion of the "gap problem" in relation to landlord and tenant law see M. Partington, *Landlord and Tenant*, Chapter 1.
[5] See *Lustgarten, op. cit.*, p. 10.

(ii) which he cannot show to be justifiable irrespective of the colour, race, nationality or ethnic or national origins of the person to whom it is applied; and
(iii) which is to the detriment of that other because he cannot comply with it."

Second, the similar section 1(1)(*b*) of the S.D.A. applies when a person discriminates against a woman under the provisions of the Act if:

> "he applies to her a requirement or condition which he applies or would apply equally to a man but:
> (i) which is such that the proportion of women who can comply with it is considerably smaller than the proportion of men who can comply with it; and
> (ii) which he cannot show to be justifiable irrespective of the sex of the person to whom it is applied; and
> (iii) which is to her detriment because she cannot comply with it."

Section 2(1) of the Act provides that section 1(*b*) has equal application to men "with such modifications as are requisite." There is no need to show less favourable treatment as with direct discrimination or victimisation. Thus, with indirect discrimination no mental element is present. It is enough to consider the effects of the requirement or condition to be discriminatory; *i.e.* detrimental so long as there is no justification for its existence.

By examining the sections we can identify four main elements:

1. application of a requirement or condition;
2. proportionately fewer people of one sex or a racial group can comply with it;
3. justification of the requirement or conditions;
4. detrimental effect.

Within these elements there are a number of other subsidiary issues, but nonetheless important, which also need to be examined. In examining these elements we will adopt the approach taken by the Employment Appeal Tribunal (E.A.T.) in *Raval* v. *Department of Health and Social Security*[6], an employment case and adapt it for a non-employment context.

## "Requirement or condition"

For a successful claim of indirect discrimination to be made a complainant must be able to show he cannot comply with a "requirement or condition". Clearly the term condition was used by the

[6] [1985] I.C.R. 685 (E.A.T.).

statute in order to have application to conditions of employment—employment issues being the main concern of the Acts—but has equal application to conditions of a tenancy agreement or other such contract. A typical example would be where an applicant to a local housing authority could not satisfy a tenant selection criterion.

Bindman, writing in 1979, suggested that there may be difficulty in establishing that a "requirement or condition" has been applied. This obligation on the complainant to prove the existence of a requirement or condition "could severely narrow the scope of indirect discrimination if interpreted to mean that there must be some express or specific statement". Where a mere practice, or state of affairs, can properly be regarded as a "requirement or condition" is still an open question. It should so be regarded in conformity with the U.S. Model.[7]

The courts have adopted the wider view suggested by Bindman. The terms "condition or requirement" overlap and were employed jointly by the statutes in order to widen the individual scope of the terms to include anything which may fall within their ordinary natural meanings.[8]

If we look at the ordinary meanings of the words as defined by the *Oxford English Dictionary*, their scope appears to be fairly wide. We must though confine the ordinary meanings of the words to the context of the Acts.

> "*Condition* Something demanded or required as a prerequisite to the granting or performance of something else; a provision, a stipulation; in a legal document a provision on which its legal force or effect is made to depend; a restriction, qualification or limitation."
>
> *Requirement* That which is called for or demanded; a condition which must be complied with.

In *Holmes* v. *Home Office*[9], the E.A.T. said the "Requirement" and "Condition" are plain, clear words of wide import and in *Clarke* v. *Eley*[10] it was suggested that "requirement" meant a provision which had to be fulfilled in order for a person to obtain a benefit. Accordingly, as Palmer and Poulton state,

> "the courts and tribunals have agreed that a wide interpretation should be given to 'requirement' and 'condition' in order to implement the object of legislation. This, they have said, is in line with the American cases ... and with the purpose of the legislation, which is to eliminate practices which have a disproportionate impact ..."[11]

[7] See G. Bindman, *Indirect Discrimination and the Race Relations Act* (1979) N.L.J. 408.
[8] See *Clarke* v. *Eley (I.M.I.) Kynoch* [1982] I.R.L.R. 131 (E.A.T.).
[9] *Supra.*
[10] I.M.I. Kynoch, supra.
[11] *op. cit.*, p. 53.

Therefore, "requirement" perhaps relates to a provision outside a contract. On the other hand a "condition" suggests a contractual obligation, but not necessarily so and may also therefore include a non-contractual obligation. Requirements or conditions may be explicit or implied, and they may be written or unwritten. It is enough that, say, a landlord places an obligation or imposes a criterion on a tenant for there to exist a requirement or condition. Similarly, it is enough that a requirement "not made explicit or in clear terms" is in the landlords' or lenders' mind.[12]

Harjit Grewal in *The Race Discrimination Handbook*, says a "requirement or condition simply means a 'must'—something which has to be complied with." A test or yardstick amounts to the same as a requirement or condition and according to Popplewell J. in *Hampson* a distinction "made between a requirement or condition and test or yardstick" is not a valid one. He went on to say "a yardstick has to be used to measure comparability but it does not prevent comparability from being a condition." For a decision to be perverse it must be shown that the wrong test had been applied.[13]

As already suggested, "indirect discrimination is unlawful whether or not the effect of the requirement or condition is appreciated and whether the effect is intended or not."[14] Whether an omission in relation to this part of section 1(1)(*b*) of both Acts has to be deliberate is open to question. The application of a "requirement or condition" suggests a positive act and it is difficult to see how an omission may as such apply to indirect discrimination. If this view is, indeed, a correct interpretation of the provisions then a significant *lacuna* exists within the legislation. Presumably the intentional exclusion of a material "requirement" could be seen as a deliberate omission. The omission would be material where its exclusion could have a disproportionate effect on the complainant because of his sex or racial group. Section 78(1) of the R.R.A. 1976 and section 82(1) of the S.D.A. 1975 clearly state that an act "includes a deliberate omission." Thus the omission in this context, seemingly would have to be intentional. Whether an accidental omission, which indirectly discriminates against a person because of their sex or racial group, was seen to be unlawful is yet to be tested. Surely the existence of such a gap is not what Parliament intended and certainly goes against the general focus on results of the indirect discrimination provisions.

Whether or not a requirement or condition creates an absolute bar is also important. The complainant needs to show he was to comply with a requirement or condition in order to gain a benefit for example to

[12] See *Thorndyke* v. *Bell Fruit (North Central)* [1979] I.R.L.R. 1 Industrial Tribunal.
[13] See *Employment Secretary* v. *Chandler* [1986] I.C.R. 436 (E.A.T.).
[14] See the *Encyclopedia of Housing* paras. 2–2632/3 and 4.

qualify for a mortgage. He must also show that the fact he cannot comply with it disqualifies him for obtaining the benefit. Therefore, the requirement or condition must amount to a prerequisite or precondition to obtaining the benefit.[15] Further, the requirement or condition has to be a mandatory requirement which constitutes an absolute bar meaning the complainant cannot comply with it. Where a criterion on access to accommodation, for example, cannot be described as mandatory and an absolute, then no unlawful discrimination arises.[16]

Additionally, the complainant must be able to show that the requirement or condition could not be complied with at the time it was imposed, *i.e.* the material time. Whether at a later date or indeed an earlier one he could comply with it is irrelevant.[17]

## "Apply equally"

The "requirement or conditions" must apply equally to others not of the same sex or racial group as the complainant. Otherwise the application of the requirement or condition may amount to direct discrimination if discriminatory content can be established. For example if it can be established that a requirement for a person to qualify for the tenancy of a vacant flat is for that person to be "white", then that is an issue of direct discrimination. If on the other hand the requirement is based on length of residence in this country it may disproportionately affect more black people than white people even though the requirement is applied equally to all applicants.

Where an individual applies for a benefit and there are no available "comparators" to determine whether a requirement or condition has been applied equally to others not of the same sex or racial group, a court will examine whether such a requirement or condition would have been applied equally. The court would need to establish the "relevant circumstances" in order to examine hypothetically whether such a requirement or condition would have been applied. Again the answer to this question will establish whether the issue is one of indirect discrimination or direct discrimination.

## "Same racial group"

In claims of indirect racial discrimination it is necessary to establish whether the complainant belongs to the "racial group" whose members

[15] See *Perera* v. *Civil Service Commission and Department of Customs and Excise* (No. 2) [1983] I.C.R. 428.

[16] See *Mear* v. *Tower Hamlets L.B.C.*, *The Times* June 3, 1988 (C.A.).

[17] See *Clarke* v. *Eley (I.M.I.) Kynoch* [1983] I.C.R. 165 and *Raval* v. *Department of Health and Social Security* [1985] I.C.R. 865 but *c.f. Turner* v. *Labour Party and Labour Party Superannuation Society* [1987] I.R.L.R. 101 (C.A.).

are disadvantaged by the condition or requirement imposed. The onus is on the complainant to show that he belongs to the racial group in question.

When defining the racial group in question there is much complexity, for example the social and economic circumstances of different ethnic groups are far from identical.[18]

Accordingly, the application of a requirement or condition may have no impact on some racial groups whilst at the same time proving to disadvantage others. A rule in a tenancy agreement relating to a tenancy in a hostel stating that no food could be consumed on the premises would certainly disadvantage Muslims who eat something immediately on breaking prayer—the timing of prayers being variable depending on the phases of the sun.

The characteristics of different racial groups and their social and economic circumstances differ enormously and it may be that an individual could belong to several such groups. For this reason it is important to establish for the purpose of a case, the correct racial group.[19] The fact that a racial group may comprise two or more distinct racial groups does not prevent it from constituting a particular racial group.[20]

This next section deals with the difficulties in establishing the distinct racial group, when examining the methods which can be adopted in determining the "relevant circumstances" of the comparison with others not of the racial group in question.

## "Relevant circumstances"

Attempting to establish indirect discrimination involves making a comparison between, say, a person of one sex and those of another in order to determine whether that person has been placed, because of a requirement or condition, in a disadvantaged position. The key to "the correct relevant comparison ... lies in correctly identifying the relevant 'circumstances' ...".[21] Indeed, the wording of the sections plainly contemplates that the relevant circumstances will subsist at the time the "requirement or condition" is applied.

Essentially, the comparison is between "pools", or racial groups of men and women defined by "the relevant circumstances".[22] The

[18] See Lustgarten *op. cit.*, pp. 47–48.
[19] See *Orphanos* v. *Queen Mary College* [1985] A.C. 761 and the excellent work by S.M. Paulter, *English Law and Ethnic Minority Customs.*
[20] R.R.A. 1976, s. 3(2).
[21] *Per* Slade L.J. in *Aziz* v. *Trinity Street Taxis* [1988] 3 W.L.R., a victimisation case but nonetheless the point about relevant comparison has equal validity.
[22] See discussion applicable to employment issues in Palmer and Poulten's work *op. cit*, pp. 56–62.

relevant circumstances of the comparison case must not be "materially different" from the case in question.[23] Accordingly, this creates a "like with like" comparison. Therefore, the case of a homeless West Indian family alleging indirect discrimination by a local housing authority must be compared with other homeless families rather than applicants generally or indeed the population at large. The relevant circumstances will be the application to the local housing authority for housing on the basis the family in question is homeless.[24]

Palmer and Poulten suggest that there are a number of further points to take into account when examining the issues of comparisons and proportions:

1. Care should be taken to ensure that the "relevant circumstances" are not themselves discriminatory,
2. The comparison is proportionate rather than absolute. As they put it the "test is whether the proportion (not number) of women who can comply is smaller than the proportion (not number) of men who can comply."
3. The results of the comparison may differ depending on the size and the nature of the groups chosen.
4. Geographical distortions may arise because of local factors, for example a "pool" selected from an inner city area may well comprise a greater proportion of ethnic minorities than a group chosen from a suburb.

## "Considerably smaller proportion"

Whether a considerably smaller proportion of the group in question can comply with the particular requirement or condition is in the main concerned with statistical findings of fact. No guidance is given in the Acts as to what is to be regarded as "considerable". A court must make a judgment on this but it is unlikely it will concern itself with issues that are seen as trivial. Accordingly, Shaw L.J. when considering a sex discrimination case indicated that the Act's provisions were "not . . . designed to provide a basis for capricious and empty complaints of differentials between the sexes." He went on to say that unlawful discrimination "involves an element of something which is inherently adverse or hostile to the interests of the persons of the sex which is said to be discriminated against".[25] Denning M.R. in

[23] R.R.A. 1976, s. 34 and S.D.A. 1975, s. 5(3).
[24] See *Orphanos* v. *Queen Mary College* [1985] and *Price* v. *Civil Service Commission* (No. 1) [1977] I.W.L.R. 1417.
[25] [1977] I.C.R. 968, at p. 973.

an equal vein suggested that "small differences in treatment" were subject to the maxim of *de minimus non curat lex.*[26]

In gathering statistical information to show that indirect discrimination has taken place, the judgment in *West Midlands Passenger Transport Executive* v. *Singh*[27], is most important. This is an employment case in which the Court of Appeal held that the complainant could have access to information on the number of applicants, successful and unsuccessful, for jobs and categorised by race. Applicants are entitled to the discovery of the number of white and non-white applicants since the

> "statistics sought were logically probative as evidence from which an inference might be drawn, that a racially discriminatory policy had been adopted which manifested itself on other occasions and that the discriminatory policy had been manifested in the present case.

This decision has very important implications for people on waiting lists, seeking mortgages and other housing related issues as well as for job humters. The decision also lends weight to the need for housing agencies to keep ethnic records and records on sex in order to review whether their practices are indirectly discriminatory or enabling them to indeed prove otherwise.

Here we have evidence of how the law relating to indirect discrimination can be effective in influencing behaviour. The Court of Appeal's decision puts an onus on the employer, landlord or indeed other housing agencies to examine their practices and policies and procedures and particularly the results of their application. Failing to do so may land them in court or open to an administrative action through one of the Commissions. Keeping records may provide reasonably probative evidence that the landlord or otherwise does not generally operate discriminatory practices. Here, the courts have added strength to the provisions, rather than offer restrictive and flimsy interpretations and may very well in the process cause agenices to sit up and take proper regard and notice.

Such record keeping may assist in highlighting historical factors which have a tendency to perpetuate the effects of past discrimination and which contrive to produce disadvantage amongst certain groups due to their sex or race.[28] A typical example may be where predominantly white and middle class housing visitors employ subjective assessments which influence whether a tenant has priority

[26] *Peake* v. *Automotive Products* [1978] Q.B. 233 at p. 236 but *c.f.* views expressed in *Ministry of Defence* v. *Jeremiah* [1980] Q.B. 87 and *Gill* v. *El Vino Co.* [1983] Q.B. 425.
[27] [1988] I.W.L.R. 730.
[28] See *Steel* v. *Union of Post Office Workers* [1977] I.R.L.R. 288 (E.A.T.) and McCrudden's important work, *Institutional Racism* (1977) 6 I.L.J. 241.

for a transfer. Making judgments based on their own value systems rather than a basic need, may well disproportionately disadvantage some groups.

For this reason, all housing agencies need to examine the exercise of discretion by their staff. It is with the use of subjective assessments that unintentional or accidental discrimination can arise. Even apparently objectively based assessments can be unintentionally discriminatory since their formulation may have been open to the same subjective value systems. There is for example a very close connection between racial disadvantagement and poverty and although it is unlikely that judgments based on income levels and wealth would be regarded by the courts as a sustainable argument for indirect discrimination, a decision made in this way will undoubtedly discriminate against ethnic minorities. Indeed, such an approach is the very undercurrent of many decisions and judgments made in our society and will continue to be so.[29] However, not all judgments made by the court need be the subject of statistical evidence. A court can decide what statistical evidence is not needed, certain facts being taken for granted.[30]

As to what constitutes a "considerably" smaller proportion there is little statutory guidance. In America the courts have used "a rule of thumb". If the success rate for women or non-whites is less than 80 per cent. than for men or whites respectively, then in general it is taken as evidence of discrimination. However, it is not rigidly applied. In Britain a difference of 20 per cent. has been held to be considerable, whereas a difference of 10 per cent. has not.[31—32]

"Nil" still amounts to a proportion. Therefore, where a rule is applied which excludes altogether a particular group, for example a racial group or women, the fact that no member of the group can comply with it means that no proportion is present to make a comparison, does not stop the comparison being made. Indeed, such a rule is highly likely to amount to direct discrimination.[33]

## JUSTIFICATION

Racial discrimination or sexual discrimination in an indirect sense cannot be determined solely on the basis that a condition or

[29] *James* v. *Valtierra* 402 U.S. 137 (1971) and discussion in Lustgarten's work *op. cit.*, pp. 8–9.

[30] See *Kidd* v. *D.R.G. (U.K.)* [1985] I.C.R. 405, (E.A.T.) but *c.f. Bilka-Kaufhaus GmbH* v. *Karin Weber Von Hartz* (No. 170/84) [1987] I.C.R. 110 (European Court).

[31] See *Moyes* v. *Borders Regional Council* (1984) S/1066/83 and *Fulton* v. *Strathclyde Regional Council* (1985) (E.A.T.) 949/83 both quoted by Palmer and Poulton. For an examination of the difficulties of statistical proof, see Lustgarten *op. cit.*, p. 50.

[33] See *Greencroft Social Club and Institute* v. *Mullen* [1985] I.C.R. 796 (E.A.T.).

requirement cannot be complied with because of a person's sex or racial group. The legislation provides the "escape" clause of justification.[34]

Consequently, where an alleged discriminator can show that he applied a condition or requirement which did indirectly discriminate because of a person's sex or racial group, but that the application of that condition or requirement was "justifiable" on a basis other than a person's sex or racial group, then the discrimination would be lawful. The burden of proof of justification rests with the alleged discriminator. Whether an indirectly discriminatory requirement or condition is justifiable is a question of fact[35] and which "requires an objective test" to be applied along with consideration of the particular circumstances.[36]

However the term "justifiable" is not to be interpreted as it has been under section 1(3) of the Equal Pay Act 1970 to mean both "necessary" and "real need". The test of "justifiable" is a much lower standard than that of necessity and does not offer as comprehensive a description as "necessity".[37] Although the S.D.A. 1975 and the Equal Pay Act 1970 should be construed and applied as a "harmonious whole" and can be regarded as two parts of a single comprehensive code directed against sex discrimination,[38] it is too big a jump to interpret the different wording of section 1(1)(*b*) and section 1(3) of the respective statutes to mean the same. The usefulness of such an approach would be to impute a similar "necessary" and "real need" meaning to the justifiable clauses of the S.D.A. and R.R.A. 1976, because both must be construed in the same manner.[39]

In order to understand the meaning of the term "justifiable" it is necessary to adopt a "purposive" approach to the legislation bearing in mind that attempts to replace the word "justifiable" with "necessary" were defeated during the passage of the legislation through Parliament. Accordingly, when considering whether a requirement or condition was justifiable the ordinary dictionary meaning of the term should be adopted. With this in mind Eveleigh L.J. in *Ojutiku and Oburoni* v. *Manpower Services Commission*[40] says:

[34] See comments of Kilner Brown in *Tower Hamlets London Borough Council* v. *Qyyum* [1987] I.C.R. 729 (E.A.T.).

[35] See comments of Hutchinsons J. in *Secretary of State for Employment* v. *Chandler* [1986] I.C.R. 436 (E.A.T.) at p. 446 and *Panesar* v. *Nestlé Co.* [1980] I.C.R. 144 (C.A.).

[36] See *Hampson* v. *Department of Education and Science* [1988] I.C.R. 278 (E.A.T.).

[37] *Per* Kilner Bram in *Gwynedd County Court* v. *Jones* [1986] I.C.R. 833.

[38] *E. Coomes* v. *Shields* [1988] I.R.L.R. 81.

[39] See the decision of the House of Lords in *Rainey* v. *Greater Glasgow Health Board* [1987] A.C. 224; *Bilka-Kaufhaus Gmbh* v. *Karin Weber Von Hartz* (No. 170/84) [1987] I.C.R. 110; *Ojutibu and Oburoni* v. *Manpower Services Commission* [1982] I.C.R. 661; and *Hampson* v. *Department of Education and Science* [1988] I.C.R. 278 (E.A.T.).

[40] *Supra* at p. 668.

> "I would turn to a dictionary definition which says 'to adduce adequate grounds for'; and it seems to me that if a person produces reasons for doing something, which would be acceptable to right-thinking people as sound and tolerable reasons for so doing, then he has justified his conduct."

One such "sound and tolerable reason" would be arguably that the condition or requirement was necessary. Otherwise it is necessary that "an objective test be applied to the position of both" parties to a complaint,[41] requiring an examination of the requirement or condition not simply "as a matter of principle but also of its effect as a matter of practice." In *Steel* v. *Union of Post Office Workers*[42] it was said that to judge whether a requirement or condition was justifiable it is necessary to weigh the need for the requirement against its discriminatory effect. The difficulty of carrying out this balancing exercise shows the problem of applying a term such as "justifiable". Hence Bindman[43] says:

> "A clearer test is that of 'necessity' while the word necessary cannot be precisely equated with justifiable, ... reference was made with approval in the *Steel* case to the American view (in the *Griggs* case ...) that practices perpetuating the effects of the past discrimination could not be justified except by 'business necessity', *i.e.* unless it was absolutely necessary for the business to operate satisfactorily and not merely desirable or convenient."

Whether the "Sound and Tolerable" reasons approach adopted in *Ojutiku*[44] provides an objective test is open to debate. And as the editorial commentary[45] says:

> "What is clear is that the evidentiary standard required to show that a discriminatory requirement was imposed for what would be regarded by 'right-thinking people' as a 'sound and tolerable reason' is far lower than that required to show that there is a 'real need' for the requirement and that it is 'necessary'."

For a defendant to claim this approach is justifiable as a "sound and tolerable reason" it must be on good grounds such as hygiene or public health. Matters of practical convenience or public image are not sufficient reasons for justification to apply.[46] Where a rule is made in the interest of safety and good management it is unlikely that discrimination will arise,[47] but the circumstances of the risks to safety

[41] See *Hampson* v. *Department of Education and Science supra* at p. 295.
[42] [1978] I.C.R. 181 (E.A.T.).
[43] *op. cit*, p. 410.
[44] [1988] I.R.L.R. 661.
[45] At p. 582.
[46] *Kingston and Richmond Health Authority* v. *Kaur* [1981] I.C.R. 631.
[47] *Peake* v. *Automotive Products* [1978] Q.B. 33.

and the measures necessary to eliminate them must also be considered.[48] The application of higher rents or charges for services would generally not be justifiable and may amount to direct discrimination.[49]

In the context of housing or service provision if a court adopted the same approach as an Employment Appeal Tribunal in examining the justification of a requirement or condition, according to M. Malone[50] the following may be taken into account,

1. Has the alleged discrimination recognised and considered the discriminatory effect of the requirement?
2. How serious is the discriminating effect?
3. What purpose is to be achieved by the requirement?
4. Is there a non-discriminatory or less discriminatory way to achieve the same objective?
5. Weighing and balancing these factors can the requirement be regarded as fair and reasonable in an objective sense?

## Detriment

If the "escape clause" of justification cannot be claimed by the alleged discriminator it still falls to be determined whether the victim has suffered a detriment as a result of the application of the indirectly discriminatory condition or requirement. It is for the complainant to show he has personally suffered a detriment.

There are two elements to this test of detriment, of *locus standi* as it has been described by Lustgarten.[51] The first element is whether the complainant "can comply" with the condition or requirement; and the second element is whether as a result of not being able to comply he has suffered a detriment.

In *Price* v. *Civil Service Commission* (No. 2)[52] it was held that it "should not be said that a person 'can' do something merely because it is theoretically possible for him to do so, it is necessary to see whether he can do so in practice." Reinforcing this view the House of Lords in *Mandla* v. *Lee*[53] felt that a literal reading of the word 'can' would have the effect of depriving members of ethnic groups from much of the protection Parliament had intended the R.R.A. 1976 to provide. Instead the word meant "can in practice" or more precisely "can consistently with the customs and cultural conditions of the racial group."

48 See *Page* v. *Freighthire Tank Haulage* [1981] I.C.R. 299 (E.A.T.).
49 *Orphanos* v. *Queen Mary College* [1985] A.C. 761 (H.L.).
50 In *A Practical Guide to Discrimination Law*, pp. 216–217.
51 *op. cit.*, p. 51.
52 [1977] I.W.L.R. 1417.
53 [1983] A.C. 548.

A "detriment may be any injury to feelings or loss of dignity and need not be confused with purely financial loss. The complainant must have suffered himself some sort of disadvantage[54] and consequently only the victim himself may bring a claim.[55] Because of this such claims are individual in nature and cannot therefore be raised by a group of people, for example a racial group against a particular landlord or other institution.

There exists no provision for housing and services cases similar to that which applies to employment complaints in relation to "some other detriment" suffered by a complainant. The provision is not restricted narrowly but covers situations where a person is "disadvantaged in the circumstances and conditions" in which they find themselves within an employment context. The application of such a provision to a wider context would have given important and flexible protection.[56]

# HOUSING EXAMPLES OF INDIRECT DISCRIMINATION

This application of a requirement or condition is often hidden away and difficult to identify. It is crucial to a successful claim that the particular discriminatory requirement or condition is clearly identifiable.[57] Some examples of indirectly discriminatory requirement or conditions which have been identified within the housing context are as follows:

(1) The application by a local authority, for example, of a requirement for access to its housing that an applicant must have been resident in its area for a specified period or gives greater waiting for longer periods of residence may be indirectly discriminatory against ethnic minorities who may be less able than other groups to comply.[58]

(2) The application of a requirement or condition that to be rehoused in a new property a person seeking rehousing must be a decant case where people in need of decant are almost exclusively white;[59] or entering into a decanting agreement

[54] *Ministry of Defence* v. *Jeremiah* [1980] Q.B. 87.

[55] A good discussion of this point is to be found in O'Donovan and Szyszczak's work, *Indirect Discrimination: Taking a Concept to Market II* [1985] N.L.J. 43.

[56] See *De Souza* v. *Automobile Association* [1986] I.C.R. 514 (C.A.).

[57] See *Francis and Others* v. *British Airways Engineering Overhaul Limited* [1982] I.R.L.R. 10 (E.A.T.).

[58] See Bindman *Indirect Discrimination and the Race Relations Act 1976* (1979) N.L.J. 408.

[59] See C.R.E., *Racial Discrimination in Liverpool City Council: Report of a Formal Investigation* (1989), p. 58.

with a group of tenants who are predominantly white that they should be rehoused, excluding other applicants from those arrangements.[60]

(3) The use of racial stereotyping[61];

(4) Assuming applicants should be steered to particular areas due to their racial origin[62];

(5) The application of a condition or requirement for the purpose of a mortgage request which treats highest earners in a household who are women differently from where highest earners are men.[63]

(6) The application of restrictions which prevent lending on a house without a front garden may well be disproportionately disadvantageous to ethnic communities.[64]

(7) The application of criteria to applicants for housing which determine a lower priority for one parent families.

(8) The adoption of practices by, for example estate agents and private landlords when letting accommodation which are designed to put off ethnic minorities or one parent families. Examples are advertising in newspapers or other places which are less likely to be read or seen by ethnic minorities or one parent families.[65]

These examples can apply equally with respect to a person's sex and in management of housing, as well as access to housing.

[60] C.R.E., *Out of Order: Report of Formal Investigation of Southwark LBC* (1990), pp. 23–27.

[61] C.R.E., *Sorry It's Gone: Testing for Racial Discrimination in the Private Rented Sector* (1990), p. 34.

[62] *Ibid.*

[63] See E.O.C., *"It's not Your Business, It's How the Society Works"* (1978).

[64] See C.R.E., *Race and Mortgage Lending: Report of Formal Investigation* (1985).

[65] See Bindman *op. cit.*

# Chapter five

# General Exceptions to Sex and Race Discrimination

## INTRODUCTION

It is important when considering whether a particular instance of discrimination is unlawful to ask first whether that type of discrimination falls within the general exceptions stated in the Acts. It is for the defendant to show that their instance of discrimination falls within such an exception.[1] In this chapter we shall, therefore, examine the general exceptions. Some of these exceptions apply to both sex and race discrimination, whereas one general exception applies only to sex discrimination. There are other general exceptions but we shall only comment on those exceptions which have direct relevance in the housing field.

## GENERAL EXCEPTIONS: RACE AND SEX DISCRIMINATION

There are two principal exceptions which apply to race and sex discrimination, the exception for charities and the exception for acts performed under statutory authority. The two other general exceptions recognised by both Acts permit some discrimination in the field of sport and in the interest of national security. Since these have no direct relevance in the field of housing we need not consider them further here and will concentrate on discrimination by charities and through acts done under statutory authority.

### Charities

Whenever a charitable instrument contains a provision which confers benefits only on members of a particular racial group, without making

[1] See *Commission for Racial Equality* v. *Prestige Group* [1984] I.C.R. 473 at p. 479.

reference to colour, or similarly confers benefits only on men, or only on women, any resultant discrimination is not unlawful.[2] A "charitable instrument" means an "enactment or other instrument passed or made for charitable purposes, or an enactment or other instrument so far as it relates to charitable purposes".[3] In the housing context purposes are charitable if they are concerned with the needs of the elderly or infirm, or are for other purposes beneficial to the community, or are for the public benefit and provide for the relief of poverty.[4] Section 34(1) of the R.R.A. 1976 ensures that any provision contained in a charitable instrument which has the effect of conferring benefits on persons of a particular colour is void and any attempt to enforce such a provision is made illegal. If such a provision exists then the act has the effect of conferring like benefits:[5]

"(a) on persons of the class which results in the restriction by reference to colour is disregarded; or

(b) where the original class is defined by reference to colour only, on persons generally."

"Defined by reference to colour only" leaves open provisions which define a racial group in other terms, for example by national origin. A charitable benefit for the "Asian residents of Handsworth" would be lawful, whereas a benefit for the "black residents of Handsworth" would confer benefits on residents of Handsworth generally.[6]

## Acts done under statutory authority

Any act of discrimination which is done under statutory authority is not unlawful.[7] Under the S.D.A. this applies only to acts or instruments passed before the commencement of the act. Whereas, under the R.R.A. the provision applies to all enactments, orders in council, instruments and to acts performed in order to comply with any condition or requirement imposed by a minister of the Crown by virtue of authority derived from an enactment. In addition, the R.R.A. permits discrimination on the basis of nationality, place of ordinary residence or length of residence in or outside of the United Kingdom, if the act is done:

[2] S.D.A., ss. 43(1) and (2) and R.R.A., ss. 34(2) and (3).
[3] S.D.A., s. 43(3), S.I. 1977 No. 528 and R.R.A., s. 34(4). For the meaning of "charitable purposes" see s. 43(4) and R.R.A., s. 34(4) and Lord Macnaughten's classification in *Commissioners of Income Tax* v. *Pemsel* [1891] A.C. 531 at p. 583.
[4] See for example *Hugh-Jones* v. *St. John's College, Cambridge* [1977] I.C.R. 848 and D. G. Cracknell's discussion in *Law Relating to Charities* pp. 35–36.
[5] R.R.A., s. 34(1).
[6] See other similar examples given in *The Enclyopedia of Housing Law and Practice* para. 2–2632/32.
[7] S.D.A., s. 51(1) and R.R.A., s. 41(1).

(a) in pursuance of any arrangements made by or within the approach of a Minister; or
(b) in order to comply with any condition imposed by a Minister.

Thus the R.R.A. would seem to "cover all possible forms of legislation or delegated legislation, *i.e.* statutes, orders in council, statutory instruments and statutory rules and orders".[8] Mr. Justice Wood went on to say that although "the protected acts can be carried out by anyone, this protection will mostly be relevant when examining the activities of bodies created by statute".[9] As Malone says in his *A Practical Guide to Discrimination Law*[10] The "most significant aspect of statutory racial discrimination is in immigration control". In immigration control, officers are required to make discriminatory decisions, there is no alternative approach. There is, though, some evidence to show that an immigration control style approach has been adopted by some local authorities when requiring "passports" before admitting people on to their waiting lists. Such an approach cannot be justified on the basis of statutory authority. Indeed, it is difficult to envisage any circumstances in which adopting such an approach could be justified. As P. Gordan *et al* in *Race Relations Rights*[11] says, "local authority departments and others demand to see passports of black people when they apply for jobs, social services, housing and so on. This is often justified on the grounds that it is necessary to check a person's immigration status to make sure they can take up employment, are entitled to state education and housing, or are entitled to welfare benefits. This is inevitably discriminatory in that it never applies to white people."

Local authorities would seem to be the main housing agency likely to claim a particular responsibility to perform acts under statutory authority, since they are primarily creatures of government. The need to comply with the "homeless" provisions of the Housing Act 1985 most readily comes to mind as an example. The Housing Corporation could similarly claim such status in circumstances when it follows ministerial guidance or complies with statutory conditions or requirements. The interests of safety provide no justification for discrimination on the grounds of sex where statutory requirements are in operation.[12]

Even though the R.R.A. provides opportunity for a wider defence, "for any act of discrimination done ... in pursuance of any enactment" than the S.D.A., it does not provide an "umbrella defence". If it did according to Wood J. "then complete protection is given even for acts

[8] *General Medical Council* v. *Goba* [1988] I.R.L.R. 425 at p. 429.
[9] *Ibid.*
[10] At p. 34.
[11] At p. 12.
[12] See *Page* v. *Freighthire Tank Haulage* [1981] I.C.R. 299 (E.A.T.).

which are grossly and inexcusably discriminatory. We cannot think that such was the intention of the draftsmen of the statute". Instead the act complained of "in its doing and in the way it was carried out must be one which was reasonably necessary" in order that the defendant could comply with any statutory "condition or requirement".[13] Relying on this judgment the effect of the provision in the Race Relations Act is consequently narrowed to be similar to that of the equivalent provision in the Sex Discrimination Act.

## GENERAL EXCEPTION: SEX DISCRIMINATION

The S.D.A. contains a general exception in the case of discrimination in the provision of communal accommodation. "Communal accommodation" means:

(a) residential accommodation which includes dormitories or other shared sleeping accommodation which for reasons of privacy and decency should be used by men only, or by women only; but which may include some shared sleeping accommodation for men, and some for women, or some ordinary sleeping accommodation[14]; and includes
(b) residential accommodation all or part of which should be used by men only, or by women only, because of the nature of sanitary facilities serving the accommodation.[15]

Consequently, it is not unlawful to discriminate in the admission of people to communal accommodation, so long as the way that the accommodation is managed, "given the exigencies of the situation, comes as near as may be to fair and equitable treatment of men and women".[16] In considering what may amount to "fair and equitable treatment" and whether this is appropriate in the circumstances account is taken of,[17]

(a) whether and how far it is reasonable to expect that the accommodation should be altered or extended, or that further alternative accommodation should be provided; and
(b) the frequency of the demand or need for use of the accommodation by men as compared with women.

[13] *General Medical* v. *Goba* [1988] I.R.L.R. 425 at p. 429.
[14] s. 46(1).
[15] s. 46(2).
[16] s. 46(3).
[17] s. 46(4).

Thus this allows for communal accommodation to be adapted in order that it may cater more equally for the sexes.

In support of this provision where a service, benefit or facility can only be effectively provided to persons using accommodation, then any resultant discrimination is not unlawful if "the woman or, as the case may be, the man could lawfully be refused the use of the accommodation".[18]

The exception concerning communal accommodation is without prejudice to the generality of section 35(1)(*c*) which applies specifically to situations where standards of modesty and decency need to be maintained. Typical examples would be in the provision of lavatories and other sanitary facilities and dormitories.[19]

[18] s. 46(5)(*b*).
[19] See Chapter 8 for fuller discussion.

# Chapter six
# Positive Action

## INTRODUCTION

Positive discrimination, or reverse discrimination as it is sometimes referred to, is unlawful. Both principal Acts afford protection against discrimination on the basis of race or sex to all people regardless of their sex or ethnic origins and effectively create a "non-discriminatory" regime.[1] For example discriminating in the favour of one sex by the application of a condition or requirement would seem to be discrimination adversely against the other. In such circumstances the group or individual affected could claim a "detriment" if adversely affected.[2] Although positive discrimination is unlawful, the Acts contain a number of provisions which allow "positive action". As the White Paper[3] puts it, 'if the principle of non-discrimination is interpreted too literally and inflexibly it may actually impede the elimination of invidious discrimination and the encouragement of equal opportunity. By "positive action" or "affirmative action"[4] we mean action which is intended to help redress any imbalance in under-represented groups.' Examples which most readily come to mind can be found in the employment scene where particular training schemes have been set up to train women or ethnic minorities for jobs where few people from these groups are employed. An example of one such scheme encouraging the training and employment of ethnic minorities in housing is the P.A.T.H. (Positive Action Training in Housing) initiative.

Although under the R.R.A. the "positive action" provisions have wide application[5] and can apply within the housing field, under the S.D.A. the provisions are restricted to the employment field.[6] Why this restriction should apply is not entirely clear. Women suffer unfavourable treatment in fields other than employment. The lack of

[1] See the White Paper, *Racial Discrimination* Cmnd. 6234 para. 57.
[2] *Jeremiah* v. *Ministry of Defence* [1980] Q.G. St (E.A.T.).
[3] *Ibid.*, para. 57.
[4] See Pannick *op. cit.* pp. 313–15.
[5] s. 35.
[6] ss. 47–49.

application to other fields demonstrates the Act's concentration on employment issues rather than demonstrating that discrimination against women in the field is non-existence.

# SPECIAL NEEDS OF RACIAL GROUPS

The special needs of particular racial groups in regard to their education, training and welfare, or any ancillary benefits can be met without such acts being unlawful.[7] This is achieved by creating a further general exception to the application of the provisions of the Act.[8] Thus privileged access to facilities and services which help to meet special needs in relation to "welfare" and any ancillary benefits is lawful. Whether the interpretation of "welfare" as a term would stretch to include the provision of accommodation is arguable. In the general sense, the provision of accommodation may not in itself meet welfare needs; on the other hand, as part of a positive approach of meeting the identified special welfare needs of a particular racial group may well qualify, especially where other welfare services are being provided. A typical example of this would be hostel accommodation where the provision of housing and welfare services go hand in hand.[9] The key would seem to be that the special welfare needs are clearly identified and that housing is provided to meet those needs in part or as a whole. Where housing alone could meet such needs may suggest the need is general rather than specific, although Lustgarten[10] gives the general example of a housing association, announcing vacancies in its flats by the circularisation of information to people in areas where there are high ethnic minority populations. What view the courts would may would seem to depend on the interpretation of the term "welfare". The Act itself offers no guidance. The ordinary and natural usage of the term is a "state of faring well or well being" and thus would generally apply to the living conditions of a particular group. "Welfare work" usually relates to the improvement of living conditions. If one takes this view then where a particular group is disadvantaged in its living conditions surely special welfare needs will arise as a result. If the provision of housing, or the provision of services or benefits or facilities in relation to housing or in addition to it, would meet welfare needs, then that provision would be directed towards meeting the special needs of the group in question and therefore lawful. After all, shelter is indisputably fundamental to the welfare of us all. This view

[7] R.R.A., s. 35.
[8] For other general exceptions see Chapter 5.
[9] See *The Encyclopaedia of Housing* paras. 2–2632/34.
[10] *op. cit.* p. 29.

would seem to be borne out by an examination of the "indirect discrimination" elements of the Act. If a housing organisation wishes to ensure it does not indirectly discriminate in letting its accommodation and in the provision of any related services, benefits or facilities, its approach would seem to necessitate some form of positive action. In general terms various racial groups have historically suffered housing discrimination. In *Racial Disadvantage in Britain*, as Smith[11] puts it, there "are dramatic differences between the minority groups and the rest of the population in terms of housing tenure and the quality of housing occupied . . .". More recent studies show that such disadvantage remains.[12] Unless some form of positive action is introduced by housing organisations these historical and present inequalities will remain unabated as the result of the continued application of indirect discriminatory practices. Thus the elimination of indirect discrimination can only be achieved through positive or affirmative action. An example might be where a housing association, although operating in an area with a sizeable population of Muslims lets very few of its properties to that particular group. Unless it takes positive steps to promote itself with the Muslim community through publicity, relationships with voluntary bodies and community groups and the translation of its literature, it is unlikely to remedy the indirectly discriminatory allocation of its accommodation. Thus in such circumstances "positive action" is a necessity even on the simple level of avoiding unlawful discrimination. If anything the law itself can introduce and even breed negative thinking and defensiveness — by allowing landlords, developers and housing agencies to do just enough to fulfill their obligations under the Act and not enter into the spirit of equal opportunity. Pat Niner and Valerie Karn comment on this point in relation to housing associations[13] and suggest such housing agencies could take the following action:

1. increase the number of ethnic minority applicants;
2. ensure that the proportion of ethnic minority applicants at least equals their representation in the local population;
3. ensure that the local ethnic minority population are fully aware of the existence of the association and what it can offer, and that they are encouraged to apply if the association can meet their needs;
4. examine the development programme of new housing to ensure that it meets ethnic minority needs.

[11] At p. 210

[12] *e.g.*, Commission for Racial Equality (CRE) *Race and Housing in Liverpool: A Research Report* (1986), Pat Niner and Valerie Karn, *Housing Association Allocations: Achieving Racial Equality* (1986) and CRE, *Homeless and Discrimination: Report of a Formal Investigation Into the London Borough of Tower Hamlets* (1988).

[13] *Housing Association Allocations: Achieving Racial Equality* pp. 149–150.

The advice would seem to be of value to all housing agencies which wish to operate under a spirit of equal opportunity and wish to eliminate indirect discrimination.

A prerequisite to such an approach would seem to be the need to keep ethnic records, monitor such records and take positive steps to deal with any evident discrimination and publish the results. There is no statutory duty, as such, to keep such records[14] but there is wide consensus in some housing sectors (particularly for local housing authorities and housing associations) that such records help to ensure that neither direct nor indirect discrimination takes place and provide evidence to prove as much. Monitoring such records can show where indirect discriminatory practices are taking effect and thus assist in the elimination of such practices, supporting any other positive action taken by the agency concerned. However, keeping ethnic records and undertaking periodic monitoring is seen as "good practice" in the Codes of Practice for the elinination of racial equality in the field of housing.[15]

## *A note on record keeping*

In 1983 the Commission for Racial Equality served a Non-Discrimination Notice[16] on the London Borough of Hackney taking the view that the council "had unlawfully discriminated against black applicants and tenants in allocations". The Commission made the recommendation that the council keep and monitor ethnic records. In the preface to its report *Race and Council Housing in Hackney: Report of Formal Investigation* (1984)[17] the Commission stated:

> "It is worth noting that an important precedent was set in issuing this non-discrimination notice against Hackney Council, in that it is the first time such a notice has been issued solely on the basis of statistical evidence. Until now, findings of discrimination have generally been centred on individual acts of discrimination. The practical difficulty of relying on this approach is that the scope for comparison, to determine whether there has been less favourable treatment on racial grounds, is necessarily narrow. When one finds less favourable treatment there will often be factors present which might appear to explain away the differences on non-racial grounds. However, when large numbers of cases are examined statistically, and less favourable treatment of a racial group is

[14] For the use of statistics see *West Midlands Passenger Transport Executive* v. *Singh* [1988] 1 W.L.R. 730 (E.A.T.).
[15] See paras. 6.1–6.4.
[16] See Chapter 13.
[17] p. 6.

established, and one then examines all possible non-racial explanations statistically, it becomes possible to say with statistical certainty whether they can in fact explain the difference. In practice, non-racial explanations start falling away when subjected to this kind of scrutiny. This is the reason why the Commission is insistent that ethnic record keeping and monitoring are essential to securing equality of opportunity, not only in the housing field, but elsewhere".

The Commission recommended that the council should, "record the ethnic origin of all persons applying for housing and being rehoused" and that the records should be analysed at quarterly intervals in relation to:[18]

"(a) the quality of accommodation offered (examining the type of property, age and quality factors including size);
(b) the quality of accommodation allocated if different from that offered; and
(c) allocation to estate or parts of estates regarded as 'difficult to let'."

For a more detailed examination of ethnic record keeping and advice on the basis of such records and methods of analysis see *Ethnic Record Keeping and Monitoring* (1985).

# POSITIVE ACTION AND WOMEN

Although, as mentioned in the introduction of this chapter the positive action provisions of the S.D.A. apply only to the employment field, there would seem to be some scope in attempting to eliminate indirect indiscrimination by positive action and such action remaining lawful. This may be essential to ensure housing agencies do not discriminate on the grounds of sex or marital status. Where for example in a shelter for homeless people, few women are housed even though there are homeless women in the area, it would seem essential to promote the shelter more fully to homeless women by whatever positive measures may eliminate indirect discrimination. However, positive action in any wider sense may well amount to reverse discrimination or preferential treatment and amount to unlawful discrimination against men.[19] Minor differences in treatment of women or men for that matter may be subject to the maxim de minimus non curat lex.[20]

[18] *Ibid.* p. 144.
[19] *Jeremiah* v. *Ministry of Defence* [1980] Q.B.D. 84 (C.A.).
[20] *Peake* v. *Automotive Products* [1978] Q.B. 233 (C.A.).

# Chapter seven
# Forms of Housing Discrimination

## INTRODUCTION

Discrimination in the context of housing can arise from the disposal or management of premises or from the provision of goods, facilities or services. Whether or not unlawful discrimination arises in a particular case also depends on whether it is subject to the specific and general exceptions of the Acts.[1] Discrimination can also arise when a landlord considers whether to give consent to an assignment or sub-letting[2] or in the application of discriminatory practices.[3] (Chapter eight).

Indeed, we have already seen in Part I that unlawful discrimination arises only if the discriminatory act or omission, condition or requirement is in relation to purposes defined by the Acts, "for the purposes of any provision of the Acts".[4] Although the provisions of the Acts are primarily concerned with the elimination of discrimination in the employment field they are also concerned with discrimination in the disposal and management of property and the provision of goods, facilities and services. Clearly discrimination can and does arise in these fields.

Besides the fields of employment, education, housing and the supply of goods and services, the Acts also contain more general provisions, with the intention of eliminating discriminatory practices.[5]

## DISCRIMINATION IN THE DISPOSAL OF PREMISES

The provisions of both Acts are written in almost identical terms, again with the intention of avoiding differences in their judicial interpretations.[6] Section 21(1) of R.R.A. reads:

[1] S.D.A., ss. 29–30 and R.R.A., ss. 20–21 see this chapter for specific exceptions and Chapter 5 for general exceptions.
[2] S.D.A., s. 31 and R.R.A., s. 24.
[3] Chapter 8.
[4] See S.D.A., s. 1(1) and R.R.A., 1(1).
[5] See Chapter 8.
[6] See White Paper, *Racial Discrimination* (1975) Cmnd. 6234, para. 68.

> "It is unlawful for a person, in relation to premises in Great Britain of which he has power to dispose, to discriminate against another:
> (a) in the terms on which he offers him these premises; or
> (b) by refusing his application for those premises; or
> (c) in his treatment of him in relation to any list of persons in need of premises of that description."

Apart from its format the section is similar to the earlier provisions in the Race Relations Act 1968.[7]

The power to dispose of premises includes granting a right to occupy[8] and would also apply in theory to premises not yet completed.[9–10] Clearly this definition is intended to be as wide as possible in order to encompass any methods or types of disposal. Certainly a right to occupy premises ensures that granting a licence would be within the scope of the Acts.[11] "Premises" takes on its ordinary natural meaning in the context of property and includes land, houses and buildings etc.[12] Generally the word "premises" is used to suggest single ownership or occupation,[13] and is also sufficiently wide to cover property other than residential accommodation, including offices, shops and other commercial and industrial property, including farm land. Indeed the R.R.A. states that unless the context otherwise requires, the term "premises" includes land of any description.[14] It is an odd omission that the S.D.A. does not include a similar reference. This may be because the S.D.A. was drafted first. Since the interpretation of the Acts is meant to be similar, the same meaning given to "premises" to include land under the R.R.A. can, it could be argued, be imputed to sex discrimination cases. Certainly the provision in the R.R.A. most closely corresponds with its predecessor in the Race Relations Act 1968 which referred to "housing accommodation, business premises or other land".[15] "Land" includes buildings or other structures along with any estate, interest, easement, servitude or right in or over land.[16]

Certainly the sale or other disposal of house plots or other units fall within the protection of the Acts, because of the inclusion of land within the definition of premises. In *Race Relations Board* v. *Haigh & Co.,*[17] a

[7] s. 5.
[8] S.D.A., s. 82(1), and R.R.A., s. 78(1).
[9–10] See *Race Relations Board* v. *Geo. H. Haigh and Co.* (1969) 119 N.L.J. 858.
[11] See *Jowitts' Dictionary of English Law* for general definition of "disposal".
[12] *Bracey* v. *Read* [1963] Ch. 88; [1962] 3 All E.R. 472; *Maunsell* v. *Olus* [1975] A.C. 373 (H.L.).
[13] *Brickwood & Co.* v. *Reynolds* [1898] 1 Q.B. 95 and *Halsbury's Statutes* Vol. 6 p. 720.
[14] s. 78(2).
[15] s. 5.
[16] See Interpretation Act 1978, s. 5, Sched. 1, see also s. 22(1) and Sched. 2, para. 5(*b*).
[17] (1969) 119 N.L.J. 858.

case under the Race Relations Act 1968, it was held that for accommodation to be protected it need not be:

(a) immediately available, or
(b) complete.

If this were the case builders, developers or intending landlords would have the ability to avoid the provisions of the Acts.[18]

However, "premises" do not include accommodation in an hotel or similar establishment which is excluded because it is covered separately under the provisions relating to the supply of goods, facilities and services.[19]

A company, association, whether or not incorporated, a trust, local authority along with an individual would be included in the definition of a "person", the definition includes a body of persons corporate or incorporate unless the contrary intention is expressed in the Acts.[20] *Quaere* whether a partnership, (estate agents and solicitors in the housing context) is a body or "persons incorporate"?[21]

Discrimination in relation to the disposal of premises encompasses the direct, indirect and victimisation provisions of the Acts.[22]

Both key provisions of the Acts[23] state that where a person disposes of premises discrimination is unlawful, subject to the general and specific exceptions (discussed below):

(a) in the terms of disposal;[24]
(b) by refusing an application;[25] or
(c) in the treatment of people in relation to a waiting list.[26]

## Terms of disposal

"Terms of disposal" would include any material consideration in relation to the disposal of premises. Tenants or other occupiers are at a distinct disadvantage in the rented sector because there exists a significant shortage of available rented accommodation. This effectively means that they are placed with little choice, and as a result possess a poor bargaining position. Arguably, the more disadvantaged a

[18] See also MacDonald *op. cit.* pp. 86–87.
[19] S.D.A., s. 29, R.R.A., s. 20(2)(*b*); and see *post.*
[20] See Interpretation Act 1978, s. 5 and Sched. 1.
[21] But see *I.T.C.* v. *Gibbs* [1942] A.C. 402 and *E.E.T.P.U.* v. *Times Newspapers* [1980] 3 W.L.R. 98 p. 101.
[22] ss. 1–4 and 82(1) S.D.A., ss. 1–2 and 78(1) R.R.A.
[23] s. 2(1) R.R.A. and s. 30(1) S.D.A.
[24] S.D.A., s. 30(1)(*G*), R.R.A., s. 21(1)(*b*).
[25] S.D.A., s. 30(1)(*b*) and R.R.A., s. 2(1)(*b*).
[26] S.D.A., s. 30(1)(*c*), R.R.A., s. 21(1)(*c*).

particular group is, then the poorer their bargaining position. Both women and ethnic minority groups are placed in this disadvantaged bargaining position and as a result indirect discrimination can quite easily arise in the terms on which premises are offered.

Not all discriminatory acts though are adversely discriminatory in nature. "Gazumping" for example effectively brings about a higher price, the higher price is obtained though for its own sake, *i.e.*, monetary gain, rather than with any discriminatory intention.[27]

Undoubtedly, it would be unlawful for a landlord to charge or demand a higher rent because of a person's ethnic group or sex. Equally it would be unlawful for a person of a particular sex or ethnic group to be subjected to more onerous conditions of sale when buying a house or more onerous conditions for example a higher interest rate, when taking out a mortgage. In a case reported by the Race Relations Board[28] a Pakistani wished to buy a house advertised "with mortgage available" but when he applied he was informed that no mortgage was available even though no enquiries into his financial position were made. Such an approach under the R.R.A. would fall foul not only of the disposal provisions of the Act but also those relating to the supply of services. Arguably, for regulated tenancies and housing association tenancies the Rent Act 1977 had ruled out the possibility of higher rentals being charged, because of the application to such tenancies of the "fair rent" system. However, rents were not always registered, restricted contracts, licensees and the like being outside the main provisions of the Act. With the introduction of open market rents under the Assured Tenancies regime of the Housing Act 1988, differential rent setting due to discriminatory motives could well return to the housing scene. As Lister and Bindman point out in *Race and Law*[29] "housing shortages create powerful financial incentives for the property owner to practise racial discrimination. Such a situation can be exploited in many ways."

Such differential rent setting can be regarded as an example of direct discrimination. Indirect discrimination on the other hand in the terms of disposal of premises may be a much more problematic issue to address. We must look at conditions or requirements employed by the parties to the agreement, the terms themselves or any preliminaries and question whether their use has a disproportionate effect on women or men or particular ethnic groups. To ban the practice within a dwelling as a condition of tenancy, religious observance for example, may have a disproportionate effect on a number of ethnic groups. Although discrimination on religious grounds in England and Wales is

[27] See comments of MacDonald *op. cit.* p. 87.
[28] See its Report for 1969–70 para. 46.
[29] p. 229.

not in itself unlawful[30] such discrimination may still indirectly affect certain ethnic minority groups, for example Muslims.[31]

Disputably, the condition of a property or the type of property will be part of the terms of its disposal, particularly for landlords with a sizable housing stock, such as local authorities and housing associations. Certainly a number of surveys concerning "race and housing" indicate that ethnic minorities tend to be housed in properties of poorer condition, inferior type[32] and in less desirable areas.[33]

Therefore where it can be shown that an individual or family have been offered inferior accommodation to other individuals and families in similar circumstances, and that this is due to reasons of sex or race, then it may be argued that there exists unlawful discrimination. What is "inferior" is often a question of personal choice. Therefore, comparisons need to be made in the light of individual preferences.

## Refusing an application

It is unlawful for a landlord, vendor or other agency involved in the disposal of premises to refuse an application on the basis of a person's sex or racial group.

Refusing an application is a particular issue with local authorities and their responsibilities to house the homeless.[34] Where people who are purportedly homeless cannot show they have a "priority need" or that they have "strong local connections" some local authorities refuse their applications for accommodation. What case law exists has been brought to court on the basis of obligations under the Housing Acts rather than by the discrimination route. But where it can be shown that a refusal of an application for accommodation is on the basis of a person's sex or racial group then unlawful discrimination may arise. An example, not entirely eliminated today, is where some local authorities refuse applications from women who have left the matrimonial home on the basis they have better rights by returning, or they have made themselves intentionally homeless, or if the local authority helped it would be itself contributing to the breakdown of the marriage.[35]

Landlords and vendors cannot argue they gave in to pressure from other tenants or residents by not letting or selling to a particular

[30] *c.f.*, in Northern Ireland *e.g.* Fair Employment (Northern Ireland) Act 1976.

[31] See discussion in Chapter four.

[32] Flats rather than houses.

[33] See D. J. Smith, *Racial Disadvantage in Britain*, part 3; N.F.H.A., *Race and Housing* and *Race and Housing; Still a Cause for Concern*; P. Niner v. *Karn*, *Achieving Racial Equality*; C.R.E. *Race and Council Housing in Hackney: Report of a Formal Investigation*.

[34] Part III of the Housing Act 1985.

[35] See C.R.E. *Race and Council Housing in Hackney: Report of Formal Investigation*, pp. 40–46 for a discussion of the racial issues.

applicant. If they give in to pressures, real or imaginary, then they will be in breach of the Acts.[36] Where individuals attempt to put pressure on, say, a landlord or vendor to discriminate, then they will also be in breach of the provisions of the Acts.[37]

Referring to transfer applications, a number of studies (see those listed as reference under Terms of Disposal section) have revealed that more ethnic minorities than whites seek transfers to accommodation more suitable to their needs. This is most likely to be as a result of being housed in poorer and inferior accommodation in the first place, in addition to a number of other factors. Where, though, rules are operated by a landlord which disallow an application for a transfer, for example because the tenant has to live in their present accommodation for three years or some other period of time, this may well indirectly discriminate against ethnic minorities. The rule would have a disproportionate effect because a relatively greater number of ethnic minorities seek transfers. Such an approach tends to perpetuate the effects of past discrimination.[38] The result is an experience more likened to *Waiting for Godot* than solving the accommodation needs of the applicants in question.

Additionally, where applications, say from women leaving the domestic home due to relationship breakdown or violence, are considered only for emergency accommodation, where other groups' applications are not so restrictively considered, then unlawful discrimination may arise. In particular it may arise because the application is not considered for the main pool of available accommodation, *i.e.*, that accommodation for which other groups may make application. This amounts to a narrowing of choice which in turn may be a detriment or less favourable treatment.[39]

The fact that an application *is* considered for one type of accommodation, particularly where that is inferior, does not preclude a claim of unlawful discrimination in relation to other accommodation which is available but for which an application was not considered. This would still amount to a refusal, a refusal need not be explicit.

## Waiting lists

Many landlords, particularly local housing authorities and housing associations, keep waiting lists of people in need of accommodation as

[36] R.R.A., ss. 30 and 31, S.D.A., ss. 39 and 40.

[37] R.R.A., ss. 31 and 33, and S.D.A., ss. 40 and 42, see Chapter 9 for more detailed discussion.

[38] See *Steel* v. *Union of Post Office Vendors* [1978] I.C.R. 181 (E.A.T.), C. McCrudden, *Institutional Discrimination* (1977) 6 LJ 241 and the discussion in Chapter 8 on Discriminatory Practices.

[39] *Jeremiah* v. *Ministry of Defence* [1979] I.R.L.R. 436 C.A.

do accommodation agencies. Such lists are necessary because the number of people seeking rented accommodation far exceeds the number of accommodation vacancies. Thus people have to wait their turn in being housed. The "waiting period" can be determined by a number of factors, often quite peculiar to the housing agencies in question. The main method in use is to judge an applicant's housing need and then assess a degree of relative priority to other applicants based on that assessment. That a "list of persons in need of accommodation" includes a local authority waiting list is beyond doubt.[40] However, where an estate agent fails to provide a list of available properties this is more likely covered under the provisions dealing with the failure to provide facilities and services.[41]

Many local authorities and housing associations attempt to be as objective as they can in assessing relative needs, some adopting "points schemes" to give numerical scores concerning an applicant's housing need. "Points Schemes" gives scores or points for a range of need factors, the cumulative points indicating the applicant's overall housing need. Urgent or unusual cases are often treated as "special cases" outside the scheme itself or dealt with on the basis of homelessness, if appropriate.

Nonetheless, in even the most ostensibly objective of schemes, discretion and subjectivity come into play which can lead to unintentional or accidental discrimination. For example, David Smith in *Racial Disadvantage in Britain* says that the inferior treatment of minorities may arise under allocations procedures not because of racial discrimination, but because of accidental factors. He comments that no matter how . . .

> "formalised the procedures are, they must involve some element of personal judgement, guesswork or apparently random selection, and there is always the possibility that these judgements might be made by prejudiced people, with the result that racial discrimination occurs"

He goes on to say that if:

> "the authority keeps no records of applicants, allocations and tenancies by ethnic groups, senior staff might not be aware that discrimination was occurring."[42]

This need to keep records has been very clearly identified in a wide range of formal investigative report recommendations issued by the C.R.E.

[40] See *Ealing London Borough Council* v. *Race Relations Board* [1972] A.C. 342 (H.L.).
[41] *Race Relations Board* v. *London Accommodation Bureau* R.R.B. Report 1973, p. 44.
[42] pp. 248–250.

Many local housing authorities have addressed these issues positively, getting rid of residential qualifications, taking care with judging priorities, employing black staff and interpreters, expelling "housekeeping standards" judgements, along with a range of other steps in keeping with the spirit of the Acts.

In the report of The Commission for Racial Equality on its *Formal Investigation into Collingwood Housing Association Ltd.* four sources of applicants were identified for the Association's accommodation (p. 21):

"(i) direct applications by persons seeking accommodation;
(ii) nominations by local authorities of council house applicants;
(iii) referral by voluntary and charitable organisations;
(iv) transfer applications from the Association's existing tenants."

A general or separate waiting list may be kept in relation to all of these sources of applicants. Both approaches are covered by the Acts.[43] There is a need to ensure no adverse treatment of applicants on a waiting list from any of these sources, or any other sources for that matter not identified in the report.

A working example of sex discrimination might be where a local housing authority gives a lower priority to one parent families than other families. The fact that the majority of one-parent families are headed by women means that women in this instance would be disproportionately affected by the operation of such an approach. Interestingly such an approach may also be indirectly discriminatory towards West Indian one-parent families because of the higher incidence of one-parent families in that particular racial group. Care must be taken to ensure that the approach adopted in applying conditions or requirements with waiting lists do not have discriminatory effects.

# EXCEPTION FOR DISPOSALS BY OWNER OCCUPIER

The provisions relating to unlawful discrimination in the disposal of premises do not apply to a person who "owns an estate or interest in the premises and wholly occupies them."[44] However, this only applies if that person does not use the services of an estate agent in disposing of the premises and does not publish an advertisement concerning the

[43] S.D.A., s. 30(1)(*c*) and R.R.A. s. 21(1)(*c*).
[44] S.D.A., s. 30(3) and R.R.A., s. 21(3).

disposal.[45] The provision is to allow wholly private or domestic transactions to proceed without breaching the provisions of the Acts.

An "estate agent" is a person "who by way of profession or trade provides services for the purposes of finding premises for persons seeking to acquire them or assisting in the disposal of premises."[46] An "advertisement" includes every form of advertisement, "whether to the public or not, and whether in a newspaper or other publication, by television or radio, by display of notices, signs, labels, showcards or goods, by distribution of samples, circulars, catalogues, price lists or other material, by exhibition of pictures, models or films, or in any way, and references to be published of advertisement shall be construed accordingly".[47] Both definitions are necessarily wide in order that agents and advertisements of all possible kinds will be included.

# DISCRIMINATION IN THE MANAGEMENT OF PROPERTY

Again the provisions of the Acts concerning discrimination in the management of property are written in similar terms. Section 21(2) of the Race Relations Act 1976, for example, says,

> "It is unlawful for a person, in relation to premises managed by him, to discriminate against a person occupying the premises:
>
> (a) in the way he affords him access to any benefits or facilities, or by refusing or deliberately omitting to afford him access to them; or
> (b) by evicting him, or subjecting him to any other detriment."

The equivalent provision of the S.D.A. 1975 is section 30(2). "Premises" and "person" have the same meaning as discussed in the previous section of this chapter. "Discriminate" means either indirect or direct discrimination and victimisation.[48]

## Access to benefits and facilities

The Acts do not simply apply to benefits and facilities provided by a landlord but include "any means by which it is in that person's power to facilitate access to benefits or facilities provided by any other

[45] *Ibid.*
[46] S.D.A., s. 82(1) and R.R.A. s. 78(1); *c.f.* definition given in s. 1(1) Estate Agents Act 1979.
[47] S.D.A., s. 82(1) and R.R.A., s. 78(1).
[48] S.D.A., s. 82(1) and R.R.A., s. 78(1).

person".[49] That other person, the "actual provider" shall also be subject to the provisions of the Acts for any unlawful discrimination.[50]

Landlords, including local authorities and housing associations, and agents of landlords are subject to these provisions. It is equally possible that discrimination occurs in the management of dwellings as it does with access to those dwellings in the first place. Thus landlords should provide an equal service to residents and tenants regardless of their sex or racial group. Not allowing women use of a communal bathroom in a housing scheme used for multiple occupation may well breach this provision. Not allowing Asians, for example, access to communal kitchen on the basis that other residents complain about cooking odours would also be unlawful.

Landlords do need to look much deeper than surface issues. Do ethnic minorities, for example, get worse treatment when it comes to carrying out repairs? Do ethnic minorities receive harsher treatment when in rent arrears, do women similarly? There are a whole range of benefits which arise out of the landlord and tenant relationship which need to be examined to ensure equality of opportunity and treatment.

For a discussion of the nature of benefits and facilities, and services for that matter see the later section in this chapter dedicated to those issues.

## Eviction and "any other detriment"

To evict a person because of that person's sex or racial group would amount to unlawful discrimination.[51] Any other detriment in this context surely means harassment whether racial or sexual by the landlord or other person managing the premises on behalf of the landlord. Although the word harassment appears in neither of the statutes, Popplewell J. in *Wileman* v. *Minitec Engineering,*[52] an employment case, referring to any other detriment under section 6(2)(*b*) of the S.D.A. (the employment equivalent to the housing provisions under discussion) said:

> "the words "sexual harassment" do not occur in the Act and are legal shorthand for an activity which is easily recognisable as "subjecting her to any other detriment."

Harassment is of much importance in the housing field, particularly in connection with race relations, and therefore a separate chapter is dedicated to the subject.[53]

[49] S.D.A., s. 50(1) and R.R.A., s. 40(1).
[50] S.D.A., s. 50(2) and R.R.A., s. 40(20).
[51] S.D.A., s. 30(2)(*b*) and R.R.A. s. 21(2)(*b*).
[52] [1988] I.C.R. 318 E.A.T. 323.
[53] See Chapter 9.

# EXCEPTION FOR RESIDENT LANDLORDS OF SMALL PREMISES

The provisions we have discussed concerning discrimination in the disposal and management of premises do not apply where the landlord or a near relative of his — the relevant occupier — resides and intends to continue to reside in the premises.[54] There are though a number of requirements which need to be met before this exception can apply:

1. The "near relative" of the person should be a wife or husband, parent or child, grandparent or grandchild or brother or sister, including such near relatives as half-sister, step-sister and sister-in-law.[55]
2. There is on the provision, in addition to the accommodation occupied by the "relevant occupier" (*i.e.* the occupier or his near relative), accommodation shared by the relevant occupier with other persons residing on the premises. The "other persons" must not be members of the household. The "shared accommodation" must not be storage space or means of access.[56]
3. The premises must be "small premises".[57] For the premises to be small premises normally there should not be residential accommodation on the premises for more than six persons in addition to the "relevant occupier" and members of his household.[58] Where premises comprise of residential accommodation for one or more households or separate letting or similar agreement, the accommodation being in addition to that used by the "relevant" occupier and his household, no more than two such households must reside in the premises.[59] In addition the "relevant" occupier and his household must be exclusive occupants of the accommodation retained for his use.[60]

There are other exceptions to the provisions against discrimination in the disposal and management of premises and these will be dealt with after considering discrimination in the provision of goods, facilities and services.[61]

[54] S.D.A., s. 32(1) and R.R.A., s. 23(1).
[55] S.D.A., s. 32(1) and R.R.A. s. 3(1)(*a*) and s. 18(1).
[56] S.D.A., s. 32(1)(*b*) and R.R.A. s. 23(1)(*b*).
[57] S.D.A., s. 32(1)(*c*) and R.R.A. s. 23(1)(*c*).
[58] S.D.A., s. 32(2)(*a*) and R.R.A., s. 23(2)9(*a*).
[59] S.D.A., s. 32(2)(*b*) and R.R.A. s. 23(2)(*b*).
[60] R.R.A., s. 32(2)(*b*) and s. 23(2)(*b*).
[61] Other more general exceptions are considered in Chapter 5.

# DISCRIMINATION IN PROVISION OF GOODS, FACILITIES AND SERVICES

Along with the more specific provisions relating to housing discrimination is the protection offered by the Acts for unlawful discrimination in the provision of goods, facilities and services.[62] Again there are a number of exceptions to these provisions, some of which will be covered in this chapter.[63]

Once more we will take the relevant section the R.R.A. and examine it and make reference to sex discrimination as we proceed. First, section 20(1) says:

> "It is unlawful for any person concerned with the provision (for payment or not) of goods, facilities or services to the public or a section of the public to discriminate against a person who seeks to obtain or use those goods, facilities or services:
>
> (a) by refusing or deliberately omitting to provide him with any of them; or
> (b) by refusing or deliberately omitting to provide him with goods, facilities or services of the like quality, in the like manner and on the like terms as are normal in the first-mentioned person's case in relation to other members of the public or (where the person so seeking belongs to a section of the public) to other members of that section."

Section 29(1) of the S.D.A. is identical except that it refers to discrimination between men and women, rather than a person who belongs to a section of the public. "Discriminate" means direct or indirect discrimination or victimisation.[64] As to "goods, services or facilities" neither of the Acts define them and we must therefore give them their ordinary and natural meanings. Some examples of facilities and services are given in Acts.[65]

## Goods

Little help is given in the Acts in stating what is meant by "goods". Lister and Bindman[66] suggest goods are, "any movable property, including merchandise or wares". This suggestion coincides with the

[62] S.D.A., s. 29 and R.R.A., s. 20.
[63] Also see Chapter 5.
[64] S.D.A., s. 82(1) and R.R.A., s. 78(10).
[65] See S.D.A. s. 29(2) and R.R.A. s. 20(2).
[66] *op. cit.* p. 260.

definition offered in the Sale of Goods Act 1979[67] which says that "goods" include:

> "all personal chattels other than things in action and money ... any things attached to or forming part of the land which are agreed to be severed before sale or under contract of sale".

*The Oxford English Dictionary* offers,

> "property or possessions; movable property; saleable commodities; merchandise, wares."

## Facilities and services

With "facilities" and "services" the Acts offer some guidance by giving the following examples,[68]

"(a) access to and use of any place which members of the public are permitted to enter;
(b) accommodation in a hotel, boarding house or other similar establishment;
(c) facilities by way of banking or insurance or for grants, loans, credit or finance;
(d) facilities for education;
(e) facilities for entertainments, recreation or refreshment;
(f) facilities for transport or travel;
(g) the services of any profession or trade, or any other local or other public authority."

The list represents a series of examples of facilities and services covered by the provisions of the Acts and is not meant to be exhaustive, providing "useful pointers to aid the construction" of the subsection.[69] Lister and Bindman[70] define "facilities" to "include any opportunity for obtaining some benefit or for doing something" and go on to say "services", "refer to any conduct tending to the welfare or advantage of other people, especially conduct which supplies their needs." These definitions are certainly consistent with the examples given by the Acts. However, the section applies "to the direct provision of facilities or services, and not to the mere grant of permission to sue facilities".[71] Neither should the provision of services or facilities be confused with the performance of a duty to control or the exercise of

[67] s. 6(1).
[68] S.D.A., s. 29(2) and R.R.A., s. 20(2).
[69] See *R.* v. *Entry Clearance Officer, ex p. Admin* [1983] 2 A.C. 818 at p. 834.
[70] *op. cit.* p. 260.
[71] Per Lord Fraser of Tullybelton in *R.* v. *Entry Clearance Officer ex p., Amin* [1983] 2 A.C. 818 at p. 834.

discretionary power arising under statute.[72] Additionally, the performance of acts "done in the course of formulating or carrying out government policy", are not services since such acts are quite different in kind from any done for a private person.[73] The subsection "contemplates actual provision of facilities which the person will use."[74]

It is worth taking a closer look at some of the examples cited in the Acts which are most relevant in the housing context:

## *(a) Access and use of public places*

Where members of the public are allowed to enter a place, not a "public place" in the usual sense of the word but rather a place open to the public, then clearly they must be allowed to use it and have access to it if they so wish without the possibility of either sex or racial discrimination.[75] Difficulties which arose following the House of Lords decision in *Charter* v. *Race Relations Board*[76] under the Race Relations Act 1968 and its non-application to social clubs (their members not being a "section of the public") have been eliminated by a specific provision which make discrimination by "associations" unlawful.[77] However, the provision applies only to discrimination on racial grounds.

On this basis the offices of building societies, banks, local authorities, and estate agents, housing associations and the like would be places which the public may have access to and use. Similarly, some community facilities such as meeting rooms, playgrounds, communal laundries and the like provided on larger local authority and housing association housing estates would also be regarded as places the public, or a section of the public, may use. However, it is doubtful these facilities would be regarded as places the public or a section of the public may use during times which they are habitually closed.[78]

## *(b) Hotel or similar accommodation*

Hotels and boarding houses are specifically regarded as facilities along with any accompanying provision of services for the purpose of the Acts. The words "other similar establishment" would narrow the

[72] See *Re Bernstein, The Guardian*, May 28, 1988, C.A. and *R.* v. *Immigration Appeals Tribunal ex parte, Kassan* [1980] 1 W.L.R. 1037 (C.A.).
[73] See *R.* v. *Entry Clearance Officer ex parte, Amin* [1983] 2 A.C. 818 at p. 834 and *Re Bernstein, supra.*
[74] See *R.* v. *Entry Clearance Officer ex p., Amin, supra.*
[75] See *Encyclopedia of Housing*, Vol. 2, paras. 2085–86.
[76] [1973] A.C. 868; see also *Race Relations Board* v. *Dockers' Labour Club and Institute* [1976] A.C. 285.
[77] See R.R.A., s. 25.
[78] See *Sandy* v. *Martin* [1974] R.T.R. 263 and *R.* v. *Shaw* [1974] R.T.R. 225.

range of other establishments included under the section to those which are *edjusdem generis* as hotels and boarding houses.[79]

Examples might include private hotels and holiday camps. Hotels for the homeless and board and lodging establishments would similarly fall under the definition. The likely question to ask about an establishment is, does the establishment provide generally similar facilities and services to a hotel or boarding house?[80]

There is some doubt as to whether a hostel would come within the provisions because of the differences between such an establishment and a hotel or boarding house. "Personal care" or support may be provided for residents which would not be available to residents in a hotel or boarding house. Additionally, access to a hostel is through a different process and may well be available to a restricted group of people rather than to the general public as is the case with hotels. If we examine the ordinary and natural meanings of the terms "hotel" and "hostel" there are distinct differences. The *Oxford English Dictionary* defines a "hotel" as a "house for accommodation of travellers; public house", similarly a "boarding house" is defined as a place "in which persons board", *i.e.* are provided with meals. On the other hand a "hostel" is a "house of residence for students or other special class". However, this definition of a hostel is not entirely confirmed by the Housing Act 1985[81] which states a:

> "hostel" means a building in which is provided, for persons generally or for a class or classes of persons,
>
> (a) residential accommodation otherwise than in separate and self-contained sets of premises; and
> (b) either board or facilities for the preparation of food adequate to the needs of those persons, or both."

The definition in general terms suggests a possible wider view of a hostel than the restricted sense given in the dictionary. It certainly also suggests that a hostel may be provided in a limited sense for a "class or classes of persons". Disputably the approach to adopt is to ask whether a particular hostel in a particular case provides facilities and services similar to a hotel or boarding house. With such an approach some hostels may well fall within the provision, other more specialist establishments will not. Similarly certain establishments which provide accommodation under a board and lodging basis for the elderly, mentally handicapped, mentally ill, the physically handicapped and other special needs groups could arguably fall within the provision.

[79] *Sandiman* v. *Breach* [1927] 7 B. & C. 96; for the meaning of "board" see *Wilkes* v. *Goodwin* [1923] 2 K.B. 86 and the recent Rent Act case *Otter* v. *Norman* [1988] 3 W.L.R. 321.
[80] See also *Encyclopedia of Housing Law*, para. 2–0836.
[81] s. 622.

However, whether they do may well depend on the level of "general care" or nursing care provided for residents. Once could not argue, that personal nursing care is provided by a hotel or boarding house. Indeed, by virtue of the Registered Homes Act 1984[82] a "residential care home" is "any establishment which provides or is intended to provide, whether for reward or not, residential accommodation with both board and personal care for persons in need of personal care by reason of old age, disablement, past or present dependence on drugs or past or present mental disorder."

Similarly the Registered Homes Act 1984 gives specific definitions for a "nursing home" and "mental nursing home" which clearly go beyond the *edjusdem generis* bounds of the meaning of hotel or boarding house or similar establishment.[83]

"Personal Care" is defined by the Registered Homes Act 1984[84] to mean care which includes assistance with bodily functions where such assistance is required. Hostels, residential care homes and nursing homes can still, though, be regarded as "premises" under the provisions relating to disposal and management of premises[85] and thus are still within the protection of the Acts. Nursing care and other professional care and provision of services would also fall under example (e), to be discussed shortly.

## *(c) Finance facilities*

Perhaps the main application of this example in the context of housing is through provision of mortgage finance by building societies, banks and other financial institutions.

An example of how discriminatory practices can come into play when providing such services is that of "red lining" certain poorer areas of towns and cities, run down inner city areas, and as a consequence operating a policy whereby lending is not provided for properties within such areas. Since proportionately more ethnic minorities than whites live in such areas the practice can amount to indirect discrimination.[86]

## *(d) Entertainment, recreation or refreshment*

Some housing projects, particularly the more specialist type of schemes, have facilities for recreation and refreshment, for example

[82] Subsections 70(1) and 70(2).
[83] See ss. 21(1), 22(1) and 22(2).
[84] See s. 20(1).
[85] S.D.A., s. 30 and R.R.A. s. 21.
[86] See the Campaign for Racial Equality report on the practices of building societies in Rochdale.

the provision of food in a sheltered scheme for the frail elderly. Thus facilities on offer should be sufficiently wide enough in scope to appeal to all residents of such projects. This requires particular thought at the design stage of such projects to ensure that the needs of both sexes and minority groups are properly taken into account. An example might be to ensure adequate cooking and dining arrangements to cater for varying religious requirements relating to diet. Care, though, should be taken to ensure "segregation" does not arise.[87] Discrimination by building societies and other financial institutions is discussed more fully in Chapter 12.

### *(e) Service of any profession or trade, or any local or other public authority*

These services and facilities have application to housing professionals including estate agents, housing managers, lawyers and the like and the staff working for local housing authorities along with such authorities themselves. This will be dealt with as part of Chapters 10 to 12.

## DISCRIMINATION: CONSENT FOR ASSIGNMENT OR SUB-LETTING

As well as it being unlawful to discriminate in the disposal and management of premises, it is unlawful to discriminate on the grounds of sex or racial origin when granting or withholding consent to a disposal by way of assignment or sub-letting of a tenancy.[88]

A "tenancy" means a "tenancy created by a lease or sub-lease, by an agreement for a lease or sub-lease or by a tenancy agreement or in persuance of any enactment." And "disposal" in this context "includes assignment or assignation of the tenancy and sub-letting with possession of the premises or any part of the premises".[89]

The provisions do not, though, apply to "small premises".[90] They do though apply to tenancies granted before the commencement of the Acts.[91]

[87] See R.R.A., s. 1(2) and generally S. M. Pouter, *English Law and Ethnic Minority Customs.*
[88] See S.D.A., s. 31(1) and R.R.A., s. 24(1).
[89] See S.D.A., s. 31(4) and R.R.A., s. 24(4).
[90] See S.D.A., 31(3) and ss. 31(2) and R.R.A., ss. 24(2) and 24(3).
[91] See S.D.A., s. 31(5) and R.R.A., s. 24(5).

"Withholding licence or consent"[92] would also include the terms upon which the licence or consent is granted.[93]

## Exceptions to housing discrimination

So far in this chapter we have discussed the main types of housing discrimination and also referred to the exception of small houses to the provisions concerned with discrimination in the disposal and management of premises and in the provision of goods facilities and services. That exception can be seen as the equivalent to the small business and private household exceptions which had until the Sex Discrimination Act 1986 applied to employment cases. It is surprising following the S.D.A. that discrimination should be allowed in the housing context to remain for these small dwellings. The assumption must be that where an individual wishes to take someone into their own home, even though the relationship is a collateral one, then that person is free to discriminate on racial or sexual grounds.

There are, though, a range of other exceptions to housing discrimination which we need to consider and these will be addressed in the remaining part of the chapter. Between the sex and racial discrimination exceptions there is little in common. We shall therefore initially consider the exceptions under the S.D.A. and move on to those which arise under the R.R.A.[94]

# HOUSING AND SEX DISCRIMINATION EXCEPTIONS

## Voluntary bodies

For voluntary bodies which do not trade for profit[95] and which have not been established by "any enactment"[96] housing discrimination[97] does not apply to the following:

(a) the restriction of membership to one sex;[98]
(b) the provision of benefits, facilities or services to members of the voluntary body where a membership is restricted to one sex;[99]

[92] See S.D.A., s. 31(1) and R.R.A. s. 24(1).
[93] See *Balfour* v. *Kensington Gardens Mansions* (1932) 49 T.L.R. 29.
[94] See also Chapter 5 for general exceptions.
[95] S.D.A., s. 34(1)(*a*).
[96] S.D.A., s. 34(1)(*b*).
[97] As defined by S.D.A., ss. 29 and 30.
[98] s. 34(20)(*a*).
[99] s. 34(2)(*b*).

(c) acts performed which are necessary to give effect when "conferring benefits on persons of one sex, only", where this "constitutes the main object" of the voluntary body in question.[1]

Benefits can be conferred in this way whether or not the body in question has a membership open to the public or a section of the public.[2]

## Further exceptions

The provision of facilities and services which are restricted to men are not rendered unlawful as housing discrimination, if:

(a) the place is, or is part of, a hospital, reception centre provided by the Supplementary Benefits Commission or other establishment for persons requiring special care, supervision or training;[3]
(b) the place is, whether temporarily or permanently, occupied for purposes of organised religion;[4]
(c) the facilities or services are shared and
  (i) if used at the same time are likely to induce serious embarrassment;[5], or
  (ii) are such that users are likely to be in a state of undress and that "a male user might reasonably object to the presence of a female user".[6]

As a result of this exception the provision of facilities or services may be restricted to men if by the nature of the facilities or services, physical contact between sexes is likely and that a person involved might reasonably object if another user was a woman.[7]

Under (a) listed above no definition of "special care, supervision or training" is offered. Where such care, supervision or training is provided it would be a question of fact whether what was provided was special. Presumably, where care, supervision or training was provided to meet the requirement of people in need of special care it is reasonable to assume such provision would be regarded as special. This approach would seem to accord with the view taken in the last chapter that the care and personal services provided in some hostels, residential care and nursing homes would take such establishments

[1] ss. 34(3) and 34(4).
[2] s. 34(2).
[3] s. 35(1)(*a*).
[4] s. 35(1)(*b*).
[5] s. 35(1)(*c*).
[6] s. 35(1)(*c*)(ii).
[7] s. 35(2).

outside the scope of the definition of hotels and boarding houses and similar establishments.[8]

# HOUSING AND RACE DISCRIMINATION EXCEPTIONS

## Family care

Section 20(1) of the R.R.A. (provision of goods, facilities and services) does not apply to arrangements where a person, whether or not for payment, takes into his home someone who is treated as part of the family. However, the person taken into the family must be a child, elderly or some other person requiring a special degree of care and attention.[9] As with the special care, supervision or training provisions of the S.D.A. referred to in the previous section,[10] no definition is given of "special degree of care and attention" and therefore each instance will be a question of fact.

## Ethnic and national associations

Discrimination by "clubs" and other non-profit making associations which have more than 25 members is unlawful.[11] Such clubs and associations cannot discriminate in the treatment of members:

(a) in the way they are offered or refused any benefits;[12]
(b) by depriving them of membership or varying their terms of membership;[13]
(c) by denying any associate members rights or varying their rights;[14]
(d) by subjecting members or associate members to "any other detriment".[15]

Typical examples in the housing field of such clubs or associations are housing co-operatives, co-ownership societies and housing associations which are constituted as industrial and provident societies.

[8] See S.D.A. ss. 29(2) and (5).
[9] R.R.A., s. 23(2).
[10] S.D.A., s. 35(1)(*a*).
[11] See R.R.A., s. 25 following the previously unsatisfactory position adopted by the House of Lords in *Charter* v. *Race Relations Board* [1973] A.C. 868.
[12] R.R.A., s. 25(3)(*a*).
[13] R.R.A., s. 25(3)(*b*).
[14] R.R.A., s. 25(3)(*c*).
[15] R.R.A., s. 25(3)(*d*).

Although such clubs and associations cannot discriminate in the treatment of their members, certain ethnic and national clubs are excepted from the provisions.[16] The test is whether a particular club exists to promote positively the interest of an ethnic, racial or national group. However, the group in question must be defined "otherwise than by reference to colour".[17] Such associations are therefore able to act contrary to the restrictions set out in section 25 so long as any act does not involve discrimination on the ground of colour.[18] Thus a housing association could exist for the benefit of Muslims, since Muslims comprise a racial group. But it would seem a housing association could not lawfully pursue activities for the benefit of ethnic minorities generally. However, a number of "black-led" housing associations have been registered by the Housing Corporation[19] on the basis that they exist to meet the special needs of racial groups in regard to welfare, *i.e.,* housing provision.[20]

Clearly, "clubs" with fewer than 25 members are exempt from these provisions and would seem to be free to discriminate.

## OVERLAP WITH EMPLOYMENT AND EDUCATION PROVISIONS

Both the S.D.A. 1975[21] and the R.R.A. 1976[22] contain exceptions which ensure that unlawful discrimination which arises under the employment or education provision is not also unlawful under the housing discrimination provisions. This eliminates duplicity in courses of action. Since discrimination in the fields of employment and education are not directly relevant in the housing field we do not need to consider these exceptions in any detail.

[16] R.R.A., s. 26(2).
[17] See s. 26(1).
[18] s. 26(2).
[19] See Housing Associations Act 1985, s. 4.
[20] R.R.A., s. 35.
[21] s. 35(3).
[22] s. 23(1).

# Chapter eight

# Related Forms of Discrimination

## INTRODUCTION

There are other forms of discrimination in the field of housing to which the Acts apply. "Other unlawful acts" will be considered in detail, in this chapter.

The "other unlawful acts" extend the provisions of the Acts and make certain forms of conduct unlawful, even though the conduct itself is not unlawfully discriminatory. The effect of conduct of this nature may very well result in unlawful discrimination, hence the concern of Parliament in relation to such acts. The "unlawful acts" or "conduct" in question relate to:

1. discriminatory practices;
2. discriminatory advertisements;
3. instructions to discriminate;
4. pressure to discriminate;
5. liability of employers and principals;
6. aiding unlawful acts.

The range of these forms of "other unlawful acts" provide an impressive battery of additional protection for those who fall victim to unlawful racial or sex discrimination. Legal proceedings for contravention of the provisions against these unlawful acts can only be brought by the Commissions.[1]

### *Discriminatory practices*

"Discriminatory practice" means the "application of a requirement or condition which results in an act of discrimination." The act of discrimination must be unlawful under the provisions of Part III of each of the Acts which we have described in previous chapters, for it to be unlawful in the housing field. Moreover, those provisions must be

[1] R.R.A., ss. 28–32 and S.D.A., ss. 37–41.

"taken with section 1(1)(*b*) of the Acts," *i.e.* the provisions relating to indirect discrimination.[2] The sections do not cover direct discrimination practices, which suggested to Lord Diplock that the R.R.A. was "curiously drafted".[3]

The application of a condition or requirement may still be unlawful if it "would be likely to result in such an act of discrimination, if it was applied to persons of a particular sex or racial group even though there had been no occasion on which the condition or requirement had been applied."[4]

Contravention of this provision arises where a person:[5]

(a) applies a discriminatory practice; or
(b) operates practices or other arrangements which in any circumstances would call for the application of a discriminatory practice.

Thus any act, even though in practice it is not discriminatory, which is designed to have a discriminatory result is rendered unlawful. Certain acts of discrimination may be so effective in their application that they never produce an actual victim. An example might be that a housing association has a reputation of only housing white applicants and therefore ethnic minorities do not bother to apply.

Similarly a housing project for overnight shelter for the homeless may have traditionally assisted men and the reputation is such that homeless women do not seek its help. Consequently, no woman would have been refused access to the hostel and therefore there has been no actual victim. Discrimination has nonetheless occurred since women are not housed there.

Where "discriminatory practices" exist, proceedings can only be brought by the Commission for Racial Equality or the Equal Opportunities Commission in their respective fields.[6] Individuals cannot therefore bring actions under these particular provisions.

## *Discriminatory advertisements*

It is unlawful to publish or cause to be published an advertisement which indicates or might reasonably be taken to indicate an intention to discriminate on the basis of race or sex.[7] These provisions were mainly intended to deal with discriminatory advertisements in the employment field, but apply also to discrimination in the housing field. The

[2] S.D.A., s. 37(1) and R.R.A., s. 28(1).
[3] See *Commission for Racial Equality* v. *Prestige Group plc* [1984] I.C.R. 473 at p. 480.
[4] S.D.A., s. 37(1) and R.R.A., s. 28(1).
[5] S.D.A., ss. 37(2)(*a*) and 2(*b*) and R.R.A., ss. 28(2)(*a*) and (2)(*b*).
[6] S.D.A., s. 37(3) and R.R.A., s. 28(3).
[7] S.D.A., s. 38(1) and R.R.A., s. 29(1).

exceptions which apply in the employment field relating to "genuine occupational qualifications" or where the advertisement applies to a job outside Great Britain, do not apply to discrimination in the provision of goods, facilities or services or the disposal or management of premises.[8] Neither does the provision concerning the use of job descriptions with a sex connotation apply in the housing field.[9]

An "advertisement" includes every form of advertisement, whether to the public or not.[10] It does not matter then that the advertisement is a restricted circulation or that it is for the eyes of a privileged few. Indeed, the latter may well amount to a "discriminatory practice" in that it could well perpetuate the effects of previous discrimination. Neither does it matter where the advertisement appears:[11]

> "whether in a newspaper or other publication, by television or radio, by display of notices, signs, labels, showcards or goods, by distribution of samples, circulars, catalogues, price lists or other material, by exhibition of pictures ... or in any other way."

The Acts though do not precisely state what is meant by advertisement. The examples cited above give an indication that the purpose of an advertisement would seem to be primarily to attract a response for the supply of goods. But clearly the intention would also cover job advertisements, advertisements for the sale of homes or attracting applicants for rented homes. Difficulties arise with public sector rented housing, where advertisements do not appear. Is for example, the promotional information relating to the operation of a local authority list a form of advertisement? It is unlikely, since the intention of the information is to describe how the waiting list operates, rather than to attract more applications for the accommodation which is or may become available.

The publisher of an unlawful discriminatory advertisement may himself be free of liability under the Acts if he can prove:[12]

> "(a) that the advertisement was published in reliance on a statement made to him by the person who caused it to be published, making it clear the advertisement would not be unlawful; and
>
> (b) that it was reasonable for him to rely on the statement."

This legal position helps the publisher in circumstances where it is difficult to determine whether a specific advertisement is or is not unlawful.

[8] S.D.A., s. 38(2) and R.R.A., ss. 29(2) and (3).
[9] S.D.A., s. 38(3).
[10] S.D.A., s. 82(1) and R.R.A., s. 78(1).
[11] S.D.A., s. 82(1) and R.R.A., s. 78(1).
[12] S.D.A., s. 38(4) and R.R.A., s. 29(4).

However, if such a person knowingly or recklessly makes such a statement which is found to be false or misleading in a material respect, that person commits an offence. The offence carries a fine of £400 upon summary conviction.[13] Where advertisements are placed may well be discriminatory in itself. Placing advertisements in journals or newspapers read only by men or white people are likely to have indirectly discriminatory results. A typical instance is the free newspaper, often local newsheets, delivered only to the homes of the "economically active." For example if a housing association advertises its properties for sale, under the various low cost home ownership initiatives, in the local press which is read in the main by the white population, because it is delivered to the more prosperous homes of the area where fewer black people live this may well result in few black people coming forward with applications to purchase. Although no discrimination in the advertisement has taken place, the result still produces discrimination. Clearly a wide placement of advertisement is one possible solution. Even though such a practice will generate greater marketing costs the effect will help ensure unlawful discrimination does not occur.

Only the Equal Opportunities Commission and the Commission for Racial Equality can bring action against discriminatory advertisements. This was because the Government felt that "some people would bring trivial and vexatious cases", if there was an individual right of complaint, and that cases "could be brought which took the Act into disrepute, and it is for that reason that we have provided for no individual compensation and have provided that only the Equal Opportunities Commission shall be able to bring such cases".[14] Although in employment cases after a finding of unlawful discrimination has been proved there exists a right to claim for compensation, no such right exists in the housing field.

## *Instructions to discriminate*

It is unlawful for a person in authority to instruct or influence another person to do an act of unlawful discrimination. It is also unlawful for such a person in authority to "procure" or "attempt to procure" the doing of such an act by another person.[15] These phrases have a wide meaning and clearly cover "the use of words which bring about or attempt to bring about a certain course of action".[16] An expression of

[13] S.D.A., s. 38(5) and R.R.A., s. 29(5).
[14] Quoted in the *Encyclopaedia of Housing Law and Practice*, paras. 2–2588/28.
[15] S.D.A, s. 39 and R.R.A., s. 30.
[16] *Commission for Racial Equality* v. *Imperial Society of Teachers of Dancing* [1983] I.C.R. 473 at p. 476.

preference for members of a particular sex or racial group would amount to "an attempt to procure".[17] For authority over another to exist "requires that there should be some relationship between the person giving the instructions ... and the person."

The provisions should not be interpreted to mean "that it is sufficient to show that the other person is accustomed to act in accordance with the wishes of persons in the same position as the person giving the instructions".[18] Although this may preclude the situation where a person within an organisation having authority over another person at the same level, where a person at a lower level is "accustomed to act in accordance with the wishes" of a superior then sufficient evidence exists to show there is a relationship involving authority. This would also apply to companies, partnerships and other corporate or uncorporate bodies who are "accustomed to act in accordance with the wishes" of an employing authority.[19]

Therefore, if a local housing authority employee was instructed by his manager to carry out an unlawfully discriminatory act then the relationship would be clearly one where authority was present. Not so clear, though, would be where the same manager asked an officer of similar authority to perform a discriminatory act. "Authority" over that other person would have to be established as fact, the wording of the Acts being quite specific. Since informal relationship of authority can exist between staff at similar levels in an organisation this interpretation seems one which is unnecessarily restrictive. An instruction or request at this level could be similar in its discriminatory effect to that of the manager and employee, yet may not technically speaking be unlawful. Although an instuction to discriminate must itself be unlawful, the instruction need not be carried out. The instruction remains unlawful. Only the Commissions are able to bring an action in relation to discriminatory instructions.

## *Pressure to discriminate*

To induce, or attempt to induce, a person to do any act which contravenes the provisions set out in Part III of the Acts is unlawful.[20] The Sex Discrimination Act is a little more specific and says that such an act which contravenes Part III is unlawful when it is done by:

(a) providing or offering to provide any benefit;[21] or

[17] *Ibid.*
[18] *Ibid.*, at pp. 476–477.
[19] *Ibid.*, "person" includes a body of persons corporate or unincorporate: Interpretation Act 1978.
[20] S.D.A., s. 40(1) and R.R.A., s. 31(1).
[21] s. 40(1)(*a*).

(b) subjects a person, or threatens to subject a person, to any detriment.[22]

As we have seen in an earlier chapter "sexual harassment" has been seen as a term used as shorthand for "any other detriment".[23] It is of interest that this detail concerning acts of inducement has been omitted from the Race Relations Act.[24]

"Induce" means in its ordinary sense "to persuade or to prevail upon or to bring about". There is no reason to believe the word should be construed in any narrower sense than that suggested by its ordinary meaning. However, it is arguable that under the Race Relations Act its meaning is wider in that it is not narrowed by the examples given under the S.D.A. Thus in the context of race relations the word "induce" would cover a "mere request to discriminate".[25]

Uner the S.D.A. it does not matter that the offer or threat is not made directly to the person in question, so long as it is "made in such a way that he is likely to hear of it".[26] An attempted inducement under the Race Relations Act is treated similarly.[27] Accordingly indirect "pressure to discriminate" is unlawful.

Where, say, a group of male tenants attempt to persuade their landlord not to let a vacant dwelling to a woman, they would be unlawfully applying pressure to discriminate.

Whether the giving or withholding of information is an "attempt to induce" is a question of fact and depends largely on the intention of the parties concerned in each particular case. Simply giving information or stating a fact may not in itself be an attempt to induce discrimination.[28] Where someone acts following discriminatory pressure even though they themselves may be motivated by non-discriminatory factors, they will have acted on racial or sexual grounds.[29]

Again only the Commissions are able to bring an action in relation to discriminatory pressure.

## *Aiding unlawful acts*

If a person knowingly aids or assists with an act which is rendered unlawful by the Acts, then that person is also considered to have

[22] s. 40(1)(*b*).
[23] See Chapters 6 and 12.
[24] See *Commission for Racial Equality* v. *Imperial Society of Teachers of Dancing* [1983] I.C.R. 473 (E.A.T.).
[25] See M. Rubenstein, *Discrimination: A Guide to the Relevant Case Law*, p. 32.
[26] s. 40(2).
[27] s. 31(2).
[28] *Commission for Racial Equality* v. *Powell and City of Birmingham District Council* E.O.R. 7 at p. 31 (E.A.T.).
[29] See *Commission for Racial Equality ex p. Westminster City Council* [1985] I.R.L.R. 426 (C.A.).

committed an act of the "like description".[30] When a person "aids" another he becomes liable from the moment the aid is given for the unlawful act to be performed.[31] "Aids" means "assisting and supporting" rather than the more usual criminal understanding of "aiding and abetting".[32]

In determining whether a person "knowingly" aids an unlawful act the onus of proof is on the prosecution.[33] Essentially it will be a question of determining that the defendant had knowledge that the act would be contrary to the provisions of the Acts.[34]

However, a person does not knowingly aid another to do an unlawful act if:

(a) he acts in reliance on a statement made to him by that other person that, by reason of any provision of this Act, the act which he aids would not be unlawful; and
(b) it is reasonable for him to rely on the statement.[35]

But if a person "knowingly or recklessly" makes such a statement which is false or misleading in a material aspect, then the person commits an offence. Upon summary conviction the offence carries a fine of up to £400.[36]

Accordingly if a landlord, for example, responds to pressure to discriminate by tenants in not housing a black applicant, then the landlord would be aiding an unlawful act and also commits a similar act as a result of this section.[37] Thus it is no defence for a landlord to say he himself is not prejudiced and that he was simply acting in accordance with the wishes of, or pressure imposed by, his tenants. A failure to act where the landlord is under a contractual or statutory duty to act may also amount to victimisation.[38]

## *Liability of employers and principals*

A "principal" is liable for any act done under his authority by an "agent", and an "employer" is liable for any act done, with or without his knowledge or approval, by an "employee" in the course of his employment.[39] The agent or employee is treated as having aided the

[30] S.D.A., s. 42(1) and R.R.A., s. 33(1).
[31] See SC.col 4500.
[32] *Greater London Council* v. *Farrar* [1980] I.C.R. 266 at p. 271 (E.A.T.).
[33] See *Gaumont British Distributors* v. *Henry* [1939] 2 K.B. 711.
[34] See *R.* v. *Taaffe* [1984] A.C. 539 (C.A.) at p. 629.
[35] S.D.A., s. 42(3) and R.R.A., s. 33(3).
[36] S.D.A., s. 42(4) and R.R.A., s. 33(3).
[37] See *R.* v. *Commission for Racial Equality ex p. Westminster City Council* [1985] I.C.R. 827 (C.A.D.).
[38] See Chapter 5.
[39] S.D.A., ss. 41(1) and (2) and R.R.A., ss. 32(1) and (2).

principal or employer.[40] Therefore all parties are liable for unlawful acts and the provisions create statutory vicarious liability.

Where an employer can show he took steps which were "reasonably practicable to prevent" the employee from committing an unlawful act, then the employer will not be liable. The defence applies where an employer can show he gave general instructions to employees to prevent unlawful acts of the kind in question.[41] Whether the adoption of a genuine "fair housing" or "equal opportunities" policy by a landlord who has employees, for example a local housing authority or a housing association, would be sufficient proof for this defence may well depend on the extent of that policy and the extent of its application.[42] However, such a defence is not open to principals in relation to the acts of their agents. Why this privileged position should be available only to employers is unclear. This may be because a principal would only seem to be liable for the acts of agents where authority, whether express or implied, has been given. Pannick argues that the provision, under the S.D.A., does not extend to "ostensible" authority, *i.e.* where a third party believes the agent is acting on the authority of the principal. Since, therefore, a principal's liability is narrower than that of an employer, then the defence of taking reasonably practicable steps to prevent unlawful discriminatory acts is unnecessary.[43]

## *Discriminatory terms in contracts*

There is no opportunity to contract out of the obligations the Acts impose, since any term in a contract which constitutes a contravention is rendered "void and unenforceable".[44] For example under section 72(1) of the Race Relations Acts a term of a contract is void where:

(a) its inclusion renders the making of the contract unlawful by virtue of this Act; or
(b) it is included in the furtherance of an act rendered unlawful by this Act; or
(c) it provides for the doing of an act which would be rendered unlawful by this Act."

The wording of the S.D.A., section 77, is identical.

However, the provision does not apply where the term discriminates unlawfully against a party to the contract, but the term shall be unenforceable against the party.[45] Such a term is, then, not made void

[40] S.D.A., s. 41(2) and R.R.A., s. 32(2).
[41] S.D.A., s. 41(3) and R.R.A., s. 32(3).
[42] See analogous discussion by Lustgarten, *op. cit.* on trade union policies, pp. 70–71.
[43] See D. Pannick, *Sex Discrimination Law*, p. 79, n. 106.
[44] S.D.A., s. 77(1) and R.R.A., s. 72(1).
[45] S.D.A., s. 77(2) and R.R.A., s. 72(2).

but does become unenforceable. In particular a discriminatory term is unenforceable by the person it would have favoured.[46]

Any person who is concerned with a contract containing an unlawful discriminatory term can apply to a county court for a revision of the contract in order that the term may be modified.[47] Such an order by a county court can make provision for the period of the contract before the order was made.[48]

The conciliation or court settlement exclusions for employment contracts do not apply to non-employment cases.[49]

[46] S.D.A., s. 77(3) and R.R.A., s. 72(3).
[47] S.D.A., s. 77(5) and R.R.A., s. 72(5).
[48] S.D.A., s. 77(6) and R.R.A., s. 72(6).
[49] S.D.A., s. 77(4) and R.R.A., s. 72(4).

# Chapter nine

# Harassment and Racial Abuse

## INTRODUCTION: WHY IS HARASSMENT IMPORTANT?

Sexual harassment and racial harassment are not specifically recognised in either of the principal statutes. This lack of statutory recognition does not mean that the law offers no protection for instances of harassment of a racial or sexual nature. For example Emslie J. has said that "sexual harassment, is a particularly degrading and unacceptable form of treatment which it must be taken to have been the intention of Parliament to restrain".[1] These sentiments can be expressed with equal force in relation to racial harassment.

Both racial and sexual harassment are degrading to their victims. Whether physical or verbal, such behaviour is unwelcome. Some people suffer racial or sexual insults quietly without complaint; they may do this because they do not wish to get on the "wrong side" of their landlord or neighbours, or simply because they have put up with such **unwelcome behaviour** for much of their lives and therefore accept it. This still does not make it **acceptable**. Personal feelings are fundamental to whether sexual or racial harassment arise. Even though a person may have put up with **unwelcome behaviour** for a number of years this does not mean they have not suffered as a result.[2]. The length of time someone puts up with harassment may though indicate that the detriment they suffered is small.[3]

There are added reasons as to why racial or sexual harassment is important as Duncan Forbes points out in the context of racial harassment because:[4]

(a) racial harassment victims are likely to be victims again;

[1] *Strathclyde Regional Council* v. *Porcelli* [1986] I.R.L.R. 134 (C.S.).
[2] *Wileman* v. *Minilec Engineering* [1988] I.C.R. 318 (E.A.T.).
[3] *Ibid.*
[4] See *Action on Racial Harassment: Legal Remedies and Local Authorities*, pp. 2–3.

(b) even home is unsafe;
(c) of the effect on the victim; and
(d) the motive of the perpetrator may be more serious than at first appears.

Harassment is often repeated. Rarely are incidents isolated. If the harassment is carried out by a neighbour or the landlord, an individual or family's personal and home security is threatened. An apparent simple act of harassment can belie a much more insidious intention. For example if a brick is thrown through the window of someone's home the only damage may be a broken window pane. This suggests the only offence is minor criminal damage. But on close examination the brick could have a note wrapped to it threatening the occupants. The brick could have been thrown through the window at a time when people were in the room. The intent could have been to assault or even kill. Thus the apparently simple act of criminal damage may have amounted to attempted assault or murder.

Taken as part of a wider campaign of harassment, involving other perpetrators such as an offence could also involve conspiracy.

## *Link with other disputes*

We have already briefly examined the link between racial and sexual harassment and "victimisation" and harassment in general as recognised by the Protection from Eviction Act 1977.[5] This close link does create the difficulty of distinguishing between different forms of harassment. A landlord may harass a tenant because he wants to get rid of them in order that he can gain vacant possession of the property so that it can be sold. That the tenant is black or a woman is not the reason for this behaviour. He will nonetheless still be committing an offence under the Protection from Eviction Act 1977. His victims may be black or women, but his motivation is not sexist or racial.

There are similar links to neighbour disputes and instances of nuisance. The relationship between racial harassment and nuisance has been successfully argued by some London housing authorities—Newham, Tower Hamlets, Camden and Islington—in eviction proceedings under Schedule 2, Ground 2 of the Housing Act 1985, against perpetrators of racial harassment.[6]

At worst, the close link described above between racial and sexual harassment and other disputes can confuse issues and consequently

[5] See Chapter 3.
[6] See in particular *London Borough of Newham* v. *McDonald*, November 23, 1988, Bow County Court (unreported), details in the Campaign for Racial Equality *Living in Terror*, pp. 27–28 and D. Forbes *op. cit.* p. 229.

fetter possible action. This is particularly so with domestic disputes. At best the link can provide possible courses of action in cases of racial and sexual harassment where the law fails to provide specific protection; in using the provisions under the S.D.A. and the R.R.A., care must be taken to ensure a racial or sexual motive can be imputed. In some circumstances, particularly where a complainant alleges victimisation the courts have failed to find in the complainants favour where it has been shown that the behaviour complained of can be explained via other motivating factors, even though these motivating factors may still amount to unacceptable behaviour.[7]

## *What is sexual harassment?*

"Sexual harassment" has been identified as a form of shorthand for the "any other detriment" provisions of the S.D.A. In *Wileman* v. *Minilec Engineering*[8], a case involving the sexual harassment of a female employee, Popplewell J. said, "the words 'sexual harassment' do not occur in the Act, and are legal shorthand for an activity which is easily recognisable as 'subjecting her to any other detriment'. Consequently where sexual harassment is alleged, the question is not 'was there sexual harassment' but was the person 'less favourably treated on the ground of her sex than a man would have been treated?'."[9] It is difficult to suggest what is meant by the term sexual harassment when no definition has been provided by statute or the courts. Certainly it must be a form of unfavourable treatment. Where such unfavourable treatment includes "a significant element of a sexual character to which a man would not be vulnerable," the treatment is on grounds of the woman's sex within the meaning of section 1(1)(*a*).[10] In the earlier case involving *Procelli* and *Strathclyde*,[11] the Employment Appeal Tribunal said "we do not find it necessary to define the expression 'sexual harassment' in precise terms. Unwelcome acts which involve physical contact of a sexual nature are obviously included. We consider that there can also be conduct falling short of such physical acts which the T.U.C. in the employment context gives examples of sexual harassment as 'repeated and unwanted statements made by someone in the workplace ... which are offensive to the worker involved, which cause the worker to feel threatened, humiliated, patronised or undermine job security or create a threatening or intimidating work environment'." It would not be difficult to adjust the wording to provide equally valid examples in the housing context.

[7] See discussion in Chapter three.
[8] [1988] I.C.R. 318 at p. 323 (E.A.T.).
[9] See *Strathclyde Regional Council* v.*Procelli* [1986] I.R.L.R. 134 (C.S.).
[10] *Strathclyde Regional Council* v. *Porcelli*,
[11] See *Strathclyde Regional Council* v. *Porcelli* [1984] I.R.L.R. 467 at p. 469.

There must, though, be a "detriment" as a result of the unfavourable treatment. However, there need not be physical or financial injury to show a person has suffered a detriment. According to Brandon L.J. in *Jeremiah* v. *Ministry of Defence*[12], "the expression 'subjecting to any other detriment' does not mean anything more than 'putting under a disadvantage'."

The extent of the detriment suffered may well have an effect on the size of any damages awarded to a victim.[13] Indeed, it would seem that personal feelings are a fundamental element in deciding whether a person has suffered a detriment. The fact that other people do not complain in similar circumstances does not mean the complainant has not suffered a detriment. If a person makes "sexual" remarks to a number of people, it has to be looked at in the context of each person. "All the people to whom they are made may regard them as wholly inoffensive; everyone else may regard them as offensive. Each individual then has the right, if the remarks are regarded as offensive, to treat them as an offence under the Sex Discrimination Act 1975."[14]

## *What is racial harassment?*

Although the term "sexual harassment" has been considered by the employment courts the term "racial harassment" has not. However, we have seen that the term "sexual harassment" is used for legal shorthand to describe an activity which amounts to subjecting a person to "any other detriment".[15] We have also seen that the expression "subjecting to any detriment" means putting someone under "a disadvantage". We have in Chapter one discussed the point that the S.D.A. and the R.R.A. should be interpreted similarly. Therefore, by this process of extension it is argued that the phrase "any other detriment" under the R.R.A.[16] can include "racial harassment" and it applies to the management and disposal of premises under both statutes respectively.[17]

What then is "racial harassment"? In the report *Living in Terror* on racial violence and harassment in housing, the Commission for Racial Equality gave the following working definition[18]:

> "Racial harassment is violence which may be verbal or physical and which includes attacks on property as well as on the person, suffered by individuals or groups because of their colour, race,

[12] [1979] I.R.L.R. 436 (C.A.).
[13] See *Wileman* v. *Minilec Engineering* [1988] I.C.R. 318 at p. 325.
[14] *Per* Popplewell J. *ibid.* at p. 326, see also comment at p. 322.
[25] See *Wileman* v. *Minilec Engineering* [1988] I.C.R. 318.
[16] See in particular s. 2(2)(*b*),
[17] See R.R.A., s. 30(2)(*b*) and S.D.A., s. 21(2)(*b*).
[18] See p. 8.

> nationality or ethnic or national origins, when the victim believes that the perpetrator was acting on racial grounds, or there is evidence of racism."

The Commission for Racial Equality (C.R.E.) argues that the victim's perception of racism is crucial. This is important say the C.R.E., because one of the concerns expressed by many victims, and by organisations working on their behalf, is that the police and other agencies such as housing departments often fail to recognise racial harassment when it occurs. As a result the offence is trivialised, the victims may receive little or no support, and the perpetrators are less likely to be identified.

Specific legal recognition of racial harassment as a crime is distinctly lacking. However, under landlord and tenant law the harassment of an occupier is a criminal offence. Section 1(3) of the Protection from Eviction Act 1977 states:

> "If any person with intent to cause the residential occupier of any premises:
> (a) to give up the occupation of the premises or any part thereof; or
> (b) to refrain from exercising any right or pursuing any remedy in respect of the premises or part thereof:
> does acts which are calculated to interfere with the peace or comfort of the residential occupier or members of his household, or persistently withdraws or withholds services reasonably required for the occupation of the premises as a residence, he shall be guilty of an offence."

This protection is given to any residential occupier—including a licensee and possibly even an illegal occupier—[19] against unlawful harassment by "any person". Therefore, the protection is available against harassment by the landlord or other people. This would include neighbours and agents of the owner of the premises. However, the intent to unlawfully deprive the occupier of possession of the premises or any associated rights must be present. Where the person concerned can show that they had reasonable cause to believe the occupier had ceased to reside in the premises then this may provide a defence.[20] Not only must intent to deprive of possession, rights or services be proved[21], but also it must be shown that "calculated acts" have been committed which interfere with the occupier's "peace and comfort".[22] For offences after January 15, 1989 the work "likely"

[19] But see *R.* v. *Blankley* [1979] Crim.L.R. 166.
[20] See *R.* v. *Davidson – Acres* [1980] Crim.L.R. 50 (C.A.).
[21] *MaCall.* v. *Abelesz* [1976] Q.B. 585.
[22] See for example *Westminster City Council* v. *Peart* (1986) 112 S.J. s. 43 (C.A.).

replaces "calculated"[23] and consequently provides a less onerous test. An omission to act does not amount to harassment[24] but may amount to "victimisation" under the S.D.A. and R.R.A.[25] These general exceptions have been strengthened by the Housing Act 1988 which introduces further protection in the case of illegal eviction and harassment and increases the amount of damages to be awarded in such cases.[26] In particular section 29 (concerning offences of harassment) removes the necessity to cause the residential occupier to give up occupation of the premises or part of the premises. However, for this provision to apply there must still be present the intent to deprive the residential occupier of rights, services or possession. Committing harassment motivated by a person's race or sex would be insufficient, unless exercised in such a way that this necessary element of intent could be proved.[27]

## *"Racial abuse" under the Race Relations Act*

Under the R.R.A. the use of a racially insulting word is not enough in itself to constitute a "detriment" and does not amount to "less favourable treatment" under section 1(1)(*a*). However, in the employment field, it may amount to less favourable treatment if the person who used the word intended that the person to whom it was directed would hear the comment or ought reasonably to have anticipated the insult would be passed on to the person or that person would hear of it in some other way.[28] If harassment through the use of offensive remarks is committed outside the course of employment then the victim will have no remedy under the Act.[29] Similarly, in the housing field, racial abuse must arise with the context of the provisions of the Act, *i.e.* in the management or disposal of premises or the supply of goods, services or facilities.

## *Racial abuse and criminal law*

Distinct, albeit limited, protection is available under criminal law to victims of racial abuse. The protection which is available is designed to produce social control primarily through the public order legislation. Prior to 1965, and the introduction of the Race Relations Act, there was

[23] Housing Act 1988, s. 29(1).
[24] See *R.* v. *Ahmad* [1986] Crim.L.R. 739 (C.A.).
[25] See Chapter seven.
[26] See ss. 27–33.
[27] For suggestions on changes in the law to correct this inadequacy see discussion by D. Forbes, *op. cit.* Chapter 15.
[28] *De Souza* v. *Automobile Association* [1986] I.C.R., s. 14.
[29] See discussion by M. D. Malone, *Sexual and Racial Harassment: A Series of Setbacks* (1987) L.S.G. 3496 at p. 3497.

no legal provision which specifically recognised "racial hatred" as an offence.[30] The offence of "incitement to racial hatred" was recognised by section 6 of the Race Relations Act 1965 and was extended by the R.R.A., s. 70 which amended the Public Order Act 1926.[31] The basic protection has been extended further by Part III of the Public Order Act 1986.[32]

"Racial hatred" means hatred against a group of persons in Great Britain defined by reference to colour, race, nationality (including citizenship) or ethnic or national origins.[33] The meanings of colour, race, etc. are discussed in Chapter four.

The Public Order Act 1986, recognises six offences in relation to "racial hatred" which are classified as an Act including or likely to stir up racial hatred or racially inflammatory material:

1. use of words, behaviour or display of written material;[34]
2. publishing or distributing written material;[35]
3. public performance of play;[36]
4. distributing, showing or playing a record;[37]
5. possession of racially inflammatory material.[38]

The test for these offences is to show the accused intended by his conduct or behaviour to stir up racial hatred, or that it was likely that racial hatred would be stirred up. Therefore, it is not necessary to show that the acts in question intended to provoke a breach of the peace nor that "racial hatred" was in fact stirred up. It is, though, necessary to show that the hatred was directed towards a specific racial group, rather than generally against ethnic minorities.

## *Harassment and the criminal law*

More general protection under the criminal law is available to victims of harassment. The most relevant protection which may be available can be classified as follows:

(a) fear of violence or provocation of violence;[39]

[30] For the application of the law against sedition see *Collins* (1839) 9 C. & P. 456 and *Burns* (1886) 16 C.O.X. C.C. 355 and the unreported case of *Count* (1947) which was concerned with racial abuse.
[31] For a criticism of s. 6 see G. Bindman, *Inclined to Racial Hatred* (1982) 132 N.L.J. 299.
[32] For a review of the history of the offence see Leopold, *Incitement to Hatred* [1982] P.L. 378.
[33] Public Order Act 1986, s. 17.
[34] s. 18.
[35] s. 19(3).
[36] s. 20.
[37] s. 21.
[38] s. 23.
[39] No breach of peace necessary Public Order Act, ss. 4(i) and 6(3).

(b) affray (threat cannot be made by words alone);[40]
(c) harassment, alarm or distress.[41]

Whether such protection is available to a victim will depend on whether the necessary mental element is present. Under the provisions of the Public Order Act 1986 the test is not whether the harassment or provocation of violence is motivated by race or sex but whether the words or behaviour are "threatening, abusive, insulting or disorderly".[42] It is also necessary to show there was the intention to provoke violence or to cause harassment, alarm or distress.[43] Acts, on the other hand, which are intended or likely to stir up racial hatred have a two-fold test. First, the words, behaviour or written material must be shown to be "threatening, abusive or insulting".[44] Secondly, such words or behaviour must have been used with the intention to stir up racial hatred[45] or would be likely, having regard to all circumstances, to stir up racial hatred.[46] Where it can be shown that such behaviour was threatening, abusive or insulting but it is difficult to show that behaviour was intended to stir up racial hatred, proceedings should be taken under sections 4(1) or 5(1).[47] For all of these offences the police have the power of arrest without warrant.[48] At Appendix 2 is a schedule of possible courses of action open to victims of sexual or racial harassment.

## *Conclusion*

The law with regard to sexual and racial harassment is convoluted and uncertain. This lack of legal clarity and recognition exacerbates the lack of positive action taken by police and housing authorities in responding to complaints. Examples of positive action grow, for example Ealing and Newham Metropolitan police authorities and local authorities introduced special schemes to deal with instances of harassment.) Uncertainty deters complainants from coming forward. Until the law changes Parliament condones the "fogginess" surrounding legal protection in cases of racial and sexual harassment. The Appeal Court has though recognised the test of harrassment opening up for victims the possibility of civil action for damages and injunctive relief.[49]

[40] See *ibid.*, ss. 3(1) and 3(3) and *Taylor* v. *D.P.P.* [1973] A.C. 964.
[41] Public Order Act 1986, s. 5(1).
[42] See s. 4(1)(*a*), 4(1)(*b*), 5(1)(*a*) and 5(1)(*b*).
[43] ss. 4(i) and 5(i).
[44] s. 18(1).
[45] s. 18(1)(*a*).
[46] s. 18(1)(*b*) but see s. 18(5).
[47] For a fuller discussion of these offences see J. Smith and B. Hogan, *Criminal Law* (1986) pp. 789–794.
[48] ss. 3(6), 4(3), 5(4) and 18(3).
[49] See *Khorasandjian* v. *Bush* (1993) N.L.J. March 5, at 32g.

# Chapter ten

# Application and Practice: Public Housing Sector Discrimination by Local Housing Authorities

## Meaning of local housing authorities

A "local housing authority" means a district council, a London borough council, the Common Council of the City of London or the Council of the Isles of Scilly.[1] The wider definition of "housing authority" means a local housing authority, a new town corporation or the Development Board for Rural Wales.[2]

## General responsibilities

Every local housing authority has a responsibility to consider the housing conditions and needs of its district "with respect to the provision of further housing accommodation"[3] and in doing so has the duty to review any information which has been brought to its notice.[4] This general obligation to consider the housing conditions and needs of its area does not translate into a specific obligation in housing a particular person or family. Instead, the allocation of accommodation and the provision of housing to meet identified needs are discretionary processes. When selecting tenants, though, a local housing authority must ensure a reasonable preference is given to:[5]

(a) persons occupying insanitary or overcrowded conditions;
(b) persons having large families;

[1] Housing Act 1985, s. 1.
[2] Housing Act 1985, s. 4(*a*).
[3] s. 8(1), *ibid,*
[4] s. 8(2), *ibid.*
[5] s. 22, *ibid.*

(c) persons living under unsatisfactory housing conditions; and
(d) persons towards whom the authority are subject to a duty under section 65 or 68 (persons found to be homeless).

## Facilitating role

To give effect to these wide obligations, section 9 of the Housing Act 1985 empowers local housing authorities to acquire, build, improve, convert, repair, manage and dispose of housing and land. This role of directly providing and managing housing is though likely to change. A changed role of "facilitating" the provision and management of housing was forecast by the White Paper, *Housing: The Government's Proposals*,[6] which introduced the Housing Act 1988,

> "The Government will encourage local authorities to change and develop their housing role. Provision of housing by local authorities as landlords should gradually be diminished, and alternative forms of tenure and tenant choice should increase. Some authorities will want to move in this direction themselves, and the Government will assist them ... Local authorities should increasingly see themselves as enablers who ensure that everyone in their area is adequately housed; but not necessarily by them."

As the White Paper goes on to say[7],

> "There will no longer be the same presumption that the local authority itself should take direct action to meet new or increasing demands. The future role of local authorities will essentially be a strategic one identifying housing needs and demands, encouraging innovate methods of provision by other bodies to meet such needs, maximising the use of private finance, and encouraging the new interest in the revival of the independent rented sector."

The provisions of the Housing Act 1988 which introduce "Tenants Choice" and "Housing Action Trusts" can be seen as key initiatives in facilitating the transfer of public owned housing stock to owner occupation and other forms of tenure and to the independent rented sector, including the housing association movement.[8] Section 161[9] of the Local Government and Housing Act 1989 states that a housing authority is not required to keep a housing stock.

[6] Cmnd. 214, see para. 1.16.
[7] para. 5.1.
[8] See Parts II and IV of the Act.
[9] Amending Housing Act 1985, s. 9.

## Responsibilities to the homeless

Local housing authorities do have specific responsibilities for the homeless. First enacted in 1977 the Housing (Homeless Persons) Act is now contained within Part III of the consolidating Housing Act of 1985. However, not all homeless people are entitled to assistance. A housing authority has to be satisfied when providing permanent housing that an applicant is according to sections 65 and 66:

(a) homeless[10];
(b) in priority need[11];
(c) not intentionally homeless[12];
(d) has a local connection[13].

A detailed discussion of the homeless provisions of the Housing Act 1985 is beyond the scope of this work.[14] Although no specific mention is made of ethnic minorities it is worth noting that women are given some recognition under the act in that section 58(1)(*a*) says a pregnant woman has a priority need for accommodation if she is homeless. Arguably women at risk through fear of violence or other abuse could be regarded as vulnerable under section 59(1)(*c*) and if so would also have a priority need. Section 58(3) makes the point a little more certain. It says:

> "A person is also homeless if he has accommodation [*i.e.* not technically homeless as specified in section 58(2)] but:
> (a) he cannot secure entry to it; or
> (b) it is probable that occupation of it will lead to violence from some other person residing in it or to threats of violence from some other person residing in it and likely to carry out the threats.

The effect of this is discussed in the next section of this chapter which deals with homelessness responsibilities and discrimination.

## General housing and homelessness responsibilities and discrimination

Local authorities could discriminate on the basis of race when allocating accommodation due to the following reasons:[15]

[10] s. 58, *ibid.*
[11] s. 59, *ibid.*
[12] s. 60, *ibid.*
[13] s. 61, *ibid.*
[14] See Arden & Hunter, *Manual of Housing Law*, 5th ed.
[15] See Commission for Racial Equality (C.R.E.) *Race and Housing in Liverpool: A Research Report*, p 79.

1. Discrimination may occur because staff act on the belief that all black households want to live in the same area.
2. Discrimination may occur by staff in the belief that black people should not be offered as good quality accommodation as white people.
3. Discrimination may occur through the selective provision of information and advice in the assessment of domestic standards.
4. Discrimination may occur because staff are pursuing the management objective of letting properties quickly.

The Commission for Racial Equality in the Non-Discrimination Notice it served on Hackney London Borough Council in May 1983 stated that the council had discriminated "against various persons of West Indian, Asian or African origin who were rehoused from the council's waiting list, rehoused as homeless cases or rehoused as a result of being decanted from their existing accommodation." The notice stated the council was responsible for the acts of discrimination by its servants under section 32(1) of the Race Relations Act 1976 and had acted:

> "in contravention of section 20(1)(*b*) read together with section 1(1)(*a*) of the Act by refusing or deliberately omitting to provide them (various persons of West Indian, Asian or African origin) with housing accommodation (provision of such accommodation being a service of the local authority) of the like quality to that offered to white persons in similar need of housing accommodation, and/or
> — in contravention of section 21(1)(*c*) read together with section 1(1)(*a*) of the Act in its treatment of them in relation to lists of persons in need of council accommodation".[16]

The decision of the C.R.E. in the Hackney London Borough Council case in issuing a Non-Discriminatory Notice is important in two respects. Firstly, it makes it clear a local authority cannot claim it is acting under a statutory authority;[17] and secondly, when local authorities are allocating tenancies they are providing services and as such the provision of those services falls under section 20 of the Act. This by extension means section 29 of the S.D.A. 1975, which is the identical provision relating to discrimination on the grounds of sex, would also apply. Again there can be no doubt that local authorities, when allocating accommodation and keeping waiting lists, cannot claim the "statutory authority" exception.

Indeed the Acts would seem to apply to all aspects of a local authority service when providing services, goods or facilities whether

[16] C.R.E., *Race & Council Housing in Hackney: Report of Formal Investigation*, p. 144.
[17] Which provides an exception to the provisions of the Act, see Chapter 10.

or not when it acts as a landlord in managing or disposing of its housing stock.

## RACIAL DISCRIMINATION AND WORK PERMITS

In the Commission's Report of a Formal Investigation into Allocations, by the Royal Borough of Kensington and Chelsea and the London Borough of Barnet in 1982, practices and policies operated by the councils' housing departments were found to be indirectly discriminatory under section 28 of the Act read with sections 1(1)(*b*), 20 and 21. The allocations related to work permit holders. The requirement imposed by the councils, said the C.R.E., "adversely affected a disproportionately larger number of foreign national residents in the areas concerned".[18] Examining work permits and passports has tended to be the practice of some local authorities when attempting to avoid responsibility for homeless non-nationals. As M. Wilson says in *Immigration and Race*[19], "L.A.'s (local authorities) are obliged to rehouse only homeless people who have been resident in the area or who have 'strong local connections,' and may insist on the need to produce a proof of residence." There has, according to Wilson, "been an increase in the number of people whose passports have been checked when applying for housing advice and assistance." In a few instances pages of passports have been photocopied and suspected "overstayers" reported to the Home Office.

The C.R.E. in its formal report on the Royal Borough of Kensington and Chelsea and the London Borough of Barnet's practices (which included comments on G.L.C. practices) recommended that the authorities should:

(a) define what information is needed about housing applicants in order to process their applications;

(b) list the variety of documents in which that information might be available; these might be birth certificates, national insurance cards, medical cards, rent books, family allowance books, driving licences, post office savings books, trade union cards or correspondence concerning services such as gas and electricity;

(c) ask all applicants which of these documents they want, or are able, to provide and leave it to them to decide whether or not to produce passports;

[18] *Ibid.*, p. 1.
[19] 1983, p. 67.

(d) issue a circular to housing departments staff explaining the council's policy on requests for passports to ensure that they understand the adverse effect which such requests can have on the perceptions of ethnic minority clients as a whole.

The formal report comments that the "Home Office have said that local authorities do not have the responsibility for the operation of immigration rules or for providing information to the Home Office. There is, therefore, no reason why local authorities need to refer individual cases to the Home Office"[20]. However, The Court of Appeal has found that a local authority is entitled to determine whether an applicant is an illegal entrant to the country and has a duty to inform the Home Office of such a decision, the decision being open to challenge by way of judicial review. Certainly this view is contrary to that held by C.R.E. and could well invite racial discrimination by local authorities.

## RESIDENTIAL REQUIREMENTS AND DISCRIMINATION

It is of course unlawful for a local authority to discriminate on the ground of a person's nationality, since this would amount to direct discrimination under section 1(1)(*a*) of the R.R.A. read in conjunction with section 3(1) which includes "nationality" as part of the definition of "racial grounds".[22]

A local authority may claim that such a "residence requirement" is "justifiable". A local authority has a general responsibility to identify and provide for the needs of its district, rather than non-local needs. This dilemma may be particularly marked in rural areas where specific schemes of low cost housing are developed to meet high local need for example in a village. The provisions relating to homelessness seem to support the argument also, since a local housing authority has only very limited responsibility towards homeless people who cannot prove a definite "local connection"[23]. To show a local connection with a particular district a homeless person must show:

(a) he is or in the past was normally resident in the district by his own choice; or
(b) he is employed in the district; or
(c) he has family associations there; or

[20] *Ibid.*, pp. 2–13.
[21] See *Dawkins* v. *Department of Environment* [1993] I.R.L.R. 284.
[22] See Chapter 4.
[23] Housing Act 1985, s. 61.

(d) there are special circumstances.[24]

In a survey undertaken by Shelter in 1983[25] of 177 local authorities 85 per cent. applied residential requirements based on residence or employment in their districts. Thirty per cent. of the 177 would only admit "residents" on to their waiting lists. Periods vary from a year to five years. Perhaps a justified example of such an approach is where social housing (housing for rent or low cost sale) is specifically provided in rural areas because of a shortage of affordable housing for local people of limited means. Similarly, local housing authorities make use of "minimum registration periods" on the waiting lists before a person or family can qualify for an offer of accommodation. Usually, the period is between six to 12 months. Taken with the period an applicant has to live in a district before registering this can simply extend the overall waiting time. In the early 1960's such an approach discriminated against members of the immigrant population since they were less able to satisfy residential requirements. Even though it can be argued that such residential restrictions apply to all newcomers to a local authority area the 1977 P.E.P. Report *Racial Minorities and Public Housing* pointed out that ethnic minority households formed a large proportion of newly arrived households in particular areas and as a result were disproportionately affected by such requirements. However, residential qualifications and minimum waiting periods may not have a discriminatory effect.[26] Most certainly the approach still discriminates against new immigrants and new nationals with limited periods of residence, for example Vietnamese refugees. It may also contravene the non-discrimination provision of the Treaty of Rome which encourages mobility of labour between member countries.[27]

## JUSTIFYING RESIDENTIAL QUALIFICATIONS

The validity of residential qualifications and minimum periods of residence will depend on their purpose and whether this is discriminatory, or if not intended to discriminate whether they have a discriminatory effect. If indirect discrimination is a result, can the requirement be justified?

If a court adopted a similar approach in the housing field as the Employment Appeal Tribunals in determining whether a residential

[24] Housing Act 1985, s. 61(1).

[25] See R. Matthews, *Restrictive Practices: Waiting List Restrictions and Housing Need* p. 11.

[26] See C.R.E. Formal report on *Race and Council Housing in Hackney* pp. 32–33.

[27] See Chapter 3.

requirement which has a discriminatory effect could be objectively justified, it might take into account the following questions:

— has the council recognised and considered the discriminatory effect of the requirement?

— how serious is the discriminatory effect? There may have been a recent influx of refugees so much so that the requirement applies detrimentally to these refugees.

— what purpose is the council trying to achieve by its residential requirement? Does the council have its requirement simply because it has always done things that way?

— is there a non-discriminatory or less discriminatory way for the council to achieve its objective?

— weighing and balancing all the above factors, should the requirement be regarded as reasonable and equitable in an objective sense?

In this way a local authority can judge whether the application of residential requirements meet its statutory responsibility to address local housing needs is appropriate and justifiable and most importantly whether it operates in a non-discriminatory way.

## RESIDENTIAL QUALIFICATIONS AND DISCRIMINATION AGAINST WOMEN

Residential qualifications can also discriminate against women. For example a woman who has left the domestic home may well wish to set up home afresh in a new area. She may wish to do this through fear of violence by her partner or fear that if she remains in the area in which she lived her partner will find her again. Their lives are bound, in some way, to overlap due to friendships, families or other associations. In such circumstances it would be difficult for her to meet requirements of residence and the "local connection" test as a homeless person or family of another local authority.[28] Links between local authorities and housing associations can help to break this problem down.

## OTHER RESTRICTIVE PRACTICES

There are other "restrictive practices" which can indirectly discriminate against women and ethnic minorities. These include

[28] *R.* v. *Bristol City Council ex p., Browne* [1979] 1 W.L.R. 1437.

restrictions against owner occupiers, income tests, housekeeping standards and offering poorer accommodation to the homeless and others in extreme housing need.

## OWNER OCCUPIER RESTRICTIONS AND DISCRIMINATION AGAINST ETHNIC MINORITIES

A practice which has been under particular criticism is that adopted by local authorities which prevents owner occupiers from registering on a waiting list, or which gives owner occupiers less priority or no priority on the waiting list. Such restrictions can be discriminatory towards ethnic minorities and women. In the case of ethnic minority groups, many such groups have a greater proportion of owner occupiers than the population as a whole, this is particularly so of the Asian population.[29] Not all owner occupiers live in "privileged conditions". As the Housing Services Advisory Group's report in 1978 on the *Allocation of Council Housing*[30—31] stated, any restrictions on waiting lists placed upon owner occupiers is "difficult to justify, since it may exclude many with genuine housing problems." Evidence is available to show that ethnic minorities have a greater proportion of their numbers living in poor housing conditions than the population as a whole. The result is almost certainly to be indirect discrimination. It is very difficult to see in what circumstances restrictions against owner occupiers registering on the waiting list could be objectively justified. Better would be for local housing authorities to allow owner occupiers to register in order that an "objective" assessment of their housing needs can be undertaken.

## OWNER OCCUPIER RESTRICTIONS AND DISCRIMINATION AGAINST WOMEN

Restrictions against owner occupiers and former owner occupiers can adversely affect the position of women where they have left the

[29] See P.E.P. Report, *Racial Minorities and Public Housing* 1977, D. Smith *op. cit.* Chapter 11, C.R.E. *Race & Council Housing in Hackney*, p. 18, C.R.E. *Race and Housing in Liverpool*, p. 14, and National Federation of Housing Associations *Race and Housing*, p. 1.

[30—31] See for example P.E.P. Report, *op. cit.*, D. Smith *op. cit.* Chapters 9 to 11, C.R.E., *Race and Housing in Liverpool* and N.F.H.A. *op. cit.*.

domestic home as a result of a relationship breakdown. Local authorities have justified this stance on owner occupiers leaving a family home on two principal counts. First, on the basis that they do not wish to provide a partner with accommodation lest this might contribute to the breakdown of the marriage relationship. By the time a woman arrives at the local authority's door seeking accommodation of her own it is highly probable the relationship has already broken down. That second, by providing a woman and any accompanying children with a new home this may well leave the husband or male partner in a property which he under-occupies. Thus, two homes will have been provided for what was once one household. In the light of growing waiting lists, local authorities have a duty, they suggest, to other people registered on their lists.

On account of this stance some local authorities have given little or no priority to women as a result of a relationship breakdown. This has been very much the case under the homelessness responsibilities of local authorities where a woman is afraid to return to the domestic or family home due to violence or threat of violence from her partner. Local authorities have attempted to avoid their responsibilities, often successfully, in a number of ways.

In *R.* v. *Ealing London Borough ex parte, Sidhu*[32] the court held that a battered woman who had taken refuge in a crisis hostel under a temporary licence was still regarded as homeless. The local authority had claimed she was no longer homeless. As was stated in the case "it was important that refuges be seen as temporary crisis accommodation, and that women living in refuges were still homeless, otherwise if women were taken out of the 'homeless' category then the Act [then the Housing (Homeless Persons) Act 1977] was being watered down and its protections would be removed from a wide class of persons that it was set up to help and for whom it was extremely important."

However, many local authorities have not regarded the provision of accommodation as the best way of resolving a relationship breakdown. Instead many have relied on a homeless woman, particularly where children are involved, gaining an injunction or a non-molestation order against her partner and for her to regain possession of the family home. However, the courts have increasingly adopted the view that their powers to grant ouster orders, in particular, should not be used to solve a local housing authority's responsibilities to provide accommodation.[33] Even though the courts have adopted this approach where a woman has the right to return to her home under the Matrimonial Homes Act 1983 some local authorities still fail to offer help unless she

[32] (1982) 80 L.G.R. 534.
[33] See for example *Warwick* v. *Warwick* (1981) 1 H.L.R. 139 (C.A.).

cannot return due to violence. As Frances Logan says in *Homelessness and Relationship Breakdown*[34] it "is therefore clear that relationship breakdown itself will not constitute homelessness even though the couple may wish to split up." This is presumably because a woman who is not in threat of violence can in theory regain possession of her home and is not vulnerable as a priority group under section 59(1)(*c*) of the Housing Act 1985. More priority may be given if she has children, although children are still being taken into care as a result of homelessness[35]. Evidence according to Logan suggests few single women are given help as homeless persons by local housing authorities[36] and she goes on to say,

> "This makes it abundantly clear that women, *per se*, are given no priority as homeless persons, but that, with very limited exceptions such as old age or illness, a woman's access to housing will be totally reliant on her having dependent children or being pregnant. It is a continuation of the philosophy ... in matrimonial law generally of creating a seeming priority for women which is in fact a priority for the bearers or carers of children, and not for women themselves."

A further approach adopted by some local authorities to avoid responsibility has been to consider a battered woman who has left the domestic or family home as intentionally homeless if she had not followed the authority's advice of gaining an injunction or ouster order.[37] However, it is unlikely a woman would be regarded as intentionally homeless where her partner failed to pay the mortgage or rent.[38] Neither would she if her marriage had broken down after repeated attempts to make it work.[39]

Violence within the domestic home is likely to place a direct responsibility on a local authority to treat an applicant as homeless.[40] There is though no need to show that violence has taken place before. The test is a lower one, *i.e.* are there "threats of violence from a person likely to carry them out".[41]

Additionally, local housing authorities should treat young homeless women as vulnerable, as Lord Ross stated although he was "not persuaded that every 16 year old is vulnerable" he went on to say

[34] p. 56.
[35] F. Logan, *op. cit.* p. 57.
[36] *Ibid.*
[37] See *R.* v. *Wandsworth London Borough Council ex p., Nimako-Boateng* (1983) 14 Fam.Law 117, but also *c.f.* the Housing (Homeless Persons) Act Code of Practice, para. 2.16.
[38] See *R.* v. *Eastleigh Borough Council ex parte, Beattie* (1982) 17 H.L.R. 168.
[39] *R.* v. *Basingstoke and Dean Borough Council ex p., Bassett* [1984] 14 Fam.Law 90.
[40] See *R.* v. *Purbeck District Council ex p., Cadney* (1985) 17 H.L.R. 534 (Q.B.D.).
[41] See *Encyclopedia of Housing Law and Practice*, paras. 1–0122 and 1–0130.

however "when you find a girl of 16 who has no assets, no means and nowhere to go and has apparently left home because of violence, I am of the opinion that no reasonable authority could fail to conclude that she was vulnerable.[42]

# OTHER SPECIFIC RESPONSIBILITIES: STATUTORY AUTHORITY

Local housing authorities have further responsibilities relating to housing. First, they have the responsibility to institute proceedings for offences relating to unlawful eviction and harassment.[43] Further they must administer as rating authorities the Housing Benefit Scheme.[44] They also have responsibilities in controlling houses in multiple occupation and common lodging houses,[45] in providing improvement grants and loans,[46] in providing assistance to home owners of defective housing,[47] in determining standards of future housing and in compulsory purchase and land compensation, slum clearance and area improvement,[48] and in administering the Right to Buy Scheme for council tenants.[49]

When providing information and services to comply with the rights of secure tenants under the "Tenants' Choice", local housing authorities are also under specific duties relating to security of tenure,[50] rights of succession,[51] rights of assignment, exchange and subletting,[52] right to carry out repairs and improvements,[53] variation of term of tenancy,[54] information about tenancies and housing allocation[55] and consultation on matters of housing management.[56]

In undertaking these duties and powers local housing authorities must have regard to the provisions of the S.D.A. and the R.R.A. As M. Ward and J. Zebedee comment on the Housing Benefit Regulations

[42] *Kelly* v. *Marklands District Council* July 12, 1985 Ct. of Sessions; *Encyclopedia of Housing Law and Practice*, para. 1–0125; for a definition of vulnerability see *R.* v. *Waveny District Council ex parte, Bowers* [1983] Q.B. 238, 4 H.L.R. 118 (C.A.).
[43] Protection from Eviction Act 1977, s.6.
[44] Social Security Act 1986, s. 28.
[45] Housing Act 1985, ss. 346, 347, 403 and 407.
[46] *Ibid.*, ss. 435 and 460.
[47] *Ibid.*, ss. 535 and 536.
[48] *Ibid.*, ss. 239, 253, 264, 582 and 604.
[49] *Ibid.*, s. 118.
[50] *Ibid.*, ss. 82–86.
[51] *Ibid.*, ss. 87–90.
[52] *Ibid.*, ss. 91–95.
[53] *Ibid.*, ss. 96–101.
[54] *Ibid.*, ss. 102 and 103.
[55] *Ibid.*, ss. 104 and 106.
[56] *Ibid.*, s. 105.

issued under the Social Security Act 1986, "In addition to the Act and regulations, other pieces of legislation circumscribe the manner in which authorities may administer the scheme," for example, "the Sex Discrimination Act 1976 and the Race Relations Act 1976 make it illegal to discriminate (either directly or indirectly) against someone, or victimise someone . . .". When undertaking such duties local housing authorities cannot claim they are doing so in defiance of discrimination law under statutory authority.[57]

# RESPONSIBILITIES IN PROMOTING RACIAL HARMONY

Section 71 of the R.R.A. says:

> "it shall be the duty of every local authority to make appropriate arrangements with a view to securing that their various functions are carried out with due regard to the need—
> (a) to eliminate unlawful racial discrimination; and
> (b) to promote equality of opportunity, and good race relations, between persons of different racial groups.
> In fulfilling this 'general statutory duty' local authorities still have to comply with the other provisions of the Act."

In its report examining the implications of section 71, the C.R.E. emphasised the need for each local authority "to carry out a review of its current policies".[58] When undertaking such a review two basic questions should be asked:[59]

(i) what is the effect of current housing policies upon the local authority's ethnic minority population?; and
(ii) what are the housing needs of the local authority's ethnic minority population and in what ways, if any, are they being met by current housing policies?

The Commission highlighted a number of issues it saw as important for a local authority to consider and implement. These included:[60]

[57] *c.f.* Home Office duties relating to immigration control, *R.* v. *Immigration Appeal Tribunal* [1980] 1 W.L.R. 1037 (C.A.), *R.* v. *Entry Clearance Officer, Bombay, ex p. Amin* [1983] 2 A.C. 818 (H.L.) where immigration control was considered an area outside the scope of the Act and advice provided by the Inland Revenue on tax relief in *Savani* v. *I.R.C.* [1981] Q.B. 458, [1981] 1 All E.R. 1121 (C.A.) which was regarded as a service under the Act; see also *General Medical Council* v. *Goba* [1988] I.R.L.R. 425 (E.A.T.) and Chapter twelve on General Exceptions.
[58] C.R.E., *Local Authorities and the Housing Implications of Section 71 of the Race Relations Act 1976*, p. 9.
[59] *Ibid.*
[60] *Ibid.* pp. 10–23.

(a) *Record keeping and monitoring* effective policy review depends on up-to-date and reliable information. Therefore records need to monitor all housing services provided by a local authority;

(b) *Allocations* to eliminate the two principal forms of disadvantage suffered by ethnic minority households in relation to the allocation of council housing. The following elements of any allocation system need to be examined to determine whether their effect was discriminatory:

 (i) residential qualifications, *e.g.,* an applicant must live in the area for five years before being considered;
 (ii) exclusions, *e.g.*, owner occupiers cannot register on the waiting list;
 (iii) priority systems, *e.g.*, does giving priority to decants or transfer cases naturally favour the white population?;
 (iv) area of choice, *e.g.*, do staff assume ethnic minorities will only be housed in certain areas. Dispersal policies or quotas, *i.e.*, only one house in five should be let to a black family, are also unlawful;

(c) *Training* there is a need for in-service training of staff to inform officers about the national and local position of the ethnic minority population and "to show the relationships between ethnic minority clients and the various housing tasks performed by a local authority";[61]

(d) *Recruitment* there was a need to recruit staff from the ethnic minority population. Here section 11 of the Local Government Act 1966 was of use since the Home Secretary can pay grants to local authorities where it was required ... to make special provision in the exercise of any of their functions in consequence of the presence within their area of substantial numbers of immigrants from the Commonwealth whose language or customs differ from those of the rest of the community;

(e) *Special housing needs* local authorities should fully recognise the special housing needs of:

 (i) black youths;
 (ii) the elderly;
 (iii) single parent families; and
 (iv) Asian women.

(f) *Housing investment programmes* H.I.P.s were introduced "to enable local authorities to present co-ordinated analyses of

[61] *Ibid.*, p. 13.

housing conditions in their area and to formulate coherent policies and programmes of capital spending on public housing".[62] Through its H.I.P. a local authority can benefit its ethnic minority population in a number of ways:

(i) by improving stock—a greater proportion of ethnic minority households are housed in the poorer local authority stock;
(ii) by providing private sector improvement grants—again a greater proportion of ethnic minority households are housed in the poorer private sector stock;
(iii) by providing assistance to housing associations, since housing associations are able to do much to help the ethnic minority population.[63]

(g) *Private sector activity* local authorities should help with private sector initiatives;
(h) *Sale of council houses* the sale of council houses and "right to buy" should not operate in a discriminatory way;
(i) *Self-help group* local authorities should assist and promote ethnic minority self-help groups.

# SECTION 71 OBLIGATIONS, UNLAWFUL DISCRIMINATION AND RACIAL DISCRIMINATION

Section 71 of the Race Relations Act 1976 imposes an obligation on local authorities to "eliminate unlawful discrimination",[64] and to "promote equality of opportunity" and good race relations.[65] A local authority must have regard to these matters in any decision it may take, *i.e.*, the section requires a local authority to "make appropriate arrangements".[66] A failure to set up appropriate arrangements would amount to a breach of the local authority's statutory duty. Therefore a failure to "develop a policy on racial harassment" may, according to D. Forbes,[67] be unlawful in two respects:

(a) where the absence of any priority means that, in practice, the authority completely disregards the need mentioned in section 71 when carrying out its functions;

[62] D.O.E. Circular No. 63/77.
[63] C.R.E., *op. cit.* pp. 18–19.
[64] s. 71(*a*).
[65] s. 71(*b*).
[66] See *Wheeler* v. *Leicester City Council* [1985] A.C. 1054 (H.L.).
[67] *Op. cit.* p. 30.

(b) where racial harassment is so widespread in the authority's area in a particular context ... that a failure to develop a policy to deal with it amounts to a complete failure to consider the need referred to in section 71 (*i.e.*, the problem is so acute that no reasonable authority could fail to have a racial harassment policy).

## SECTION 71 OBLIGATIONS AND CONTRACT COMPLIANCE

Although a local authority would be able to use its statutory duty under section 71 to justify sanctions against organisations and individuals to prevent and eliminate discrimination it is unlikely it can be used to persuade organisations and individuals to adopt its political stance on race relations.[68]

A practice in some local authorities, *e.g.*, Birmingham City Council, in recent years had been to attach terms to contracts into which they have entered, which attempt to promote good race relations through "contract compliance." An example might be that a building contractor undertaking modernisation works to a local authority estate is required to employ local labour, particularly important where a high proportion of the population on the estate in question is from ethnic minorities. However, in the Local Government Act 1988 Parliament has now made it unlawful to take into account "non-commercial matters" when considering tenders from private companies.[69] However, in order to comply with their obligations under section 71 local authorities are able to ask contractors the following questions:[70]

"1. Is it your policy as an employer to comply with your statutory obligations under the R.R.A. and, accordingly, your practice not to treat one group of people less favourably than others because of their colour, race, nationality or ethnic origin in relation to decisions to recruit, train or promote employees?
2. In the last three years, has any finding of unlawful racial discrimination been made against your organisation by any court or industrial tribunal?
3. In the last three years, has your organisation been the subject of formal investigation by the Commission for Racial Equality on grounds of alleged unlawful discrimination?

[68] For example of sanctions which can and cannot be used see D. Forbes, *op. cit.* pp. 13–15.
[69] s. 17; see also Local Government Training Board, *Managing Competition: Tendering For Local Government Services*, p. 5.
[70] *Employment Digest*, 244, April 25, 1988.

If the answer to question 2 is in the affirmative or, in relation to question 3, the Commission made a finding adverse to your organisation,

4. What steps did you take in consequence of that finding?
5. Is your policy on race relations set out:

    (a) in instructions to those concerned with recruitment, training and promotion;
    (b) in documents available to employees, recognised trade unions or other representative groups of employees;
    (c) in recruitment and advertisements or other literature?

6. Do you observe as far as possible the Commission for Racial Equality's Code of Practice for Employment, as approved by Parliament in 1983, which gives practical guidance to employers and others on the elimination of racial discrimination and the promotion of equality of opportunity in employment, including the steps that can be taken to encourage members of the ethnic minorities to apply for jobs or take up training opportunities?"

However, section 17 and Schedule 2 of the Local Government Act 1988 outlaws the use of non-commercial matters in supply or works contracts of public authorities which effectively puts an end to the furtherance of political objectives. The guidance is still of use, though, by bodies other than public authorities.

# Chapter eleven

# Application and Practice: The Quasi-Public Housing Sector

## INTRODUCTION: THE NATURE OF THE QUASI-PUBLIC HOUSING SECTOR

The quasi-public housing sector is essentially the middle ground of housing policy occupied by the housing assocations movement and its overseer, the Housing Corporation. As Alder and Handy note in *Housing Association Law*,[1] the "voluntary housing movement is sometimes regarded as the 'third force' in housing policy, providing an alternative to the public rented sector and also to private owner occupation against a background of decline in the supply of private rented accommodation." Similarly it has been suggested that housing associations constitute a "quasi-public sector of housing operations".[2]

Housing associations currently receive more than £1.7 billion annually from the government-established Housing Corporation and approximately £100m annually from local authorities. Around 40,000 to 50,000 homes for rent are provided each year, along with a further 5–10,000 homes for sale in the main, to the elderly and first time buyers. Housing associations now own more than half a million dwellings which amounts to three per cent. of the nation's housing stock. In some inner city areas their ownership can be as high as 60 to 70 per cent. of the stock in those areas.[3]

Additionally, housing associations are seen as important vehicles in implementing the housing policy initiatives of the Housing Act 1988.[4] Housing associations may well:

(a) become landlords of tenants who opt to change landlords under Tenant's Choice[5];

[1] 2nd Ed., 1991 Sweet & Maxwell, p. 3.
[2] Arden & Hunter: *Manual of Housing Law*, 5th ed., p. 000.
[3] See Alder and Handy *op. cit.*, Chapter 1. Over 60,000 new houses were produced in 1992.
[4] See the White Paper, *Housing: The Government's Proposals* Cmnd. 214.
[5] Housing Act 1988, ss. 83–114.

(b) be newly formed tenants co-operatives under the Tenant's Choice provisions;
(c) be involved on the disposal and redevelopment of properties as a result of the formation of Housing Action Trusts[6];
(d) be newly formed by local authorities to enable the voluntary transfer of public sector housing stock
(e) expand due to the new financial regime introduced for registered housing associations which provides for greater use of private finance.[7]

Along with government funding and the position of privilege in relation to government housing policy comes government intervention. Intervention is exercised through the Housing Corporation which was originally established in 1964 to assist and promote housing association activity.[8] Since 1974, however, the Corporation's role has been much wider and has included the function of supervision and control of housing associations eligible for public subsidies. Indeed all housing associations, subject to a few specialised exceptions, must first register with the Housing Corporation to be eligible for public subsidy.[9] Essentially, only registered charities which have housing amongst their objects or registered industrial and provident societies which are exclusively restricted to permissible housing or related purposes are statutorily eligible for registration.[10] Conceivably other bodies are able to fall within the "generic definition" of a housing association. Section 1(1) of the Housing Associations Act 1985 says:

> "housing association" means a society, body of trustees or company:
>
> (a) which is established for the purpose of, or amongst whose objects or powers are included those of, providing, constructing, improving or managing, or facilitating or encouraging the construction or improvement of housing accommodation; and
> (b) which does not trade for profit or whose constitution or rules prohibit the issue of capital with interest or dividend exceeding such rate as may be prescribed by the treasury, whether with or without differentiation as between share and loan capital.

In addition to the statutory requirements for eligibility to register with the Corporation as a housing association there are administrative criteria which have to be satisfied. In particular, the Corporation will

[6] ss. 60–92, *ibid.*
[7] s. 50 *ibid.*, and see White Paper *ibid.*, paper s. 4.5–4.8.
[8] Housing Act 1964, s. 1.
[9] Originally Housing Act 1974, s. 13, now Housing Associations Act 1985, s. 5.
[10] Housing Associations Act 1985, ss. 4(1)–4(3) as amended by Housing Act 1988, s. 48.

examine whether there is a need for a new association and whether existing registered associations can adequately fulfil the need identified by the emerging association. Notably, as a result of this approach the Housing Corporation will register housing associations which intend to meet the needs of ethnic minorities and other associations which have been established to support newly established and emerging black-led housing associations.[11]

Accompanying the registration arrangements detailing eligibility for public funding are arrangements for the supervision and control of registered housing associations by the Housing Corporation.[12] It is through these arrangments and the provisions of public funding that the government is able to intervene in the activities of housing associations. The arrangements have been said to constitute "draconian, largely unappealable and occasionally unenforceable powers of supervision and intervention".[13] Superimposed upon these statutory arrangements, the Corporation has the discretion to increase its powers of control by the adoption of detailed administrative requirements. This discretion is one which is used extensively, particularly through the issue of Housing Corporation Circulars and in the annual allocation of public funds to regions of the country and then to individual housing assocations.

# THE HOUSING CORPORATION AND HOUSING FOR WALES

The Chairman, Deputy Chairman and 13 other members of the Housing Corporation's Board are appointed by the Secretary of State and are bound to follow his directions.[14] The Corporation does not act as servant or agent of the Crown,[15] and in this respect, then, is an independent public corporation.

## Responsibilities to avoid unlawful discrimination

From the position it holds, the Housing Corporation (and Housing for Wales), can wield considerable influence over the activities of

[11] See Housing Corporation Reports of 1986, 1987 and 1988; for a detailed examination of the registration requirements see Alder and Handy *op. cit.*, Chapter 8.
[12] Housing Associations Act 1985, ss. 9, 13–17 and 24–32 and s. 36A introduced by Housing Act 1988, s. 49.
[13] Alder and Handy *op. cit.* p. 5.
[14] Housing Associations Act 1985, Sched. 6, paras 2–7; for similar provisions relating to Housing for Wales see Housing Act 1988, Sched. 5 paras 2–4.
[15] *Ibid.*, para. 193.

registered housing associations and the needs which are met by the provision of new housing. Indeed the Corporation has two prime responsibilities in respect of unlawful discrimination in addition to its wider obligations under the two principal Acts. First, section 71 of the R.R.A. which relates to the elimination of unlawful discrimination and promotion of good race relations by local authorities[16] also applies to the Housing Corporation and Housing for Wales.[17] Secondly, the Housing Corporation (and Housing for Wales hereafter included in a "Housing Corporation") has the power to issue guidance as to management of accommodation by registered housing associations.[18]

The role of the Housing Corporation in preventing discrimination amongst housing associations can be examined under the following headings:

- statutory duty under R.R.A., s. 71;
- power to issue Management Guidance;
- general policy: Circular HC22/85.

## *Statutory duty under the Race Relations Act 1976, s. 71*

Section 75(5) of the Housing Associations Act 1985[19] extends the general functions of the Corporation to include the "general statutory duty" to:

> "... make appropriate arrangements with a view to securing that their various functions are carried out with due regard to the need:
>
> (a) to eliminate unlawful racial discrimination; and
> (b) to promote equality of opportunity, and good relations between persons of different racial groups."[20]

Since the subsection has been added to section 75, which enumerates the functions of the Corporation, we need look no further initially than that section to understand the extent of the duty. The section says the Corporation has the following general functions:[21]

(a) to promote and assist the development of registered housing associations and unregistered self-build societies;

[16] See Chapter 15.
[17] Housing Act 1988, s. 56.
[18] *Ibid.*, s. 49 creating Housing Associations Act 1985, s. 36A.
[19] Added by Housing Act 1988, s. 57.
[20] R.R.A., s. 71.
[21] s. 75(1).

(b) to facilitate the proper performance of the functions, and to publicise the aims and principles, of registered housing associations and unregistered self-build societies;

(c) to maintain a register of housing associations and to exercise supervision and control over registered housing associations;

(d) to undertake, to such extent as the Corporation considers necessary, the provision (by construction, acquisition, conversion, improvement or otherwise) of dwellings for letting or sale and of hostels, and the management of dwellings or hostels so provided.

The Housing Corporation has in addition specific functions, for example, the administration of grants to housing associations which is now undertaken as a direct function rather than as agent of the Secretary of State.[22] The wording of section 71 suggests that its general duty applies to all functions undertaken by the Housing Corporation rather than those stated in section 75.

Similarly as with local authorities the Housing Corporation must make "appropriate arrangements" to ensure the duty imposed by section 71 is carried out. In this respect, the Corporation will need to introduce arrangements covering the aspects of its work which have been similarly considered for local authoritiies.[23] In addition, these appropriate arrangements need specifically to take into account the following functions:

(a) promotion and assistance;

(b) proper performance of registered housing associations;

(c) registration, monitoring and control; and

(d) the administration of grant funding.

It has been suggested that the short-term success of section 71 duties will be seen by the:

- Improvement in the representation of black people on the Corporation Board.
- Improvement in the number of black people employed in the top Housing Corporation jobs and a fair representation throughout the hierarchy generally.
- Publication of monitoring statistics which show both housing association performances on all key race equality indicators and progressive improvements.

[22] Housing Act 1988, s. 50, repealed Housing Association Act 1985, s. 75(1)(*d*).
[23] See Chapter 10.

- Success and growth of the black housing association movement and of the adequacy of Housing Corporation support.[24]

And in the long term the measure will "be the degree to which good quality and affordable (affordable by black people relative to their income) housing is provided for people in housing need."[25]

The points referred to above make the position very complex since the administration of grant funding involves:

1. the allocation of resources regionally and then to individual associations, through an Approved Development Programme;
2. the assessment of eligible costs for individual schemes, through the complex Total Cost Indicator Cost T.C.I. system; and
3. the actual payment of grant to specific projects by way of a competitive bidding process assessed against which is made on a value for money basis.

The ability of individual associations to compete on this value for money basis can largely be a function of size due to economies of scale and bargaining power. The vast majority of black-led housing associations are newly formed and therefore small. Their ability to compete is therefore extremely limited. The Housing Corporation makes continued public statements about protecting the programmes of these emerging associations but the increasingly competitive regime does little to help.

## *Cost ceilings and indirect discrimination*

In 1985 the C.R.E. stressed its concern over the apparent discriminatory effect of the T.I.C. system in that the system "was biased against the provision of single family dwellings in general, and larger single family dwellings in particular." As a result, the system allegedly failed to provide "single family dwellings in the Southall London Borough Council area and since there was 'a disproportionate need for this type of accommodation living in the Southall area' the system 'unfairly discriminated against ethnic minority households'."[26]

The T.I.C. approach required that the "aggregate costs of each approved project are compared with national costs in order for the Housing Corporation to determine whether the project represents

[24] See A. Misra, *The Verdict on Race is — We could do Better*, Voluntary Housing 22, no. 1, p. 10.

[25] See n. 24.

[26] See C.R.E. *Total Indicative Costs: A case of Indirect Racial Discrimination*, Introduction.

'value for money'.[27—28] The new T.C.I. system attempts to carry out a similar "value for money" assessment, whilst at the same time setting a cost ceiling for each project.

As a result of the findings of the C.R.E. study a special uplift of T.I.C. was allowed to ensure the system did not unintentionally discriminate in the way described. There are similar, although as yet unconfirmed, fears that the new T.C.I. approach does not sufficiently ensure that larger dwellings can be provided and that the new funding regime introduced by the Housing Act 1988 for housing associations generally favours the production of smaller dwellings. This will be a subject the Housing Corporation will need to keep under review if it is to satisfy the obligations imposed by the statutory duty under section 71 of the R.R.A.

## *Imposing statutory duty on registered housing associations*

The statutory duty imposed by section 71 relates to all the Corporation's functions. One such function, as we have already indicated is to ensure the proper performance of the functions of registered housing associations.[29] There seems ample scope under this obligation to pass on the general duty to housing associations. The requirement, which is all it can amount to, will not have the same force as with the Corporation since it will merely amount to a form of administrative control. However, coupled with the Corporation's power to issue management guidance to registered housing associations such an approach could well have significant administrative impact.

## *Issuing management guidance*

A new section, section 36A, was added to the Housing Associations Act 1985 by section 49 of the Housing Act 1988, enabling the Corporation to issue management guidance to registered housing associations. To give this provision sufficient teeth, the Corporation can have regard to such guidance when deciding whether to use its powers to secure the proper managment of an associations affairs.[30] The guidance can be general or specific[31] and before being issued or revised the Corporation has the duty to consult bodies which it sees are representative of housing associations and it must obtain the approval of the Secretary of State.[32]

[27—28] *Ibid.*, p. 3.
[29] Housing Assocations Act 1985, s. 75(1)(*b*).
[30] *Ibid.*, s. 36A(1).
[31] s. 36A(2).
[32] s. 36A(4).

Guidance can be issued by the Corporation on the following matters:[33]

(a) the housing demands for which provision should be made and the means of meeting those demands;
(b) the allocation of housing accommodation and determining priorities between individuals;
(c) the terms of tenancies and the principles upon which the level of rent should be determined;
(d) the standards of maintenance and repair and the means of achieving such standards; and
(e) consultation and communication with tenants.

In the "Tenants' Guarantee", the Housing Corporation has already issued such guidance and requires registered housing associations to consider the following:

> "Policies and procedures must provide equality of opportunity to all sections of society, taking particular and full account of the race relations and sex discrimination legislation."[34]

The guidance notes point out that "there must be a common qualifying age for men and women seeking sheltered accommodation," and say that "among other good practices, associations are expected to keep records of applicants' own definition of their ethnic origin, and monitor them".[35]

The Guidance Notes go on to say:

> Registered housing associations will be required to comply with the code of practice on race relations in the field of rented housing being prepared by the Commission for Racial Equality. Associations should also conform with best practice to avoid any kind of discrimination and to promote equality of opportunity both in access to accommodation and the provision of services to all members of the community who may be disadvantaged by race, sex or disability.[36]

The issue of the code of practice by the C.R.E. will be dealt with in Chapter 18 and a copy of the draft code of practice is attached at Appendix III.

Under this power to issue guidance there does seem to be particular scope for the Housing Corporation to be very specific about equal opportunities requirements and about the need to eliminate unlawful race and sex discrimination and other forms of undesirable discrimination against other disadvantaged and minority groups.

[33] s. 36A(3).
[34] B3.2 p. 2.
[35] B3.4 p. 5.
[36] H. p. 5.

## *General guidance: circular HC22/85, race and housing*

In Circular HC22/85, *Race and Housing*, the Housing Corporation asserted its unequivocal policy on equal opportunities in housing which it formulated in 1982:[37]

> All eligible groups shall have the same opportunity. Because minority groups are over-represented among those in most urgent housing need, special initiatives to assist those minority groups are likely to be necessary.

The report went on to say that the Corporation expected all associations working in areas with ethnic minority populations to adopt the recommendation's in the N.F.H.A.'s reports *"Race and Housing"* and *"Race and Housing: Still a Cause for Concern".* Where co-ordination between existing associations and ethnic minority groups fails to meet identified needs or "associations are unable or unwilling to work with ethnic minority groups, the Corporation will consider registering a new association".[38]

The five year programme launched in 1985 to create new black housing associations displays that the Corporation was dedicated to a policy of support (see HC Circular HC22/85). A growing number of "black" housing associations which concentrate in providing housing for black people in need have been registered, although the Corporation has been criticised for making insufficient funds available to these emerging organisations.[39] As mentioned earlier the Corporation's introduction of a competitive regime for housing associations and in particular its apparent intent on reducing the number of developing housing associations potentially undermines the commitment in supporting black-led housing associations which has been displayed since 1985.

# THE VOLUNTARY HOUSING MOVEMENT

## Diversity of voluntary housing movement

We have, in the preceding section of this chapter, already examined the legal definition of a housing association and found that constitutionally these associations can be a society, body of trustees or

[37] Para. 2.
[38] *Ibid.*, para 5.2.
[39] See later in this Chapter support by housing associations for emerging black housing associations.

a company. In fact there exists a great variety of types of associations within the voluntary housing movement. There are some 2,700 housing associations registered with the Housing Corporation and it has been estimated some 4,000 are in existence including non-registered associations; of these, the vast majority, approximately 60 per cent. are industrial and provident societies which have charitable status. The remaining are registered charities, either trusts or guarantee companies, industrial and provident societies which are non-charitable and which may be mutual or non-mutual, and a minority of companies limited by guarantee. But within these legal forms is hidden a wide range of philosophies and aims.[40] The wide variety of "species and sub-species"[41] creates a housing movement which some see as being one of its main strengths[42] and others see as a weakness.[43]

## General housing responsibilities

Unlike local authorities,[44] housing associations have no statutory duty to consider the housing conditions of the districts within which they operate nor to provide any particular kind of housing. They are not creatures of statute, they are of their own invention. The duties of a housing association in providing housing to meet social needs arises out of constitutional objectives or more likely out of the need to register with the Housing Corporation to be eligible for public subsidy. This latter point in turn limits the permissible objects of an association either to charitable purposes or to prescribed housing related purposes.[45] Until section 50 of the Housing Act 1988 came into force, housing association grants had seemed restricted to eligible housing projects, *i.e.* ones which provide dwellings for letting or provides a building for use as a hostel or dwellings for low cost purchase.

Now housing associations may claim grant in respect of expenditure incurred by them in connection with housing activities.[46] No doubt the guidance in D.O.E. Circular 170/74 will still need to be followed. It stresses that Housing Association Grant is only available for housing projects designed to provide accommodation for people whose needs and circumstances justify the provision of housing to be substantially subsidised by the taxpayer.[47] Regardless of these requirements the

[40] See Alder and Handy, *op. cit.*, Chapter 1, for greater discussion.
[41] *op. cit.* p. 19.
[42] See C. Baker, *Housing Association.*
[43] Housing Services Advisory Group, *Housing Associations: Working Paper of the Cohen Committee.*
[44] See Housing Act 1985, s. 22 and Chapter 10.
[45] Housing Associations Act 1985, s. 4, as amended by Housing Act 1988, s. 48.
[46] *Ibid.*, s. 50(1).
[47] Para. 29.

receipt of Housing Association Grant does not in itself create a statutory duty.[48]

## Specific housing responsibilities

### *The homeless*

Under section 72 of the Housing Act 1985, where a local housing authority requests a registered housing association to assist them in the discharge of their statutory duties with regard to the homeless and those threatened with homelessness, the association "shall co-operate in rendering such assistance ... as is reasonable in the circumstances."

It is unclear from this provision what is the extent of the duty to render assistance. Clearly the assistance requested must be "reasonable in the circumstances," it must not be assistance which no reasonable authority would seek. Whether or not this extends to requesting an association to provide accommodation rather than the local housing authority is arguable. An example might be where an association meets the needs of a particular group of people, perhaps the elderly, and an applicant to the authority who is homeless falls into that group. In such circumstances the association may well be in a better position to provide accommodation, and possibly support, more suited to the applicants needs.[49]

Although little used, the power to seek assistance may well create a specific duty for a particular association to help an authority discharge its statutory obligations towards a homeless person or family. When associations provide assistance they must bear in mind the points already discussed in the previous Chapter concerning discrimination by local authorities in discharging their duties towards homeless women and ethnic minorities.

### *Suitable alternative accommodation*

Before the enactment of the Housing Act 1980 (now incorporated in consolidating Housing Act 1985), it was felt unnecessary to regulate the activities of registered housing associations. They were regarded as being "motivated by an interest to provide housing for the poorer classes", and "could be trusted to exercise their discretion ... in a social and humanitarian manner".[50] Legal protection for tenants was

[48] See *Peabody Housing Asssociations* v. *Greene* (1979) 38 P. & C.R. 644 at p. 654.
[49] See D.O.E. and D.H.S.S. Joint Circular 116/77 and Code of Practice.
[50] *Per* Cumming-Bruce L.J. in *Governors of the Peabody Donation Fund* v. *Higgins* [1983] 2 W.L.R. 1091.

minimal. It was likely that a housing association would fail to rehouse someone who was displaced from their accommodation.

Since 1980, housing associations have only been able to gain possession of dwellings against secure tenants under a number of grounds set out in Schedule 2 to the Housing Act 1985.[51] Under Grounds 9–11 of Part II of the Schedule and Ground 12–16 of Part III an association has an obligation to provide, or else show availability of, suitable alternative accommodation. Under Grounds 12–16 the court must also consider whether it is reasonable to grant an order for possession.[52]

## *Nomination arrangements with local authorities*

Regardless of the rhetoric in the voluntary housing movement housing associations are under no statutory obligation to enter into arrangements with local housing authorities for prospective tenants to be nominated to specific properties. Yet in practice such nominations are very much regarded as local authority rights[53] and are often conditions of Housing Corporation finance and incorporated in conditions of sale of local authorities land. In the latter two circumstances section 76 contractual obligations may well arise.

Little guidance is available on the nature of such nomination arrangements and details have been left to housing associations and local authorities to agree between themselves. This has led to a plethora of arrangements. The lack of statutory or official guidance seems to be intentional — "the kind of arrangements made will vary from place to place and from time to time" — states Circular 170/74. Housing Corporation Circular 16/80 indicates that the generally accepted 50 per cent. agreement that most associations have with local authorities should not be a hard and fast rule and that associations should negotiate alternative arrangement, particularly for special projects. D.O.E. Circular 73/67 gave warning about the extent of nomination rights: "Whilst it is important to ensure that the benefit of subsidy goes to help those who need it . . . local authorities should exercise their right with discretion. For the authority to nominate tenants for all vacancies can destroy the whole point of an independent association".[54]

In its report of the *Formal Investigation into Collingwood Housing Association Ltd* the C.R.E. stated that it would be reasonable to expect that nominations "would include ethnic minority applicants at least in

[51] See Alder and Handy, *op. cit.*, Chapter 4.
[52] On suitability see Alder and Handy, *op. cit.*, p. 262.
[53] See D.O.E. Circular 170/74.
[54] See Institute of Housing, *Working Together* (1983) warning about extremes.

proportion to the size of the local authority minority population".[55] There was need for detailed discussion where nominations fell short of this basic requirement. Additionally, local authorities need to "take steps to ensure that ethnic minorities in their area were made aware of the opportunities for rehousing" through housing associations.[56]

Associations should hold "systematic and regular consultations" with local authorities. A recommended approach on nominations is for local authorities to make regular nominations of applicants who are incorporated within a waiting list until a suitable void property is available. In this way there is little danger that a local authority will fail to meet its quota of nominations.[57]

It is good practice for local housing authorities to keep and analyse ethnic records on nominations. As P. Niner and V. Karn say,[58] unless a local authority "assesses its ethnic records in an effective way, its potential contribution to increasing the number of black housing association tenants will not be fulfilled."

## *Discrimination by housing associations: paucity of information*

Very few studies have been undertaken which have examined whether housing associations unlawfully discriminate in the disposal and management of their housing stock. What studies have been carried out[59] relate to issues of race. Little or no information is therefore available on possible sex discrimination by housing associations. This paucity of information therefore means that little can be done by analysing their record in the field. However, it should be stressed that many associations — for example Leeds Federated Housing Association, Merseyside Improved Housing Association Ltd., Friendship Housing Association Ltd. and Focus Housing Trust — have positive and progressive policies relating to equal opportunities, which involve keeping records and monitoring performance. Such associations are able to set examples for others within the movement and elsewhere to follow. Many associations provide accommodation on a special needs basis to meet the needs of women, ethnic minorities and other disadvantaged groups. Examples are refuges for women, Asian women in particular, and sheltered schemes for the Asian elderly. Care though needs to be exercised to ensure such special schemes are not in practice distinctly special. Such needs should be met through the

[55] Para. 8.34.
[56] *Ibid.*
[57] *Ibid.*, para. 8.35.
[58] *Housing Associations : Achieving Racial Equality*, p. 14 Summary.
[59] *e.g.*, C.R.E. *Formal Investigation into Collingwood Housing Association Ltd*, P. Niner & V. Karn, *op. cit.* and the N.F.H.A. *Race and Housing* series of reports.

provision of general housing as far as possible to avoid any possibility of stigma arising with the particular client group.

## Selection of tenants

### *General background*

The selection of tenants is for housing associations one of the main activities where there is considerable use of discretion. Confronted with the difficulty of excessive demand, housing associations are faced with having to make value judgements about who gets housed. A survey of housing accommodation tenants carried out in 1984 showed that:

1. 94 per cent. of households had a net weekly income less than the national average;
2. 67 per cent. of households relied on state benefits as their main source of income;
3. 50 per cent. of the economically active heads of households were out of work;
4. 32 per cent. were pensioners;
5. 21 per cent. of single people, excluding the elderly, were from ethnic minorities;
6. 76 per cent. of households qualified for housing benefit payments;
7. 48 per cent. were single people;
8. 47 per cent. of families were headed by a single parent;
9. 11 per cent. of tenancies were granted to ethnic minorities.[60]

The survey dealt only with new tenants and the picture with regard to existing tenants is somewhat different. *Household and Family Composition*, a report from H.M.S.O., based on the 1981 census, gave for the first time information about housing associations as a separate housing tenure. The survey showed that tenants of housing associations are mid-way, as a socio-economic group, between owner occupiers and local authority tenants.[61]

With the voluntary housing movement's recent emphasis on meeting special housing needs and in providing new housing for rent and for sale in the inner cities it is expected that new tenants and purchasers are more likely to come from disadvantaged groups, *i.e.* those in greater need indicated above. It can be seen that housing associations let 11 per cent. of their tenancies to ethnic minorities and some 47 per cent. to households headed by a single parent. This indicates that

[60] N.F.H.A., *Voluntary Housing* (1985) Vol. 17, no. 11.
[61] See also *New Society* (1984) at p. 220.

generally the needs of ethnic minorities and women with children are being met. Over time it is likely, if these present trends continue, that the socio-economic make-up of tenants will be similar to that of local authority tenants. Certainly the more housing associations concentrate on meeting housing need the more likely that the needs of disadvantaged groups will be more fully represented in their lettings.

## *Waiting lists*

Housing associations like local authorities keep "waiting lists" of people seeking accommodation. The first difficulty an applicant faces is being admitted onto a waiting list. Associations may keep general waiting lists for specific types of property, *e.g.* three bed houses, or specific areas. Some even keep "enquiry lists", which act as a waiting list to be admitted onto a waiting list. These various approaches are adopted in order to keep waiting lists to a manageable size and in proportion to the number of vacancies the association has over a given period. Faced with excessive demand for a limited supply of accommodation some method of filtering or assessment is needed. As a result the process of being admitted onto a waiting list can be in practice somewhat opportunistic in nature. If an applicant applies at a time when a waiting list is open they may well be able to register on the list. Otherwise they may be refused admission, regardless of priority compared to applicants already registered. The process may well favour those people who are more aware of the housing system and housing opportunities available and disfavour the disadvantaged of society who are less aware of such opportunities. Many associations therefore attempt to keep open waiting lists even though the resource implications are considerable. Applicants come from four main sources:

(i) direct applications by person seeking accommodation;
(ii) nominations by local authorities of council house applicants;
(iii) referrals by voluntary and charitable organisations; and
(iv) transfer applications from an associations existing tenants.[62]

Housing associations provide accommodation on a basis of housing need and for a person or family to be admitted onto a waiting list they must display housing need in some shape or form. Various needs are readily identified by housing associations and these are used to make up a set of criteria whereby the overall need of each application is measured.[63] Following the introduction of the Housing Act 1988,

[62] See C.R.E., *Report Into Formal Investigation of Collingwood Housing Association*, p. 21.
[63] See HC Circular 16/80 and Tenants Guarantee.

housing associations are no longer able to let secure tenancies at fair rents, except in special circumstances[64], therefore, Housing Corporation guidance is provided in its Tenants' Guarantee which supersedes the advice contained in HC Circular 16/80 relating to letting fair rent properties.

The guidance contained in the Tenants' Guarantee emphasises that the "essential purpose of registered housing associations is to provide accommodation for those who are inadequately housed or homeless, and for whom suitable housing is not available at prices within their means, or at all, elsewhere in the local market".[65] Additionally registered housing associations should:

1. When determining their priorities for the provision of accommodation and when offering tenancies, take account of housing demand and conditions in their area.
2. Consult and co-operate with local housing authorities, especially about their responsibilities for homeless persons and other statutory housing obligations, and with other relevant public bodies such as social services departments and health authorities.
3. Collaborate with voluntary and community organisations to make their housing service publicly known.
4. Respond to tenants requirements for mobility, and to participate actively in national and local mobility and exchange schemes.
5. Make publicly available their policies and procedures for selecting tenants and allocating tenancies[66], and
6. Ensure such policies and procedures are open, fair and based on housing need. Associations should make publicly and freely available a summary of:
   a. who is eligible for their accommodation. In most cases this must exclude people on their governing bodies, or employed by them, or their close relatives.[67] Any further restriction imposed by the rules of charitable associations;
   b. how members of the public may apply for tenancies, including any arrangements for nominations or referrals from the local housing authority and other organisations;
   c. their policies and procedures for deciding on priority as between applicants; and

[64] Housing Act 1988, s. 35.
[65] Para A1.
[66] See also Housing Act 1985, s. 106.
[67] Housing Associations Act 1985, s. 15.

d. their policies and procedures for responding to tenants wishing to move (whether or not by way of exchange of dwellings) to other dwellings let by that association or another landlord.[68] Copies should be sent to the Corporation, relevant local housing authorities and other organisations, such as local advice centres, advising the public on access to housing. Copies should also be given to people who apply for accommodation.

7. Translate, where appropriate its policies and procedures.
8. Base these allocation policies upon the severity of an applicants' housing needs.
9. Pay particular attention to the specific housing needs experienced by particular groups which *inter alia* include:
    (a) single parent families;
    (b) people from ethnic minorities;
    (c) women suffering domestic violence; and
    (d) disabled people.
10. Ensure policies and procedures provide equality of opportunity to all sections of society, taking particular regard of race relations and sex discrimination legislation.
11. Establish procedures which can be objectively demonstrated.[69]
12. Prepare annual summaries of lettings activities to include the number and types of lettings to different types of applicant and make these available to inquirers.
13. Do not deter low income applicants by requiring more than one or two weeks rent in advance or by asking for premiums or deposits.[70]

However the guidance is scant, especially on equal opportunities and it is to be hoped that more detailed guidance will be issued along the lines of that contained in H.C. Circular 16/80.

Once an applicant has been accepted onto a waiting list there is a further process of selection which attempts to determine priorities where there are two or more eligible applicants to consider for a particular vacancy. This process of selection should be based on the criteria in the particular association's policy and in many cases may be similar to the needs criteria used by local authorities.

[68] *c.f.* generally requirements for letting all its tenancies set out in Housing Act 1985, s. 106.
[69] See the requirements relating to statistical evidence in *West Midland Passenger Transport Executive* v. *Singh* [1988] 1 W.L.R. 730 (C.A.).
[70] See generally H.C. "Tenants Guarantee".

## Legal requirements

### *Constitutional requirements*

Of fundamental importance to a housing association when selecting tenants is its constitutional object. The constitution will contain some provision which may specify or limit the type of person the association is able to assist. It may very well refer to people of "necessitous circumstances" or the "poor" or may instead refer to a particular group within society such as the elderly or disabled or a more narrowly defined class such as the widows of ex-seamen. To assist applicants outside the object of the association would be for the association to act *ultra vires.*

The need to fall within charitable objectives must also be borne in mind.[71] Where a charitable housing association has within its constitution a rule which provides for the conferring of benefits by reference to colour, the provision relating to colour must be disregarded.[72] Therefore a housing charity can confer benefits on ethnic minorities if it defines the particular group by reference to a characteristic other than colour, *i.e.* ethnic origin or nationality.

Additionally, an association having 25 members or more cannot discriminate on racial grounds in relation to its present members or prospective members and access to its benefits facilities or services,[73] unless its main object is to confer benefits of membership on "persons of a particular racial group defined otherwise than by reference to colour".[74] This exception enables "bona fide social, welfare, political and sporting organisations whose main object is to confer benefits on a particular ethnic or national group to continue to do so".[75] Benefits, "whatever they may be" can be conferred in this way on members[76] and consequently the benefit of the grant of a tenancy can apply as an exception. Whether granting benefits to a particular group is the main object of an association will depend on (i) the essential character of the association, and (ii) all relevant circumstances, including, in particular, "the extent to which the affairs of the association are so conducted that the persons primarily enjoying the benefits of membership are of the racial group in question.[77]

"Association" is not specifically defined but the phrase "any association" is used "however described, whether corporate or

[71] See Housing Associations Act 1985, Schedule 2, Grounds 11 and 13–15.
[72] R.R.A., s. 34.
[73] R.R.A., s. 25.
[74] R.R.A., s. 26(1).
[75] See White Paper, *Racial Discrimination* Cmnd. 6234, para. 73.
[76] R.R.A., s. 26(21).
[77] *Ibid.*

incorporate, and whether or not its activities are carried on for profit.[78] However, the term does not include a trade union, employers' or trade or professional body.[79]

Similarly, it is lawful for members of a particular racial group to have access to facilities or services to meet their special needs with regard to education, training or welfare, or any ancillary benefit.[80] The section appears wide enough to allow positive discrimination in the provision of temporary accommodation, although it is doubtful whether it would extend sufficiently to cover the provision of a house.

Voluntary bodies which by definition would include housing associations[81] are able to;

(a) restrict membership to persons of one sex; and
(b) provide benefits, facilities or services to such members.[82]

A voluntary body is one (a) the activities of which are carried on otherwise than for profit, and (b) which was not set up by any enactment.[83]

Further, there are exceptions which permit discrimination on the basis of sex for:

(i) establishement for persons requiring special care, supervision or attention;
(ii) facilities likely to be used by both sexes and which could result in embarrassement or objection, *e.g.* changing rooms or lavatories; and
(iii) dormitories or other shared sleeping accommodation.[84]

## *Support for black-led housing associations*

This position allowing exceptions for voluntary bodies, associations and charities, leads to the favourable consideration of special housing associations, in particular those which have been formed to meet the needs of black people. The first such housing association to be registered by the Housing Corporation was Ujima Housing Association Ltd which was registered in 1980.

By the end of 1987, some 38 black associations were registered by the Corporation, some having objects which were directed towards

[78] R.R.A., s. 25(1).
[79] See s. 25(1)(*c*); generally *c.f.* the position before the Act came into force *Dockers Labour Club and Institute* v. *Race Relations Board* [1976] A.C. 285, and *Charter* v. *Race Relations Board* [1973] A.C. 868.
[80] R.R.A., s. 35.
[81] S.D.A., s. 34(1).
[82] S.D.A., s. 34(1).
[83] *Ibid.* s. 34(1).
[84] *Ibid* s. 35.

specific ethnic minority needs. The registration can be seen as part of the Housing Corporation declared five year programme to register five black associations which have in the main a large black proportion. Hence associations have been registered throughout the country, including the East and West Midlands, North West and Merseyside and North East. However, 21 of the 38 are registered for the London area.

Similarly, there are examples of initiatives where existing housing associations have offered direct or indirect support to new emerging housing associations. The West Yorkshire Housing Associations Group established the West Yorkshire Housing Associations' Trust to sponsor and support black associations in the area, providing grant funding and management and development support. The Trust was registered with the Housing Corporation as a housing association to ensure donations from the parent associations would not impinge upon their constitutional objectives and statutory restrictions on their activities overviewed by the Housing Corporation. Although, a similar initiative in the West Midlands did not receive such widespread support from existing housing associations, some of whom were unhappy about providing their own resources to support new and emerging black-led associations. However, one Birmingham based association, the Birmingham Friendship Housing Association Ltd., sponsored and supported the Mashriq Housing Association, a community based association wishing to work in the Saltley area of Birmingham, which has now registered with the Housing Corporation. Little support, though, was given by other local housing associations.

## *Statutory requirements*

The Housing Act 1980 introduced certain duties to publicise allocation rules. These apply to registered housing associations other than co-operative housing associations.[85] They apply to *all* housing accommodation and not just the secure tenancies with which the Act was concerned.

A registered housing association must[86] publish a summary of its rules as we have discussed earlier on in this Chapter. There is direct statutory obligation to comply with the requirements which are established by individual housing associations set out in the rules contained in their policies and procedures. This is clearly a matter of public law and is therefore enforceable by means of an application for judicial review in the High Court. A prospective applicant for accommodation would have sufficient *locus standi* being within the

[85] Housing Act 1985, ss. 106 and 114.
[86] *Ibid.*, s. 106(1).

range of beneficiaries of the statute.[87] It is unlikely that the statutory obligation confers a *private* right of action for damages upon any individual and therefore the judicial review procedure is the *only* available remedy, thus denying access to the local county court.[88]

The substantive power to allocate tenancies does not derive from statute but from the general powers of the association. It is therefore not a public law power. The fact that a housing association operates within a statutory context for public purposes and with public money, although it has the effect of circumscribing the activities which the association can pursue, does not turn a landlord and tenant relationship into one of the public law.[89] However, some doubt has been cast on this somewhat formalistic approach by *R.* v. *Wear Valley District Council, ex p. Binks.*[90] If the allocation of tenancies is a private law matter it is unlikely that a disappointed applicant would have a remedy in the courts since a decision to refuse accommodation would not as such affect his legal rights. On the other hand, it is arguable that an applicant who is placed on a waiting list has achieved a *legitimate expectation* that he/she will be offered accommodation. This would confer at least a right to a fair hearing in accordance with the rules of natural justice. The notions of natural justice and legitimate expectation are not confined to public law.[91] The purpose of the distinction between public and private law in this context is confined to establishing whether challenge must be by means of special application for judicial review procedure. It is also worth remembering that the Attorney-General may initiate litigation in the form of a relator action. Moreover a local authority could also initiate proceedings against a housing association on behalf of the inhabitants of its area under section 222 of the Local Government Act 1972. This may well be an appropriate course of action where there is evidence to suggest a housing association is operating unlawful sex or race discrimination practices. Although in practice it is more likely to be expedient for the C.R.E. or the E.C.C. to undertake a formal investigation of the association concerned.

Additionally a registered housing association must make available to any applicant for accommodation, at all reasonable times, and without charge, details of the personal particulars which it has recorded as relevant to the application, *but only those supplied by the applicant.*[92] Thus an association could record its own secret and idiosyncratic

[87] See *I.R.C.* v. *National Federation of Self Employed and Small Businesses Ltd* [1982] A.C. 617.
[88] *Cocks* v. *Thanet District Council* [1983] A.C. 286.
[89] See *Peabody Housing Association* v. *Green* (1978) 38 P. & C.R. 644.
[90] [1985] 2 All E.R. 699.
[91] *McInnes* v. *Onslow-Fane* [1978] 1 W.L.R. 1520.
[92] Housing Act 1985, s. 106(5).

particulars about applicants. This limited provision well illustrates the attitude of English law to the matter of access to official information. Many associations, though, do in practice make information much more freely available. Although the Data Protection Act 1984 requires associations who operate a computerised system to provide information of *any* personal details kept on the system, it does not extend to manual records.

## *Race discrimination and allocations: C.R.E. recommendations*

In its report on the *Formal Investigation into the Collingswood Housing Association Ltd* the C.R.E. made a number of recommendations on good allocation practice which were adopted by the Association.[93] Generally the C.R.E. found no evidence of instances of unlawful discrimination by the Association but it was "not entirely satisfied with some of the explanations which were given". Additionally, the C.R.E. felt that certain practices undertaken by the Association were directly discriminatory because "in particular circumstances some black applications could be excluded on racial grounds from the Association's housing".[94] Because there was no evidence that a particular black person was discriminated against there could be no claim of direct discrimination under section 1(1)(*a*) of the R.R.A. Neither were such practices covered by the protection given by the Act in section 28 (unlawful discriminatory practices). The section had application only in relation to indirect discrimination since it had to be read with section 1(1)(*b*) of the Act.

This difficulty in application of the Act suggests a need to review the legislation. No doubt a similar problem of application could arise under the S.D.A.[95]

Recommendations of the C.R.E. included the following:

1. There should be objective selection criteria and systematic procedures for their implementation, otherwise "subjective judgements of officials become particularly important and there is an increased risk of personal prejudices, including racial ones, affecting allocations decisions".[96]
2. It was bad practice to "normally try to assimilate immigrants rather than create groups" or to take the view "that immigrant families would be more acceptable to existing tenants if there was only one on a particular scheme" or to adopt a policy

[93] See pp. 27–37 of the Report.
[94] *Ibid.*, p. 28.
[95] See comment of C.R.E., Formal Investigation Report, pp. 28–29.
[96] *Ibid.*, para. 8.3.

because of the "prospect of resistance from existing tenants".[97]

3. Even though an official made comments which were unconsciously and unintentionally racist there is a risk that officials, particularly when training visiting and allocations staff, could influence staff with such views.[98]
4. Care should be taken not to give "special consideration to applicants who wanted to move to be near members of their family. In circumstances where all or almost all of the tenants on a particular scheme are white, and where the great majority of schemes are located at some distance from areas of ethnic minority residence, preferential treatment of this kind will largely be confined to whites".[99]
5. Although there is a need to consider the requirements of particular groups of especially needy persons such as single parents — otherwise sex discrimination may arise — account should be taken of the "special needs which might exist within the local minority community." Of importance could be (i) young black West Indians amongst whom there is known to be a disproportionately high level of homelessness, and (ii) elderly Asians in need of sheltered housing" where they can enjoy the support of other members of their own community".[1]
6. Associations should keep a system of recording the colour or ethnic origin of all applicants and that these records should be monitored.[2]
7. Care should be taken to build sufficient large dwellings to ensure housing was provided which would appeal to the ethnic minority communities. Otherwise, because a greater proportion of Asian and West Indian families are in need of large family homes compared to white population, "it would seem likely therefore that the proportion of Asian and West Indian families who could be housed ... would be smaller than the proportion of English families".[3]
8. There was a need to examine carefully local housing needs including needs of existing ethnic minority communities.[4] Positive efforts are needed for associations to make contact with "local representatives of ethnic minority communities" and other local agencies.[5] Advertising schemes should not

[97] Para, 8.6.
[98] Para 8.7.
[99] Para 8.12.
[1] Para 8.14.
[2] Paras 8.16–8.17.
[3] Para 8.18.
[4] Para 8.21.
[5] Paras 8.22 and 8.23.

be simply by a sign board at the site of a particular scheme, since if the scheme was outside the areas of where ethnic minorities lived it was unlikely they would be aware of the housing opportunities the particular scheme offered.[6]

9. Visiting staff should be fully and effectively trained including "instructions in race relations and in the implications of the R.R.A." Otherwise there was a risk that "visiting officers could be unconsciously biased because of their ignorance of the cultural traditions of ethnic minority families".[7]

More complete advice on how to address these recommendations along with implementing other aspects of good practice are well documented in the N.F.H.A. *Race and Housing* series of reports.[8]

[6] Paras 8.24–8.29.

[7] Para 8.30.

[8] See also C.R.E., *Draft Code of Practice for the elimination of racial discrimination and the promotion of equal opportunities in the field of rented housing* and P. Niner and V. Karn, *op. cit.*; see also Chapter six.

# Chapter twelve

# Application and Practice: Private Housing Sector

## INTRODUCTION

In the private housing sector there are a wide range of housing agencies involved in the provision, disposal and management of housing and the provision of related goods, services and facilities. The agencies range from building societies, estate agents, builders and developers right through to people selling their own homes and private landlords. In this chapter we shall discuss the main private housing sector agencies, and comment in particular on policies and practices which could be seen as discriminatory and also comment on aspects of good practice.

## Estate agents and accommodation agencies

An "estate agent" means "a person who, by way of profession or trade, provides services for the purpose of finding premises for persons seeking to acquire them or assisting in the disposal of premises.[1] An "accommodation agency" falls within that definition by the nature of its trading activities. Much of the early case law under the R.R.A. concerned the activities of estate agents and accommodation agencies. In *Race Relations Board* v. *Rita Foden*[2], the Homestead Accommodation Agency deliberately withheld addresses of available accommodation from a Mr Talwar on the ground of his colour. Such treatment was clearly unlawful discrimination and the victim received damages for loss of opportunity. Further in *Race Relations Board* v. *Hooper and Jacksons*[3], a South London estate agent apparently refused to sell a house to a person on the ground of his colour.

[1] R.R.A., s. 78(1), S.D.A., s. 82(1).
[2] [1972] Race Relations Board Annual Report p. 37.
[3] [1972] R.R. Board Annual Report pp. 37–8.

However, after inspection by officials from the Race Relations Board it was clear from documentation that no discrimination had arisen since the refusal was not based on the prospective purchaser's colour. The defendant was ordered to pay costs.[4]

Estate agents and accommodation agencies are liable for their own discriminatory practices, but can also be liable for discriminatory acts of their employees[5] unless they have taken all "reasonable practicable steps" to prevent the discriminatory acts arising.[6] Care must be taken with advertisements[7], when receiving instructions for sale or disposal[8] and when instructing staff relating to the disposal and management of premises.[9] Additionally a person who knowingly assists another in an act of unlawful discrimination will be treated as having committed the act in question himself or herself, unless proof can be given that reliance was placed on a statement believed to have been made in good faith.[10]

## *C.R.E. formal investigation into Cottrell & Rothan Estate Agents*

In 1978 the Commission for Racial Equality began to investigate alleged racially discriminatory practices operated by Cottrell and Rothan Estate Agents, whereby the agents recorded details of the requirements of black applicants for their services on pink cards and those of white applicants on white cards: instructions such as "no pink cards" would then be noted on the internal records relating to those properties for which the vendors had given discriminatory instructions to the agency. It was clear that discrimination of this nature had been carried on over a period of many years.[11] After investigation, the Commission issued a Non-Discrimination Notice under section 58 of the R.R.A. stating to the agents that on various dates since June 1977:

(a) it or its servants or agents provided less favourable service to certain applicants by withholding from them, on ground of race or colour, details of certain properties which were available for sale through its offices and denying them the opportunity to view and to offer to purchase those properties, in contravention of section 20 of the Act;

[4] For further discussion and other cases see I. MacDonald *op. cit.* pp. 85–6 and R.R.B. Annual Reports 1969–75.
[5] R.R.A., s. 32(1) and S.D.A., s. 41(1).
[6] R.R.A., s. 32(3) and S.D.A., s. 41(3).
[7] R.R.A., s. 29(1) and S.D.A., s. 38.
[8] R.R.A., s. 30 and S.D.A., s. 39.
[9] R.R.A., s. 31 and S.D.A., s. 40.
[10] R.R.A., s. 33(1) and S.D.A., s. 42(1).
[11] C.R.E. Formal Investigation Report, pp. 1–2.

(b) it instructed its servants or agents, in contravention of section 30 of the Act, to discriminate, in contravention of section 20, by refusing or deliberately omitting to provide certain applicants on grounds of race or colour its services of the like quality in the like manner and on the like terms as were normal to other members of the public, the instruction having been given or remaining in force since June 13, 1977;

(c) it, its servants or agents, accepted and followed discriminatory instructions from vendors, and in assisting them thereby to discriminate unlawfully in the disposal of residential accommodation in contravention of section 21, it or its servants or agents contravened section 21 by virtue of section 33 of the Act.[12]

Despite the agents' attempts to get the notice set aside through an application for judicial review because allegedly the Commission's investigation was not undertaken in accordance with natural justice, the Divisional Court found that the notice should stand.[13]

The Commission also recommended that the estate agents should:

(a) not accept or record discriminatory instructions from vendors, landlords or other agents, and when asked to do so should explain the provisions of the R.R.A.;

(b) in their standard letter to vendors, setting out their policy, should include a reference to the firm's policy to adhere to the provisions of the R.R.A.;

(c) through the partners of the firm, monitor the sales operation in their respective offices to ensure that staff were acting in accordance with instructions not to discriminate.[14]

In addition, vendors who had instructed Cottrell and Rothan to discriminate were also warned about the illegality of their acts. Since the acts of discrimination had taken place long before the incidents came to light and since none of them was likely to sell their present property for some time, the Commission accepted "signed written assurance against any future discrimination of the same kind".[15]

## *Mr G. D. Midda and D.S. Services Ltd.*

During the late 1970's, the Commission for Racial Equality received allegations that the proprietor Mr G. D. Midda of D.S. Services Ltd., a Birmingham accommodation bureau, had instructed his staff "to ask

[12] C.R.E., *op. cit.* p. iii.
[13] See next Chapter for fuller discussion.
[14] *Ibid.*, p. 17.
[15] *Ibid.*, p. 17.

landlords whether they had any preferences concerning the racial origins of tenants they would accept".[16] The Commission, after investigation, found that the bureau had contravened the R.R.A.:

(a) by discriminating in the service provided to black persons seeking accommodation;
(b) by instructing staff to so discriminate;
(c) by discriminating in accommodation they were letting on behalf of landlords; and
(d) by attempting to procure landlords to discriminate in the letting of their property.[17]

The contravention was recited when the Commission served a Non-Discrimination Notice under section 58 of the R.R.A.

## *Allen's Accommodation Bureau*

The only investigation into an accommodation bureau in London conducted by the Commission was into the activities of Allen's Accommodation Bureau during 1979–80. Mr Ajao (who is of Scottish and Nigerian ethnic origin) had been told by the agency on several occasions that there were no vacancies, even though his work colleagues were told that accommodation was available. On one visit Mr Ajao was told by a member of staff that there was a vacant bedsitter but the landlord would not take black tenants.

During the subsequent investigation by the Commission the Bureau "agreed that it accepted and acted upon discriminatory instructions given by landlords" because:

(a) landlords could pick and choose whichever tenants they liked, because there were more people looking for accommodation than units of accommodation avaialable; and
(b) the bureau did not see it as its duty to persuade landlords not to discriminate but rather accepted the situation as it was. If the bureau ignored the instructions of landlords, the result would be embarrassment, both for the bureau and black applicants, and a waste of the applicants' time and money.[18]

Needless to say the Commission found the Bureau had contravened the R.R.A.:

(a) by discriminating in the service it provided to black persons seeking accommodation;

[16] C.R.E., *A Guide for Accommodation Bureaux*: Individual Cases and Formal Investigations.
[17] *Ibid.*, p. 29.
[18] *Ibid.*, p. 30.

(b) in instructing staff to discriminate;
(c) by knowingly aiding landlords to discriminate in the letting of their properties.

## *Richard Barclay and Co.*

After a complaint by a temporary employee of Richard Barclay and Co., the C.R.E. undertook in 1987 a formal investigation into the activities of the Clapham office of the estate agency. The Commission found that unlawful discrimination had taken place in that the agency had only two prospective buyers with Asian names on its records, representing 0.1 per cent. of its total customers. The agency though proposed no changes to its methods of training staff.

The Commission intend to monitor the position over the next five years to ensure no further discrimination takes place. Otherwise a complaint will be made to the Director of Fair Trading which could result in a ban on the agency's continued operation and further action may be taken under the R.R.A.[19]

## *Orders by the Director of Fair Trading*

The Director General of Fair Trading has the power to make an order prohibiting "unfit persons from doing estate agency work" where the Director is satisfied that that person "has committed discrimination in the course of estate agency work".[20] A person shall be deemed to have committed discrimination in this context:

(a) where a finding has been made against him in proceedings under section 66 of the S.D.A. or section 57 of the R.R.A. (under individual enforcement provisions through the courts) and the finding has become final;[21]
(b) where a non-discrimination notice has been served on him under either of the principal Acts and the notice has become final;[22]
(c) if he is for the time being subject to the restraint of an injunction or order granted against him for persistent discrimination;[23]

[19] See Estate Agents Act 1989, s. 3(1)(*b*), Sched. 1 and C.R.E., *Racial Discrimination in a London Estate Agency: Report of a Formal Investigation into Richard Barclay and Co.* (1988) pp. 5 and 12–14.
[20] R.R.A., s. 3(1)(*b*).
[21] *Ibid.*, paras. 2(*a*) and (*e*) and Sched. 1.
[22] *Ibid.*, paras. 2(*b*) and (*f*).
[23] *Ibid.*, paras. 2(*c*) and (*g*).

(d) if there has been a finding against him under section 72(20)(*a*) of the S.D.A. or section 63(2)(*a*) of the R.R.A., for contravention of the provisions of the Acts relating to discriminatory advertisements, instructions to discriminate and pressure to discriminate, and that the finding has become final.

Any of the findings, notices, injunctions or orders must relate to Part III of the Acts, *i.e.*, discrimination in fields other than employment. Therefore, even where an estate agent has been shown to have unlawfully discriminated against employees or prospective employees such finding can have no impact on the right of the agent to continue to operate. Surely, though, if an agency discriminates against its own employees that approach may well be reflected in its general activities and may be reasonably probative of discriminatory practices in the provision of its services. Further, findings or notices referred to above can only be taken into account for a period of five years from the point at which they become final.[24] "Estate agency work" means "things done by any person in the course of a business (including a business in which he is employed) pursuant to instructions received from another person who wishes to dispose of or acquire an interest in land".[25]

Essentially the approach applied by the Estate Agents Act "imposes a system of negative licensing—*i.e.*, a person can practise until he his forbidden to do so.".[26]

## *C.R.E. recommendations for accommodation bureaux*

The C.R.E. have recently published the following recommendations stating that bureaux should adopt, implement and monitor equal opportunites policies for the service they provide. In particular such a policy should:

- set out the bureau's commitment to equality of opportunity in a written statement. For example:

"the policy of this bureau is to provide to all members of the public on the same terms and conditions, without regard to considerations of race [and sex]. No landlord, landlady, applicant for accommodation or tenant will be treated less favourably because of race, colour, nationality, or ethnic or national origins [or sex]."

[24] Sched. 1, para. 3.
[25] Estate Agents Act 1979, s. 1(1).
[26] B. Harvey and D. Parry, *The Law of Consumer Protection and Fair Trading* (1987) p. 180.

A comprehensive policy statement would also summarise the action needed to achieve the aims set out in the policy;

- allocate responsibility for the implementation of the policy to the manager or proprietor of the bureau;
- notify existing landlords and landladies, for whom the bureau acts, in writing setting out the policy, as well as new landlords and landladies seeking to use the services of the bureau. (This could be done by including reference to the policy statement in a standard letter to landlords and landladies setting out the bureau's terms.);
- ensure that the policy is known and understood by all staff, by writing to existing staff and to new staff when they are appointed. Any breach of the policy should result in disciplinary action. Guidance and training should also be given on the implications of the policy;
- review periodically criteria for the provision of services provided by the bureau and take appropriate action where practices involve or might lead to unlawful discrimination;
- ensure that staff do not comply with any discriminatory instructions they receive from clients and inform such clients that acts of the kind suggested amount to unlawful discrimination. This would similarly apply where existing tenants and neighbouring residents put pressure on the bureau with a view to not letting accommodation to persons on sexual or racial grounds;
- monitor the operation of the policy by:

  (a) checking records of vacant accommodation on file to ensure there are no discriminatory instructions or odd comments or codes indicating discriminatory preferences in instructions;

  (b) carrying out occasional random checks to ensure that persons using the services of the bureau to find rented accommodation have been given details of all appropriate vacancies. If not, it should be determined whether this is due to sexual or racial discrimination;
- ensure that unlawful acts of discrimination by clients are reported to the relevant Commission. This should normally be done after first drawing the matter to the attention of the persons concerned and where they are not prepared to refrain from such behaviour;

- improve the service provided to women, black persons and other ethnic minorities; for example, by advertising in the ethnic minority press, or in areas of considerable minority settlement, by employing women and members of ethnic minority groups and in particular someone who speaks the predominant minority language of the area.[27]

# LANDLORDS AND PROPERTY COMPANIES

It is only lawful for a landlord to discriminate when letting accommodation where:

(a) the landlord or a near relative (husband, wife, parent, child, grandparent, grandchild, brother or sister) lives and intends to continue to live on the premises; however, it need not be their only home;[28] and
(b) the landlord or a near relative shares with the tenant relevant accommodation, *i.e.* bathroom or kitchen or lounge; and
(c) the premises are "small premises", which means that in addition to the accommodation occupied by the landlord or a near relative, there should be no more than two "separate lettings", or in the case of a boarding house there should be no more than six occupants.[29]

Even in these circumstances it is desirable that discrimination should not take place. Estate agents and accommodation bureaux cannot rely on the small premises exception as a defence in providing discriminatory services. Their services are not covered by the exception.

It is unlawful discrimination for a landlord to state to a black person that a flat had been taken "just ten minutes ago" when it is still found to be available when a white person enquired shortly afterwards.[30] Similarly it is unlawful discrimination where a prospective tenant is refused a tenancy because of the colour of her boyfriend[31] or because one of the prospective joint tenants of a flat was black.[32]

[27] See generally C.R.E., *A Guide for Accommodation Bureaux, Landladies and Landlords* (1989).
[28] Bailey v. *Bryant* (1858), 1 E. & E. 340.
[29] R.R.A., s. 22 and S.D.A., s. 32.
[30] See *Juttla* v. *Stacewicz* quoted in C.R.E., *A Guide for Landladies and Landlords*, p. 30.
[31] See *Cooke* v. *Szabo*, quoted in C.R.E., *op. cit.* p. 31.
[32] See *Tobierre* v. *Morrell*, quoted in C.R.E., *op. cit.* p. 32; see also other examples relating to 'bed and breakfast' accommodation in London against Racism in Housing, *Anti-Racism for the Private Rented Sector* (1988) at pp.72–74.

Unlawful discrimination also arises where a single woman is refused the opportunity to take over accommodation, since such a refusal is on the ground of her sex.[33]

## *C.R.E. recommendations*

The C.R.E. have recommended that all landlords and landladies "should ensure that there is no unlawful discrimination and that there is equality of opportunity in the services they provide to tenants and potential tenants" and that they "should adopt, implement and monitor an equal opportunity policy".[34] Clearly this may be more difficult for the smaller landlord with few resources and therefore he or she will ensure equality of opportunity by whatever means is appropriate.

A policy should:

- set out the landlords' commitment to equality of opportunity in a written statement;
- allocate responsibility for the policy and its operation to a senior manager;
- ensure the policy is known and understood by all staff and that staff receive appropriate training;
- ensure the policy is known to all tenants and potential tenants;
- review existing practices and procedure and change any which could result in unlawful discrimination;
- ensure effective action is taken to combat racial or sexual harassment against tenants and provide support for victims;
- regularly monitor the operation of the policy, keeping effective records and in particular examining two main areas:
  (a) access to housing; and
  (b) quality of housing let;
- identify and meet the special needs of women, black and ethnic minority tenants or prospective tenants.

The London Against Racism in Housing Campaign[35] make further recommendations for the owners of "bed and breakfast" hotels:

- "They should make special efforts to appoint managers who have undergone anti-racist training and, for managers in post,

[33] See *Taylor* v. *Burnett and Hilltree Park Limited* (1983) quoted in E.O.C. Annual Report (1983) at p. 8.
[34] C.R.E., *op. cit.* at p. 22.
[35] *Op. cit.* p. 77.

those who have not undergone anti-racist training should be encouraged to do so without delay."

- "They should ensure that all residents and staff know of the company's anti-racism policy."
- "They should enact anyone who perpetrates racial harassment against another resident but ensure that this policy is not unfairly used to threaten or intimidate black and other ethnic minority residents in the hotel."
- "All complaints of racial harassment must be fully investigated and, where a member of staff is found to be the perpetrator, action must be taken."

## BUILDERS AND DEVELOPERS

Most certainly, as owners, builders and developers would be liable under the legislation if they were to unlawfully discriminate. They will also be liable for the unlawfully discriminatory act of their employees[36] and of their agents.[37] Therefore, builders and developers will be responsible for unlawfully discriminatory acts done in their name by estate agents, solicitors or employees.

In particular section 30 of the S.D.A. and section 21 of the R.R.A. state it is unlawful to dispose of premises on the basis of sex or race.[38] This is important in relation to builders and developers because they may well only grant a right to occupy, or right to purchase at the time a plot is reserved by a prospective purchaser. The power to dispose of premises accordingly includes the granting of a right to occupy[39] and any other form of disposal. It is likely that such a power would apply to premises not yet built. Indeed "premises" includes land of any description under the R.R.A., s. 78(2). Oddly, the S.D.A. does not include a similar definition. However, relying on the similar interpretation of the two Acts and the meaning of "premises" in the context of property which includes land, houses and buildings it is submitted the same definition can be used under the S.D.A.[40]

One matter of importance for builders and developers is that it has been held that the disposal of house plots or similar units come under the protection of the earlier Race Relations Act 1968. In *Race Relations Board* v. *Haigh & Co.*[41], it was held that to come under the protection

[36] R.R.A., s. 32(1) and S.D.A., s. 4(1).
[37] R.R.A., s. 32(2) and S.D.A., s.41(2).
[38] See Chapter 3.
[39] S.D.A., s. 82(1) and R.R.A., s. 78(1).
[40] See discussion Chapter 8.
[41] (1969) 119 N.L.J. 858.

of the Act accommodation need not be immediately available or complete. Neither can a builder or developer justify discrimination because he feels selling a house to a one parent family or a black family for example could have a detrimental effect on the sales of other houses. This is simply giving in to a perceived prejudice or pressure to discriminate from prospective purchasers.[42] Thus assumptions on sales and profitability must be made relating to the real world and not a world where purchase by some groups and individuals is restricted in order to improve profitability. Care must be taken to ensure sales staff do not operate dispersal sales policies relating to ethnic minorities. These have been held as discriminatory in other housing fields.[43]

Builders and developers must also take care not to discriminate in the terms they provide for prospective purchasers. A trend over the last decade has been for developers and builders to provide other services and facilities relating to house purchase such as mortgage finance advice and purchase of existing properties from purchasers in order to break lengthy house purchase chains. The points under discussion on mortgage finance provision later in this chapter need also to be borne in mind by builders and developers.

## *Questions of policy*

The following are useful questions builders and developers can ask themselves to ensure unlawful discrimination does not arise when selling properties:

1. Does the company have an equal opportunities policy stated in writing?
2. Are members of staff, particularly sales staff and agents aware of the policy and have they been appropriately trained?
3. Is a senior manager within the company responsible to ensure the equal opportunities policy operates effectively?
4. Do records show that sufficient properties are sold to ethnic minorities and women (single women and one parent families, and joint sales to men and women)?
5. Are property types built in appropriate areas which would appeal to all sections of the community (depending on the aims of the company)?
6. Are services and facilities provided on an equal opportunities basis, in particular mortgage finance and advice?

[42] S.D.A., s. 40 and R.R.A., s. 31.
[43] See C.R.E. *Report of Formal Investigation into Walsall M.B.C.* (1985).

# PRIVATE SALES OF HOUSES

Generally a private vendor is required to follow the terms of the Acts in the same way as any other owner who wishes to dispose of their property. They will be responsible for their own acts of unlawful discrimination on the grounds of race or sex and their agents[44] and must take care not to give discriminatory instructions.

However, in very limited circumstances a vendor selling a private house is exempt from the general provisions of the Act relating to the disposal of premises.[45] The exemption arises where a person who owns an estate or interest in the premises and wholly occupies them[46] and where he does not use the services of an estate agent[47] for the "purposes of the disposal" of the premises or "publishes or causes to be published an advertisement in connection with the disposal".[48] Essentially, the exemption allows purely private or domestic sales to proceed without the provisions of the Acts coming into play and would still allow the service of an estate agent in determining the value of the premises, *i.e.* a service not directly "for the purposes of the disposal."

# MORTGAGE LENDING

Discrimination in providing mortgage finance on the basis of sex or race is unlawful.[49] Mortgage lending has been the subject of investigation by both Commissions. Since the provision of a mortgage is probably the main means of gaining access to housing for most of the population of England and Wales, owner occupation now accounting for some 64 per cent. of the total housing stock, it is critical that the lending practices of building societies, banks and local authorities should operate in a non-discriminatory way.

## *Mortgage lending and sex discrimination*

In 1982 it had been the Equal Opportunities Commission's intention to undertake a formal investigation into the practices and lending policies of the Provincial Building Society. But after the Society decided to seek judicial review of the Commission's decision in this respect the formal investigation was dropped and a joint review by the Commission and Society was undertaken instead. The joint report

[44] S.D.A., s. 41 and R.R.A., s. 32.
[45] S.D.A., s. 39 and R.R.A., s. 30.
[46] *Quaere*: Whether interest includes "equitable interests", in particular licences?
[47] S.D.A., s. 82(1) and R.R.A., s. 78(1).
[48] S.D.A., s. 30(3) and R.R.A., s. 21(3).
[49] S.D.A., s. 29 and R.R.A., s. 20.

*Mortgage Lending and Practice* (1982) was the result of the review and it contained a number of recommendations to the Provincial Building Society:

1. Sufficient space should be provided on the mortgage application form, to enable full details of at least two applicants to be shown at the beginning of the form including information concerning income.
2. A separate mortgage enquiry procedure should be established which enables a record to be maintained of that category of mortgage enquiry which envisages a full mortgage interview at a later date.
3. Reference enquiries should be precisely worded so that replies received are strictly objective and factual.
4. Wherever possible lenders should arrange with insurers for joint insurance policies to be available to borrowers.
5. A full explanation of the requirements of the S.D.A. to be included in staff training courses.
6. Examination of situations where a woman's salary or part-time earnings provide the main basis of a mortgage to be included in staff training courses prompting discussions of avoidance of sex discrimination.
7. A comprehensive explanation of the S.D.A. to be incorporated in the Society's mortgage manuals with reminders at relevant points within the text.

These recommendations were suggested along with the main conclusion of the joint review which "demonstrated that a clear and precise statement of lending policy within the terms of section 29 of the S.D.A. provides a secure foundation for the provision of mortgages in a way which does not discriminate on grounds of sex."

In fact recommendation six had been the subject of a separate survey carried out in 1978 by the Consumers' Association Survey Unit on behalf of the Commission. The survey revealed that almost a third of the cases examined "where the wife earned more than her husband, the building society branches visited refused to take her income as the main basis for calculating the mortgage," and that more than a third of the branches "discriminated in some way against a couple with a higher-earning wife." Almost half the mortgage brokers who were asked "advised shoppers that they would be unlikely to get a mortgage based on the income of a higher-earning wife".[50]

Along with the joint report *Mortgage Lending and Practice* the Commission issued *The Provision of Mortgages: Guidelines on Good Practice*. A copy of these guidelines is provided at Appendix four.

[50] See pp. 6–7.

## *Mortgage lending and race discrimination*

In 1985 the Commission for Racial Equality published *Race and Mortgage Lending* a report on its formal investigation into the allocation of mortgage in Rochdale for the period 1977 to 1981. Although the Commission did not find any practices or rules which were intended to discriminate against Asians, it did "identify practices which indirectly discriminated against them. Indeed, most Societies did not have detailed local lending policies and left decisions on where and how to lend to the discretion of local branch managers".[51] The report went on to say:

> "One effect of local discretion is that 'rule of thumb' practices develop. These derive from experience of local conditions and, in general, are unobjectionable. Our investigation, however, showed that these 'rules', such as the practice of not lending on a house without a front garden, became convenient ways of allocating mortgages for particular types of property and excluded whole classes of property as unmortgageable. When mortgage facilities are in short supply, those 'rules' can be used as a form of rationing. If the type or location of the property excluded is that which members of an ethnic minority because of their circumstances have to buy, the effect of a locally devised 'rule of thumb', which cannot be justified on commercial grounds, may be disproportionately disadvantageous to that community. The 'rule', therefore, becomes discriminatory."[52]

The C.R.E. arrived at a number of conclusions:

1. A "blanket" policy or practice of lending only on properties which have front gardens is indirectly discriminatory.[53]
2. If a building society operates a policy or practice of not lending against cheaper properties this would disproportionally affect the chances of Asian applicants obtaining mortgages.[54]
3. If a building society has a practice of applying a condition or requirement that lending should not be made against properties in inner areas or improvement areas of Rochdale, then such rules are indirectly discriminatory.[55]
4. Similarly if a building society refuses to lend on properties located in multi-racial areas, on the grounds of the racial

[51] p. vii.
[52] *Ibid.*
[53] pp. 33–36.
[54] pp. 36–38.
[55] pp. 37–38.

composition of the population in such areas, then that policy is directly discriminatory.[56]

## *C.R.E. recommendations to lending agencies*

The Commission as a result of the formal investigation made a number of recommendations:

a. lending agencies should make arrangements to draw up, and formally adopt and communicate to all employees an equal opportunity policy to ensure there is not direct or indirect discrimination in the provision of mortgages. A short statement should appear on the mortgage application form;
b. a senior officer should be given the responsibility to ensure compliance with the Act and the stated policy;
c. lending policies and criteria should be reviewed to ensure direct or indirect discrimination does not occur. Instructions should, accordingly, be given to members of staff, particularly with regard to the application of discretionary practices;
d. agencies with whom the lender has close associations should be aware of the stated equal opportunities policy;
e. ethnic records should be kept and monitored;
f. monitoring should include a review of the following factors:

   (i) age of property
   (ii) type of property;
   (iii) front garden;
   (iv) price of property;
   (v) area of property—in particular areas of ethnic minority concentration;
   (vi) joint family applications;
   (vii) investor status;
   (viii) terms of mortgage offer;
   (ix) reasons for refusal of applications;

g. staff should be trained on the implications of the Act and the stated policy for their work, including the need for keeping and monitoring records of ethnic origin;
h. information regarding lending criteria should be available, in translated form, to potential mortgage applicants.

[56] pp. 39–41.

# Chapter thirteen

# Enforcement through Administrative Action: The Role of the Commissions

## INTRODUCTION

Under the Race Relations Act 1968 the only means of enforcing the anti-discrimination provisions of the Act were through the administrative action of the Race Relations Board. Administrative action as the only means of enforcing the provisions of the R.R.A. and the S.D.A. was eschewed for a combination of administrative action through two new Commissions and individual action through tribunals or the courts depending on the nature of the complaint. Hence the 1975 Act was described as

> "a new and radical approach, combining the right of individual access to legal remedies with the positive and strategic functions of a powerful Equal Opportunities Commission, responsible for enforcing the law in the public interest on behalf of the community as a whole".[1]

Individuals who feel they have been the victims of conduct made unlawful by the Acts may institute proceedings (other than for claims about discriminatory practices, advertisements, pressure or instructions) in an industrial tribunal (employment cases only) or in a designated county court. The Commissions have a role also in enforcing the provisions of the Acts and their administrative actions are the only available remedy for claims about discriminatory practices, advertisements, pressure or instructions.[2] In addition, though, the Commissions have other powers of enforcement and these will be discussed in this chapter.

[1] White Paper, *Equality for Women*, Cmnd. 5724, para. 81.
[2] S.D.A., ss. 37(3) and 72 and R.R.A., ss. 28(3) and 63; see also Chapter 8.

## *Role of the Commissions*

The duties of the Commissions are:

(a) to work towards the elimination of discrimination;
(b) to promote the equality of opportunity between men and women generally (E.O.C.), and equality of opportunity and good relations between persons of different racial groups generally (C.R.E.); and
(c) to keep under review the workings of the Acts and make recommendations to the Secretary of State for their amendment.[3]

Broadly speaking the functions of the Commissions can be said to include the following:[4]

(a) to conduct investigations in areas covered by the Acts and to take action to eliminate unlawful practices;
(b) to assist and represent individual complainants in appropriate cases;
(c) to conduct enquiries into matters outside the scope of the legislation which may affect the relative positions and opportunities of the sexes (E.O.C.) and ethnic minorities (C.R.E.), and to make recommendations;
(d) to review the operation of the legislation and make recommendations;
(e) to conduct research and to take action to educate and persuade public opinion.

## *Composition and constitutions of the Commissions*

Both the Commission for Racial Equality and the Equal Opportunities Commission are composed along similar lines. Each Commission may comprise between eight and 15 Commissioners[5] appointed for a term of office of up to five years by the Secretary of State[6] and at remuneration set by him[6a], one of whom will be a chairman appointed by the Secretary of State.[7] Appointments may be full time or part time.[8] Commissioners can be appointed following a period of office[9] and in practice this has happened often. Commissioners have been usually

[3] S.D.A., s. 53(1) and R.R.A., s. 43(1).
[4] See *e.g.*, *Equality for Women*, para. 109.
[5] S.D.A., s. 53(1) and R.R.A., s. 43(1).
[6] S.D.A., Sched. 3, para. 3(2) and R.R.A., Sched. 1, para. 3(2).
[6a] S.D.A., Sched. 3, para. 4 and R.R.A., Sched. 1, paras. 5 & 6.
[7] S.D.A., s. 53(2) and R.R.A., s. 43(2).
[8] S.D.A., s. 53(1) and R.R.A., s. 43(1).
[9] S.D.A., Sched. 3, para. 3(6) and R.R.A., Sched. 1, para. 3(6).

appointed for periods of two to three years and thereafter re-appointed up to a total of six years. Commissioners may resign during their term of office[10] or their appointment may be terminated by the Secretary of State due to:

(a) non-attendance;
(b) bankruptcy;
(c) incapacity.

The Secretary of State may change the minimum and maximum number of Commissioners permitted by the statutes.[11] Extra appointments of Commissioners can be made by the Secretary of State to assist in carrying out a formal investigation.[12]

Each Commission is a body corporate[13] and is "not an emanation of the Crown, and shall not act or be treated as the servant or agent of the Crown".[14] Accordingly, the Commissions cannot claim any Crown privileges.[15] Nor does property belong to the Crown.[16] Similarly staff are not treated as civil servants[17] even though appointment of staff is subject to the approval of the Minister of the Civil Service.[18]

Although the first appointments to the C.R.E. were all white since then there has been a better representation of ethnic minorities as Commissioners.[19] Since the E.O.C. was established there has been a rough balance between men and women appointed as Commissioners, with slightly more women than men. The Commission at the time of writing however does not have a Commissioner from an ethnic minority group—such an appointment may well result in closer links between the two Commissions.

## *Powers of the Commissions concerning enforcement*

The powers of the Commissions in relation to enforcing the Acts can be stated briefly as follows:

(a) in carrying out their duties, the Commissions may conduct formal investigations in any matter they discover conduct in contravention of the Acts;[20]

[10] S.D.A., Sched. 3, para. 3 and R.R.A., Sched. 1, para. 3(4).
[11] S.D.A., s. 53(3) and R.R.A., s. 43(3).
[12] S.D.A., s. 57(2) and R.R.A., Sched. 1, para. 7.
[13] S.D.A., Sched. 3, para. 1 and R.R.A., Sched. 1, para. 1.
[14] S.D.A., Sched. 3, para. 2(1) and R.R.A., Sched. 1, para. 2(1).
[15] S.D.A., Sched. 3, para. 2(2)(*a*) and R.R.A., Sched. 1, para. 2(2)(*a*).
[16] S.D.A., Sched. 3, para. 2(2)(*c*) and R.R.A., Sched. 1, para. 2(2)(*c*).
[17] S.D.A., Sched. 3, para. 2(2)(*b*) and R.R.A., Sched. 1, para. 2(2)(*b*).
[18] S.D.A., Sched. 3, para. 8 and R.R.A., Sched. 1, para. 8.
[19] See C.R.E. Annual Report 1987.
[20] S.D.A., s. 57 and R.R.A., s. 48.

(b) issuing non-discrimination notices;[21]
(c) instituting legal proceedings in respect of persistent discrimination;[22]
(d) the sole right to institute legal proceedings in respect of discriminatory practices, advertisements, instructions and pressure;[23]
(e) assisting individual complainants in cases where special circumstances or factors justify giving assistance;[24]
(f) issuing codes of practice in relation to employment and rented housing—only C.R.E. has power to issue codes of practice in relation to rented housing.[25]

## *Conduct of formal investigations*

Each Commission has the power to institute "formal investigations" and must conduct a formal investigation if required to do so by the Secretary of State. Investigations of this nature can be conducted for any purpose connected with the Commissions' respective duties.[26] Formal investigations may be quite specific and directed towards alleged unlawfully discriminatory acts of particular individuals or organisations, the so called "belief" investigations because they are investigated in the belief that unlawful discrimination has taken place.[27] They may well be "general", where the activities of named persons are not part of the investigation. As such they may be initiated as a result of a strategic examination of particular discrimination issues. For example the C.R.E., in its *Report of the Formal Investigation into Race and Council Housing in Hackney*[28] says: "Our formal investigation into the allocation of council housing in the London Borough of Hackney was initiated as one aspect of the C.R.E.'s programme of work in the public housing field." Indeed, an investigation of a general nature may well be prompted by individual complaints. The Commissions must nominate one or more Commissioners to conduct a formal investigation and, as commented above, may specifically appoint additional Commissioners to assist with the investigation. The nominated Commissioners may be delegated full powers relating to the conduct of the formal investigation.[29]

[21] S.D.A., s. 67 and R.R.A., s. 58.
[22] S.D.A., s. 71 and R.R.A., s. 62.
[23] S.D.A., s. 72 and R.R.A., s. 63.
[24] S.D.A., s. 75 and R.R.A., s. 66.
[25] S.D.A., s. 56A as amended by R.R.A., Sched. 4, para.1; R.R.A., s. 47 as amended by Housing Act 1988, s. 137.
[26] S.D.A., s. 57(1) and R.R.A., s. 48(1).
[27] See comments of Griffiths L.J. in *R.* v. *C.R.E. ex p., Hillingdon L.B.C.* [1982] 1 Q.B. 276 at 292.
[28] p. 17.
[29] S.D.A., s. 57 and R.R.A., s. 48.

The formal investigation is of great importance to both Commissions in their armoury of enforcement powers as Lord Diplock has commented "not least important of the powers exercised by the Commission is the power to conduct formal investigations."[30]

## *Terms of reference*

The C.R.E. and E.O.C. are required to draw up terms of reference for a "general" investigation or a "belief" investigation directed at "named persons".[31] Where the Secretary of State requires a formal investigation to take place, terms of reference are drawn up in consultation with the relevant Commission.[32]

## *Requirements before formal investigation can proceed*

Before either Commission embarks upon a formal investigation it must satisfy a number of requirements.[33] The requirements depend upon whether the terms of reference of the investigation are general or relate to activities of named persons.

## *General investigations*

Once the terms of reference have been drawn up the Commissions have a duty to give general notice of the holding of the investigations.[34] A "general notice," in relation to any person, means a notice published at a time and in a manner which would ensure that it is seen within a reasonable time by persons likely to be affected by it.[35] A general notice appearing in relevant national or local newspapers or journals would seem to be sufficient.

## *Named persons or "belief" investigations*

In circumstances where named persons are the subject of the investigation a special procedure applies.[36] The Commissions must inform named persons of any specific acts of discrimination thought to be unlawful by:

[30] On C.R.E. in *R.* v. *C.R.E. ex p., Hillingdon L.B.C.* [1982] A.C. 779 at 784.
[31] S.D.A., s. 58(2) and R.R.A., s. 48(2).
[32] S.D.A., s. 58(2) and R.R.A., s. 49(2).
[33] S.D.A., s. 58(1) and R.R.A., s. 49(1).
[34] *Ibid.*
[35] S.D.A., s. 82(1) and R.R.A., s. 78(1).
[36] S.D.A., s. 58(3) and R.R.A., s. 49(3).

(a) informing the person of their belief and of their proposal to investigate the act in question;[37]
(b) offering the person an opportunity of making oral or written representations, or both;[38]
(c) where a person takes the opportunity of making oral representations allowing representation by:
    (i) counsel or a solicitor;
    (ii) some other person of his choice, not being a person to who the commission object on the ground he is unsuitable.[39]

The view taken by the Court of Appeal in *R,* v. *C.R.E. ex p., Hillingdon L.B.C.* is that the opportunity to make oral or written representation with regard to the proposal to hold a formal investigation is an arguable one. The wording of the particular sections[40] suggests the opportunity arises in order that representations against the alleged discriminatory act which is believed to be unlawful. This latter view does seem to be the more likely interpretation, otherwise the "opportunity" to make representations is one of generality against the investigation rather than one which specifically addresses the issue, *i.e.* the alleged discriminatory act, which gives rise to the investigation. How can representation be made against the investigation if the specific discriminatory act cannot be addressed.[41]

The C.R.E. have suggested there are two varieties of named person investigations:

1. a named person investigation where no specific discriminatory act is stated and where the general notice procedure stating the named person applies; and
2. a named person investigation where a discriminatory act is stated and the preliminary notice procedure has to be applied.

Lord Diplock again giving the judgment in the House of Lords took the view that the first variety did not exist legally and therefore the Commission in a named persons investigation must always follow the preliminary notice procedure.[42] Since the Commissions may vary the terms of reference of an investigation once started,[43] it would seem appropriate to initiate a general investigation where particular discriminatory acts have not been identified or where a Commission

[37] S.D.A., s. 58(4) (*a*) and R.R.A., s. 49(4)(*a*).
[38] S.D.A., s. 58(4)(*b*) and R.R.A., s. 49(4)(*b*).
[39] S.D.A., s. 58(4) and R.R.A., s. 49(4).
[40] S.D.A., s. 58(4)(*b*) and R.R.A., s. 49(4)(*b*).
[41] *c.f.* Lord Diplock's view in the *Hillingdon* case at 779.
[42] See *R.* v. *C.R.E. ex p., Prestige Group plc* [1984] 1 W.L.R. 335.
[43] S.D.A., s. 58(5) and R.R.A., s. 49(5).

does not wish to state them until further investigation, then change the terms of reference to those relating to a named person investigation. When terms of reference are changed the requirement to service of preliminary notices and offer opportunities to make representation still arise.[44] The whole effect though gives rise to a "preliminary inquiry" rather than simply a preliminary stage to the full investigation.

Furthermore in a named persons investigation "the Commission's belief as stated in the terms of reference defines and limits the scope of the full investigation".[45] This is an unnecessarily restrictive view since it suggests the investigation should be confined to named acts as well as named persons, thus removing the possibility of investigation of other unnamed discriminatory acts which may be identified during the course of inquiries. However, it would seem that the Commissions would be able to investigate "kinds of acts" similar to those prescribed by the terms of reference, otherwise this "would impose upon the investigating powers of the Commission letters that Parliament could never have intended".[46] Additionally, if the Commissions "are of the opinion that from individual acts which raise a suspicion that they may have been influenced by racial [or sex] discrimination an inference can be drawn that the persons doing those acts were also following a more general policy of racial [or sex] discrimination, the Commission[s] are entitled to draw up terms of reference wide enough to enable them to ascertain whether such inference is justified or not".[47] But this depends on drawing up terms wide enough to encompass "beliefs" which may not have been formulated before the investigation began, but which have been formulated during the process of the investigation. If the terms of reference are not wide enough to encompass the newly suspected acts then the Commissions are not able to investigate without changing the terms of reference without going again through a "preliminary inquiry". This would seem an unnecessarily complex and long-winded process which Parliament surely could not have intended. Admittedly, the first rule of natural justice, *audi alteram partem*, should be observed but surely this is achieved at the stage when the relevant Commission serves its appropriate notice of intention to investigate. The potential merry-go-round process conjured up by the need to change terms of reference to allow investigation of newly suspected acts of discrimination which show themselves as an investigation proceeds, is generated purely by the restrictive interpretation of the relationship between acts and terms of reference stated by the Court of Appeal.

[44] *Ibid.*
[45] *Hillingdon* case *per* Lord Diplock at 786.
[46] *Ibid.* pp. 86–7.
[47] *Ibid.* at 791.

## *Formal investigation*

For the formal investigation itself the Commissions can require people to produce information or attend the investigation by serving a notice on the person in question so long as the information or evidence in question could be required by the High Court.[48] If a person fails to comply with such a notice or a Commission has reasonable cause to believe that he will not comply with it the Commission can apply to the county court for an order requiring compliance.[49] Further, a person commits an offence if he:

(a) wilfully alters, suppresses, conceals or destroys a document which he has been required by a notice or order to produce; or

(b) in complying with a notice or order, he knowingly or recklessly makes any statement which is false in a material particular.

Such a person will be liable on summary conviction to a fine.[50]

However, such notices can be served only where:

(a) service of the notice was authorised by an order made by the Secretary of State; or

(b) the terms of reference state that the Commission believe that a person named in them may have done or may be doing acts of all of any of the following descriptions:
    (a) unlawfully discriminatory acts;
    (b) contravention of the provision relating to discriminatory practices;
    (c) contravention of the provisions relating to discriminatory advertisements, instructions, and pressure.

The Commissions' investigatory powers are confined to those defined acts.[51]

Therefore, in "general investigations" the Secretary of State must authorise by order the use of the Commission's subpoena powers. Otherwise subpoena powers may be used freely, except, following the *Hillingdon* judgment, that freedom to require people to appear or provide written information may well be restricted to matters relating to the acts specified in the terms of reference of the investigation.

A fine seems a small penalty for the destruction of relevant documentation relating to alleged unlawful discriminatory acts. And if

[48] S.D.A., ss. 59(1) and 59(3) and R.R.A., ss. 50(1) and 50(3).
[49] S.D.A., s. 59(4) and R.R.A., s. 50(4).
[50] S.D.A., s. 59(6) and R.R.A., s. 50(6).
[51] S.D.A., s. 59(2) and R.R.A., s. 50(2).

documentation is destroyed before a notice or order has been issued, there is no penalty whatsoever. During an investigation or once it is completed the relevant Commission may, if their findings suggest it, make recommendations:

1. to any person whose policies or practices or any other matter should be changed with a view to promoting equality of opportunity between the sexes or persons of different racial groups; or
2. to the Secretary of State for changes to the law or otherwise.[52]

The findings of the Commission following a formal investigation shall appear in a report, delivered to the Secretary of State, if he ordered the investigation initially, who in turn will publish it. However, the Secretary of State can require that there should be no report published.[53] This seems an odd legislative provision. Why undertake a formal investigation into for example practices which are discriminatory and not publish the findings? This may relate to the restrictions placed upon the Commissions relating to the disclosure of information during the formal investigation, which intend to protect the interests of "informants".[54] In particular when preparing a report for publication or for inspection the Commission can exclude, so far as is consistent with their duties and the object of the report, any matter which related to the private affairs of any individual or the business interests of any person where the publication of that matter might in the opinion of the Commission, prejudicially affect that individual.[55]

## *Non-discriminatory notices*

The service of a non-discrimination notice is far from straightforward. If during the course of a formal investigation the Commissions become satisfied that a contravention of the Acts has taken place they are empowered to serve a non-discrimination notice on the person concerned.[56] However, it looks highly unlikely that a Commission is able to serve such a notice on a person during a "general" investigation. Since the *Prestige* and *Hillingdon* judgments such powers would seem to only arise during "named persons" investigation. Presumably where discriminatory practices, and for that matter advertisement, instruction or pressure, are found to be in operation the

[52] S.D.A., s. 60(1) and R.R.A., s. 51(1).
[53] S.D.A., ss. 60(2) and 60(3) and R.R.A., ss. 51(2) and 51(3).
[54] S.D.A., s. 61(1) and R.R.A., s. 52(1).
[55] S.D.A., s. 61(3) and R.R.A., s. 52(3).
[56] S.D.A., s. 67(1) and R.R.A., s. 58(1).

Commissions are empowered to serve a non-discrimination notice since the service of such a notice is the only means legislatively available to eradicate such practices.[57] The notice can be served whether or not proceedings have been brought in respect of the particular discriminatory act or acts.[58]

Before a non-discrimination notice can be served on the person in question, the relevant Commission must first:

(a) give notice that they are minded to issue a non-discrimination notice, specifying the grounds on which they contemplate doing so; and
(b) offer an opportunity of making oral or written (or both) representations within a period of not less than 28 days specified in the notice; and
(c) take account of any representations made.[59] However the right to make representations does not extend to cross-examination of witnesses who gave evidence to the Commission. The hearing of oral representations is not a judicial function but an administrative one and therefore does not require the formality of cross-examination of witnesses. The rules of natural justice at this stage required no more than that the Commission should act fairly.[60]

Once this pre-notice stage is completed and the Commission are satisfied on the balance of probabilities that the person is committing, or has committed, discriminatory acts they may serve a non-discrimination notice requiring the person:

(a) not to commit any such acts; and
(b) where compliance involves changing practices or other arrangements:
    (i) to inform the Commission that changes have been effected and what those changes are; and
    (ii) to take such steps as may be reasonably required by the notice for the purpose of affording that information to other persons concerned.[61]

In addition, a non-discrimination notice may also require the person on whom it is served to furnish the appropriate Commission with such other information reasonably required by the notice in order to prove the notice has been complied with.[62] The notice may specify the

[57] S.D.A., ss. 37(3) and 67(1) and R.R.A., ss. 28(3) and 58(1).
[58] S.D.A., s. 67(1) and R.R.A., s. 58(1).
[59] S.D.A., s. 67(5) and R.R.A., s. 58(5).
[60] *R.* v. *C.R.E. ex p., Cottrell and Rothan* [1980] 1 W.L.R. 1580.
[61] S.D.A., s. 67(2) and R.R.A., s. 58(2).
[62] S.D.A., s. 67(3) and R.R.A., s. 58(3).

"manner and form in which, any information is to be furnished to the Commission" and the time at which, up to five years after the notice has become final, the information should be provided.[63]

Essentially the service of a non-discrimination notice is a means of preventing further discriminatory acts from taking place. It is not a means to provide remedy for discriminatory acts which have taken place in the past, instead it prevents, or attempts to prevent their recurrence. Therefore as Lustgarten[64] has commented "the Commission have no power to compel the discriminator to take any positive steps."

There is a right of appeal against the service of a non-discrimination notice which must be made within six weeks after the service of the notice.[65] The appeal in the housing field must be made to a designated county court,[66] which if it feels the appeal is well founded may quash any requirement stated in the notice or substitute different requirements.[67] The court may examine not only the reasonableness of requirement in the notice but may also examine the facts ascertained by the Commissions during the course of their investigation including considering evidence from witnesses and their cross-examination.[68]

A non-discrimination notice becomes final once the right to appeal period has expired or once the county court has ratified the notice or else altered its requirements or when an appeal is withdrawn or abandoned.[69] Once it has become final it remains in force for the next five years and failure to observe its requirements renders the recipient liable to proceedings by the Commissions for an order or injunction enforcing its requirements.[70] The relevant Commission must keep a register at its offices of notices which have become final. Any person is entitled to inspect the register and to obtain copies of any of its entries on payment of a fee determined by the Commission.[71]

The process of serving a non-discrimination notice has rightly been described by Lord Denning as "so elaborate and so cumbersome that it is in danger of grinding to a halt" and saying that the Commission for Racial Equality "have been caught up in a spider's web spun by Parliament from which there is little hope of their escaping".[72] Nor have the courts helped in their interpretation of the statutes by assisting in

[63] S.D.A., s. 67(4) and R.R.A., s. 58(4).
[64] *op. cit.* p. 247.
[65] S.D.A., s. 68(1) and R.R.A., s. 59(1).
[66] S.D.A., s. 68(2) and R.R.A., s. 59(2).
[67] S.D.A., ss. 68(2) and 68(3) and R.R.A., ss. 59(2) and 59(3).
[68] *C.R.E.* v. *Amari Plastics Ltd.* [1982] 1 Q.B. 1194.
[69] S.D.A., s. 82(4) and R.R.A., s. 78(4).
[70] S.D.A., s. 71 and R.R.A., s. 62; see also Non-Discrimination Notice of C.R.E. in its *Formal Report on Racial Discrimination in a London Estate Agency, Richard Barclay & Co.* (1988) pp. 13–14.
[71] S.D.A., ss. 70(1) and 70(2) and R.R.A., ss. 61(1) and 61(2).
[72] *C.R.E.* v. *Amari Plastics Ltd.* [1982] I.C.R. 304 at 313.

simplifying this elaborate and cumbersome process. If anything, the courts have added to its complexity.

In enforcing the provisions of the Acts the Commissions are unable to bring individual cases to court, unless taking out non-compliance proceedings. Only individual victims can pursue actions in court and even then are unable to take out proceedings relating to discriminatory practices, advertisements, instructions and pressure: these are the subject of administrative action by the Commissions. This limitation on the powers of the Commissions in instituting court proceedings means they must always follow the cumbersome process of the formal investigation. As Pannick[73] has commented: "Giving the E.O.C. [and the C.R.E.] power to commence legal proceedings in their own name would be a more effective method of enforcing anti-discrimination law than leaving such action solely to individual victims."

## *Persistent discrimination: enforcement of non-discrimination notice*

At any time up to five years after a non-discrimination notice has become final or a person has been found guilty by a tribunal or county court of unlawful discrimination, it appears to a Commission that unless restrained the discriminator is likely to commit further discriminatory acts, the Commission may apply to a county court for an injunction restraining the person from doing so S.D.A., s. 71(1) and R.R.A., s. 62(1). If the court is satisfied that the application is well founded it may grant an injunction or order on the terms applied for or on more limited terms.[74] Accordingly, care must be taken in wording the injunction or order since if it is too wide the court may well set it aside or limit it in such a way that it is rendered ineffective.[75]

## *Review of anti-discrimination law and enforcement*

The effectiveness of this enforcement power depends on the ability of the respective Commissions to be able to monitor compliance of notices and court orders. Criticism[76] has been made of the inability of the E.O.C. for the inadequacy of resources and the evidence which is available to show, certainly in the employment field, that discriminators do not necessarily change their practices.[77] The C.R.E. has stated its intention of monitoring Richard Barclay & Co. Estate Agents, for a

[73] *op. cit.* p. 284.
[74] *Ibid.*
[75] See Lord Denning's comments in *R.* v. *C.R.E. ex p., Hillingdon L.B.C.* [1982] 1 Q.B. 276 at 287.
[76] In Ellis *Sex Discrimination Law* (1988) p. 269.
[77] See Leonard, *Pyrrhic Victories* (1987 H.M.S.O.).

period of up to five years.[78] Reluctance to pursue formal investigations and enforcement proceedings may well be due to the fetters placed upon the Commission as a result of the *Hillingdon*, *Prestige* and *Amari Plastics* cases. Indeed, both Commissions have commented on the cumbersome process involved and agreed for a change in the legislation to introduce procedures which are more straightforward and certain in operation and to shorten effectively the overall period it takes to conclude an investigation. As the E.O.C. have stated in *Legislating for Change? Review of the Sex Discrimination Legislation* (1986):

> The proceedings for an investigation should, in the Commission's view, ensure that the Commission can carry out a speedy and effective investigation and that any individual being investigated has an adequate opportunity to defend himself and state his case. The present procedure, particularly the provision for representation by an individual to investigate in accordance with section 58(3A) of the Act fails to achieve either of these objectives.

The C.R.E. has made similar overtures, perhaps more emphatically, bearing in mind the difficulties it has faced with the courts.[79]

## *Special enforcement arrangements*

The Commissions have special powers and functions relating to discriminatory practices, advertisements, instructions and pressure. Essentially, as briefly touched upon already, legal proceedings or administrative action relating to these specific discriminatory acts can only be instituted by the Commissions. In the case of discriminatory practices the Commission have to launch a formal investigation in the way we have already generally described. The same process of enforcement applies.

Similarly the same approach is available to the Commissions to deal with discriminatory advertisements, instructions and pressure. But in addition the Commissions, and only the Commissions, may apply to a county court to investigate proceedings for contravention of these provisions of the Acts.[80] The proceedings can be:

(a) an application for a decision whether the alleged contravention occurred; or
(b) in order to prevent a further contravention, an application to a county or sheriff court for an injunction or order.[81]

[78] See paras. 5 and 6 of the Non-Discrimination Notice, *op. cit.* p. 14.
[79] See C.R.E., *Review of the Race Relations Act 1976: Proposals for Change* (1985).
[80] S.D.A., ss. 71(1) and 71(3) and R.R.A., ss. 63(1) and 63(3).
[81] S.D.A., s. 71(2) and R.R.A., s. 63(2).

These powers are available whether or not the person concerned is the subject of a non-discrimination notice or a court finding.[82]

## *Assistance to complainants*

Both Commissions have the power to assist an "aggrieved person" in determining whether to institute legal proceedings and helping such a person to formulate and present their case in the most effective manner.[83] However, such help may only be rendered where:

(a) the case raises a question of principle;
(b) it is unreasonable, because of the complexity of a case or the position of the individual in relation to the alleged discrimination, to expect the person to deal with the case unaided;
(c) some other special consideration applies.[84]

The assistance rendered may include: giving advice, attempting to procure settlement, arranging advice by a lawyer, arranging representation or other assistance.[85] The Commissions have to decide whether to give assistance within two months from receiving application.[86] They can by notice extend this period to three months.[87] Nonetheless the decision whether or not to give assistance remains discretionary. Where the Commission incur expenses in giving assistance, the recovery of those expenses shall constitute a first charge for the benefit of the Commission on any cost or expenses which become payable to the applicant, subject to any charges under the Legal Aid Schemes.[88]

## *Codes of practice*

Both Commissions may issue codes of practice which contain guidance for:

(a) the elimination of discrimination in the field of employment;
(b) the promotion of equality of opportunity in that field:
  (i) between men and women; and
  (ii) between persons of different racial groups.[89]

For some time the Commission for Racial Equality has been considering introducing a code of practice, without statutory force, in

[82] See Chapter 9 for a fuller discussion of these forms of housing discrimination.
[83] S.D.A., s. 75(1) and R.R.A., s. 66(1).
[84] *Ibid.*
[85] S.D.A., s. 75(2) and R.R.A., s. 66(2).
[86] S.D.A., s. 75(3) and R.R.A., s. 66(3).
[87] S.D.A., s. 75(4) and R.R.A., s. 66(4).
[88] S.D.A., ss. 75(5) and 75(6) and R.R.A., ss. 66(5) and 66(6).
[89] S.D.A., s. 56A and R.R.A., s. 47.

the field of rented housing for the elimination of racial discrimination and the promotion of equal opportunity.

During the passage of the Housing Bill 1988 through Parliament the C.R.E. successfully lobbied for a statutory power to issue codes of practice in the field of rented housing. The result is that section 47 of the R.R.A. has been amended.[90] Section 47(1) now includes the following paragraphs:

> "(c) the elimination of discrimination in the field of housing;
> (d) the promotion of equality of opportunity in the field of rented housing between persons of different racial groups."

In addition subsection (3A) has been added which says:

> "(3A) In the course of preparing any draft code of practice relating to the field of rented housing for eventual publication under subsection (2) the Commission shall consult with such organisations or bodies as appear to the Commission to be appropriate having regard to the draft code."

The Commission must consider representations it receives relating to draft codes of practice it publishes and modify the draft accordingly.[91] Thus when issuing the draft of its first code of practice in the field of rented housing early in 1989 the Commission consulted a wide range of agencies involved in the field.

Once modified a draft code of conduct has to be transmitted to the Secretary of State who shall:

(a) if he approves of it, lay it before both Houses of Parliament; and
(b) if he does not approve of it, publish details of his reasons for withholding approval.[92]

For a period of 40 days the draft code of practice is subject to the negative resolution procedure before the House. If no such resolution is passed the Commission must issue the code in the form of the draft and the code will come into force at the date by order of the Secretary of Sate.[93] Such an order, by way of statutory instrument[94] may contain such transitional provisions or savings as appear to the Secretary of State to be necessary or expedient.[95] The Commission may modify existing codes of practice but must follow the same procedure as for issue of new code of practice.[96]

[90] Housing Act 1988, s. 137 and Local Government and Housing Act 1989, s. 161.
[91] R.R.A., s. 47(2).
[92] *Ibid.*, s. 47(4).
[93] ss. 47(4)–(7).
[94] s. 47.
[95] s. 47(8).
[96] s. 47(9).

## *Status of a code of practice*

A failure on the part of any person to observe a code of practice shall not itself render that person liable to legal or administrative proceedings. But in any proceedings before a county court any code of practice which has been issued shall be admissible in evidence. Where a provision of a code of practice appears to the court to be relevant to "any question arising in the proceedings it shall be taken into account in determining that question".[97] As the C.R.E. stated in its first draft code of practice in the field of rented housing:[98]

> The code does not impose any legal obligations itself, nor is it an authoritative statement of the law—this can only be provided by the courts and tribunals. If, however, its recommendations are not observed, this may result in breaches of the law where an act or omission falls within any of the specific prohibitions of the Act. Moreover, the code's provisions are admissible in evidence in any proceedings under the R.R.A. before the courts, and if any provision appears to be relevant to a question arising in the proceedings, it must be taken into account in determining that question.

A failure to adhere to the codes of practice, where the issue is relevant to that under consideration, may be probative of discrimination taking place. This though must be viewed in the circumstances of the case in question.

Oddly, the code of practice does not have to be so taken into account by the Commission in questions which arise as part of its own administrative proceedings when undertaking formal investigations. However, no reasonable body should fail to take account of its own publically stated guidance.[99]

## *Code of practice in the fields of housing and rented housing*

The codes of practice issued by the C.R.E. have two aims:

1. to provide detailed guidance on the operation of the R.R.A. to the field of rented housing and the elimination of racial discrimination; and
2. to give examples of good practice in the implementation and promotion of equal opportunities.[1]

[97] s. 47(10).
[98] Para. 1.2.
[99] *Associated Provincial Picture Houses* v. *Wednesbury Corporation* [1948] 1 K.B. 223.
[1] Para. 1.1 of the Code.

As well as looking at the specific provisions of the Act relating to discrimination in the housing field the Code also outlines:

- Equal Opportunity Policies;
- Particular problem of racial discrimination and disadvantage in housing:
  - A. Access to housing;
  - B. Quality of housing;
  - C. Service delivery;
- Racial Harassment;
- Strategies for Good Practice, included:
  - (i) ethnic record keeping and monitoring;
  - (ii) use of ethnic records: measurement and targeting;
  - (iii) training;
  - (iv) positive action.

The Codes throughout gives examples of racial discrimination in housing and sets out recommendations and action plans. A copy of the Code for Rented Housing is included in Appendix three. The Code of Housing is almost identical.

Presumably, the power to issue a code of practice relating to the field of rented housing has only been extended to the C.R.E., is that fewer incidents of discrimination relating to sex have been evidenced. Additionally, the E.O.C. did not lobby for the power to be extended to its field of operation.

# Chapter fourteen

# Individual Enforcement

## INTRODUCTION

A claim by a person "the claimant", that another person "the respondent", has committed an act of discrimination against the claimant which is unlawful as set out in Part III of the Acts, may be made by the subject of civil proceedings in tort.[1] Proceedings can be brought only in a designated county court with the same remedies as are available in the High Court.[2] A designated county court is one so designated by an order made by the Lord Chancellor.[3] There is a right of Appeal to the Court of Appeal.

### *Time limitations*

A complaint to a designated county court must be made within six months from the point at which the alleged discriminatory act took place.[4] The six months period expires in accordance with the following rules:

(a) a deliberate omission occurs at the time the person in question decided upon it. Unless there is evidence to the contrary, a person is taken to have decided upon an omission:
   (i) when the person does an act inconsistent with doing the act he is said to have omitted; or
   (ii) at a time when the person, if he meant to do the act in question, might reasonably be expected to have done it;

(b) An act spread over a period of time is treated as having taken place at the end of the period in question;

[1] S.D.A., s. 66(1) and R.R.A. s. 57(1).
[2] S.D.A., s. 66(2) and R.R.A., s. 57(2).
[3] S.D.A., s. 76(1) and R.R.A., s. 67(1).
[4] S.D.A., s. 68(2) and R.R.A., s. 76(2).

(c) Where the unlawful act is a term in a contract the act applies throughout the life of the contract.[5] See also *Calder* v. *James Finlay Corp. Ltd.*[6]

However a court can consider a complaint which is out of time if the circumstances of the case suggest it is just and equitable to do so.[7] It is up to the court "to do what it thinks is fair in the circumstances".[8] If a person has applied to the C.R.E. for assistance in the case, the time limit can be extended by two or three months, due to the Commission's time scales for considering applications for assistance.[9]

Although an act which has occurred outside the limitation period cannot be the subject of a claim[10] it can be admissible as evidence where it is relevant to a further act which is made the subject of a complaint within the limitation period.[11]

## *The questions of procedure and discovery*

Both Acts provide a procedure whereby a complainant may ask questions of a person who may have discriminated against them. This is to assist the complainant in deciding whether to institute proceedings and if so to formulate and present the case in the most effective manner.[12] As the Home Office Guidance on the Acts states:[13]

> The exchange of questions and answers will focus attention on what would have to be shown in order to prove unlawful discrimination, but the main purpose is to establish as far as possible both the facts of the grievance, and in particular, the reasons why the respondent took the action complained of. In some cases the exchange of information may show the complaint to have been groundless, or based on a misunderstanding. In others it may result in a settlement so that legal proceedings are unnecessary. Where proceedings are instituted it should help to simplify them by identifying in advance what is agreed and what is indispute between the parties.

As such the questions and answers are admissible as evidence.[14] There exist standard forms which are available, along with guidance notes, free of charge from the Commissions.

[5] S.D.A., s. 76(6) and R.R.A., s. 68(7).
[6] November 24, 1982 E.A.T. Scot and *Ammes* v. *I.L.E.A.* [1977] I.C.R. 308 E.A.T. at 311.
[7] S.D.A., s. 76(50) and R.R.A., s. 68(6).
[8] *Hitchinson* v. *Westward Television Ltd* [1977] I.C.R. 279 at 282.
[9] R.R.A., ss. 66(4) and s. 68(3).
[10] Subject to exceptions allowed in S.D.A., s. 76(5) and R.R.A. s. 68(6).
[11] *Din* v. *Carrington Viyella Ltd.* [1982] I.C.R. 256 at 261 E.A.T.
[12] S.D.A., s. 74(1) and R.R.A. s. 65(1).
[13] Sex Discrimination 1985 para 8.8 and Racial Discrimination 1977 para. 8.7
[14] S.D.A., s. 74(2) and R.R.A., s. 65(2) and *Quinn* v. *Williams Furniture Ltd.* [1981] I.C.R. 328.

If the court finds that without reasonable excuse the respondent to the questions deliberately omitted to reply within a reasonable time, or the reply was equivocal or evasive, then the court may draw any inference from that fact it feels just and reasonable, including an inference that the respondent did in fact commit an unlawful act.[15]

The questions procedure is not intended to replace the general principle relating to the discovery of documentation. This still applies to discrimination cases. Therefore it is not "intended to be a substitute for, but an addition to, the complainants" rights to discovery and inspection of documents'.[16] In fact the questions procedure can be used once proceedings have been instituted.[17] However, an order for discovery is not available where the county court "is of the opinion that it is not necessary either for disposing fairly of the proceedings or for saving costs".[18] Where personal documents are concerned these should only be ordered to be disclosed where it is essential in the interests of justice that the need for confidence should be overridden and that such disclosure "is necessary for fairly disposing of the proceedings" and "whether the necessary information has been or can be obtained by other means, not involving a breach of confidence".[19]

## *Burden of proof and standard of proof*

Rarely is there direct evidence of discrimination. Instead, what "affirmative evidence" is available will usually consist of inferences which are drawn from the primary facts of a particular case.[20] The burden of proof lies with the complainant in cases of direct discrimination. As Phillip J. has said "there is no doubt that, although the Act of 1975 is silent upon the burden of proof, the formal burden of proof lies upon the applicant".[21] Further in employment cases, if the primary facts indicate that there has been discrimination of some kind, the employer is called on to give an explanation and, failing clear and specific explanation being given by the employer to the satisfaction of the industrial tribunal, an inference of unlawful discrimination from the primary facts will mean the complaint is a success.[22] Therefore it should "be recognised that in the course of the case the evidential

[15] S.D.A., s. 74(2) and R.R.A., s. 65(2).
[16] Per Salmon L.J. in *Science Research Council* v. *Nasse* [1980] A.C. 1028 at 1069.
[17] See for example Sex Discriminations (Questions and Replies) Order 1975 (S.I. No. 1975 2048), amended by Sex Discrimination (Questions and Replies) (Amendment) Order 1977 (S.I. 1977 No. 844).
[18] C.C.R., Ord. 14, r. 2(2).
[19] *Nasse* v. *Science Research Council* [1979] I.R.L.R. 465 at pp. 467–8.
[20] See *Khanna* v. *Ministry of Defence* [1981] I.R.L.R. 331 (E.A.T.) and *Wallace* v. *South Eastern Education and Library Board* [1980] I.R.L.R. 193 (N.I.C.A.).
[21] *Oxford* v. *D.H.S.S.* [1977] I.C.R. 884 at 887.
[22] *Khanna*, above at 658–9.

burden may easily shift to the respondent".[23] Thus, "it is a burden which may move easily to the respondent, as a result of the evidence of the applicant".[24] Therefore, unless the respondent is able to satisfactorily explain or provide evidence to show unlawful discrimination has not taken place, the applicant's case will succeed. Where a satisfactory explanation is provided the burden of proof shifts again to the applicant since he or she bears the burden of proof throughout the proceedings even though it may momentarily shift to the respondent.[25] Additionally, although in direct discrimination cases the burden of proof lies with the applicant "it would only be in exceptional or frivolous cases" that a court would find it unnecessary to hear what the respondent had to say.[26] Because the standard of proof is based on a "balance of probabilities," it is important that respondents explain clearly the basis of the apparent inequality of treatment and where a court or tribunal accepts the respondents' explanation it should be specific about its reasons for doing so.[27] In cases of indirect discrimination the burden of proof requires the complainant to provide evidence to show a requirement or condition has been applied by the respondent which has a disproportionate effect on the applicant because of his race or sex. If the evidence presented by the applicant shows that this is the case it is then for the respondent to rebut the evidence or show the application of the requirement or condition is justifiable.[28]

The applicant need not show there was an intention or motive to discriminate. In a recent sex discrimination case Lord Goff of Chievely said:[29]

> There is discrimination under the statute if there is less favourable treatment on the ground of sex ... the intention or motive of the defendant to discriminate, though it may be relevant as far as remedies are concerned (see s. 66(3) of the Act of 1975), it is not a necessary condition to liability; it is perfectly possible to envisage cases where the defendant had no such motive, and yet did in fact discriminate on the ground of sex.

Accordingly, it is unnecessary for the applicant to show that the sole reason for less favourable treatment was motivated because of sex or

[23] *Oxford* v. *D.H.S.S.*, above at 886.
[24] Per Phillips J. *Humphrey* v. *St. George's School* [1987] I.C.R. 546 at 549.
[25] See *Saunders* v. *Richmond Upon Thames B.C.* [1977] I.R.L.R. 362.
[26] *Ibid.*, at 887 for a critique of the legal burden of proof see D. Pannick, *The Burden of Proof in Discrimination Cases* (1981) 131 N.L.J. 895.
[27] *Wallace* v. *South Eastern Education and Library Board*, [1980] I.R.L.R. 193 at 195 N.I.C.
[28] See Chapter 6.
[29] *R.* v. *Birmingham City Council, ex parte., Equal Opportunities Commission* [1989] 25 E.O.R., 32 at 33.

race. Instead it is enough to show sex or race was an "important factor" or a "substantial and effective cause" or a "substantial reason".[30] Of course the respondent may well wish to show that race or sex was not a factor at all and if this can be satisfactorily rebutted the burden of proof will shift back to the applicant.

In *Chattadhyay* v. *Headmaster of Holloway School*[31] Browne-Wilkinson J. explained that there is not usually available to the applicant "any evidence of overtly racial discriminatory words or actions used by the respondent" ... He went on to say that it was for that very reason the law has established that "if an applicant shows that he has been treated less favourably than others in circumstances which are consistent with that treatment being on racial grounds, the industrial tribunal [or court] should draw an inference that such treatment was on racial grounds, unless the respondent's can provide a satisfactory innocent explanation."

It does now seem to be accepted that statistical evidence relating to the respondents actions in similar circumstances to the case in question is discoverable. As a result since such "statistics are logically probative as evidence from which an inference might be drawn" where they showed a racially discriminatory policy was in operation on other occasions it was a reasonable inference to draw that the discriminatory policy has been manifested in the applicants case.[32] Indeed the C.R.E.'s Code of Practice in the rented housing field strongly recommends "that local authorities, housing associations and co-operatives, Housing Action Trusts, Tenants' Choice landlords and private landlords and landladies keep ethnic records and monitor them on a regular basis".[33] Such an approach by housing agencies will provide admissible evidence to show that discriminatory practices are or are not in operation and allow resulting inferences to be drawn.

## *Admissibility of evidence*

Although an action cannot be commenced if it is six months after an alleged discriminatory act occurred[34] the circumstances and facts about such acts can still be submitted as evidence if they are relevant or related to later acts which are themselves the subject of legal proceedings. However, no damages or relief can be obtained for the earlier act.[35]

[30] *Owen & Briggs* v. *James* [1982] I.C.R. 618 at 623–6.
[31] [1982] I.C.R. 132 at 137.
[33] See *West Midland Passenger Transport Executive* v. *Singh* [1987] I.R.L.R. 351 (E.A.T.).
[33] Para. 6.1.
[34] See above.
[35] See *Din* v. *Carrington Viyella (Jersey Kapwood) Ltd.* [1982] I.C.R. 256 (E.A.T.).

Clearly if statistical evidence is discoverable then it is admissible in proceedings.[36] Similarly, evidence concerning the attitude of the alleged discriminator before the act in question is also admissible. For example if the applicant was treated with hostility by the respondent, the evidence of that hostility would be admissible since it may show circumstances consistent with a racist or sexist attitude, even though there may exist an innocent explanation. The existence of such hostility calls for an answer.[37]

Neither, is there any distinction between attitude, for example evidence of hositility, before or after the alleged discriminatory act. Either can be consistent with a racist or sexist attitude. Thus evidence of events after the alleged act is admissible if it is "logically probative of a relevant fact".[38]

## *Remedies*

Where a county court finds in favour of a complainant the same remedies are available as are available in the High Court.[39] Therefore the court may award any of the following remedies:

1. an order declaring the rights of the parties;
2. an injunction which effectively is an order of the court requiring an individual or other body to perform, to refrain from committing, or not to commit specified discriminatory acts;
3. damages.

An award of damages in respect of an unlawful act of discrimination may include compensation for injury to feelings whether or not compensation is made in any other respect.[40] Additionally an award may consist of compensation in relation to any expenses incurred or loss sustained by the complainant, for example loss of earnings. However, an award of compensation is limited for forseeable damage which arises directly from the unlawful act of discrimination, in particular any pecuniary loss which is "properly attributable" to the unlawful act.[41] Compensation is not payable for damage which is far too remote, *i.e.* where the discriminator could not possibly foresee such consequences.[42] Therefore injury to feelings unrelated to the unlawful discriminatory act cannot be "properly attributable" and

[36] *West Midlands Passenger Transport Executive* v. *Singh*, above.
[37] *Chattopodhyay* v. *The Headmaster of Holloway School* [1981] I.R.L.R. 487.
[38] *Ibid.*
[39] S.D.A., s. 66(2) and R.R.A., s. 57(2).
[40] S.D.A., s. 66(4) and R.R.A., s. 57(4).
[41] *Coleman* v. *Skyrail Oceanic Ltd.* [1981] I.R.L.R. 398 (C.A.).
[42] *Wileman* v. *Minilec Engineering Ltd.* [1988] I.C.R. 318 at 329.

cannot be taken into account in making an award.[43] Compensation for harassment must be related to the degree of detriment suffered and since personal feelings are specifically involved in such cases the assessment must be both objective — how other reasonable people of the same group would have felt — and subjective — how did the particular person feel about the harassment.[44] There may be exceptional cases in which exemplary damages would be appropriate since a claim for compensation for unlawful discrimination "should be dealt with in like manner as a claim in tort",[45] and therefore "exemplary damages are appropriate where there has been a cynical calculation that the wrongful act could be done with such advantage that the advantage would outweigh any subsequent penalty."

Finally, with regard to damages in respect of unlawful indirect discriminatory acts, *i.e.* those falling with section 1(1)(*b*) of the Acts, no award will be made if the respondent satisfactorily shows that the requirement or condition in question was not applied with the intention of treating the complainant unfavourably on the basis of sex or race.[46]

## *Legal advice and assistance and legal aid*

Actions taken by individuals in sex or race discrimination cases qualify under the Legal Aid Act 1988 for aid or assistance subject to the appropriate financial status of the perosn concerned.[47] Legal aid is available for proceedings, relating to sex or race discrimination, in the county court and appeals to the High Court if the Legal Aid Board can be persuaded it is reasonable representation should be provided.[48] As the Legal Aid Handbook states[49]:

> "Proceedings brought under the R.R.A. and the S.D.A. may carry little potential benefit to the applicant in purely financial terms but considerable benefit from the point of view of the applicant's personal status. The proceedings that may be brought under the Acts are directed towards financial compensation, and in the light of distress caused to the applicant by the discrimination complained of it may be considered that that applicant has shown reasonable grounds for taking proceedings, notwithstanding that the potential financial benefit is insignificant."

[43] *Coleman, ibid.*
[44] *Snowball* v. *Gardner Merchant Ltd.* [1987] I.C.R. 719 (E.A.T.) and also *Wileman* v. *Minilec Engineering Ltd.* [1988] I.C.R. 318.
[45] Per Lawthen L.J. in *Skyrail Oceanic Ltd.* v. *Coleman* [1981] I.C.R. 864.
[46] S.D.A., s. 66(3) and R.R.A. s. 57(3); see also *Orphans* v. *Queen Mary College* [1985] I.R.L.R. 349 (H.L.).
[47] ss. 9 and 15.
[48] Civil Legal Aid (General) Regulations 1989, regulations 28 and 29.
[49] 1992, p. 24.

However, where aid or assistance can be provided by one of the Commissions, particularly the C.R.E. because of the greater extent of its powers in the housing field, it is likely that the Legal Aid Board will refuse representation unless it can be demonstrated support is not specifically available from the Commissions.[50]

[50] *Ibid.*, reg. 30(1)(*a*).

# Appendix I

# Accord Housing Group Limited and its subsidiaries

## EQUAL OPPORTUNITIES POLICY

## 1. Statement of policy

Accord's main objective is to provide housing and associated amenities for people in greatest need, on a fair and equitable basis. In society, certain groups and individuals are unfairly discriminated against. For this reason, Accord is committed to taking positive steps to help redress the effects of unfair discrimination and disadvantage in order to ensure that equality of opportunity becomes an integral feature of all its activities.

This statement sets out Accord's commitment to eliminating unfair discrimination from all aspects of its work, to outline policy priorities and to give the mechanisms for implementing, monitoring and co-ordinating progress towards the achievement of those policy objectives.

Accord Housing accepts and encourages applications for accommodation and employment from all sections of the community regardless of race, colour, ethnic or national origin, religion, sexuality sex, lifestyle, disability, age, marital or employment status.

## 2. Scope of policy

Accord's equal opportunities policy applies to all aspects of our work particularly:

- (a) the provision of housing and services;
- (b) recruitment, employment and training;
- (c) the employment of housing developers, consultants, contractors and suppliers;

(d) membership of the association and its management committee.

## 3. Policy objectives

The objectives of the equal opportunities policy are to eliminate unfair discrimination and take positive action in relation to:

(a) access to Accord's housing, the quality, size and location of accommodation offered to people in need and how long people wait to be offered accommodation;
(b) the provision of maintenance and other related services;
(c) the protection of tenants' rights in relation to racial and other forms of harassment;
(d) recruitment and selection procedures and ensuring equality of opportunity for all job applicants;
(e) the provision of relevant training and development opportunities;
(f) the way Accord procures the design and development of new housing;
(g) the recruitment of members of the association and its committee members to ensure that there is fair representation from the target groups;
(h) the provision of a copy of this policy statement to contractors and consultants to ensure they are fully aware of Accord's equal opportunities policy. Any contractors or consultants used by Accord will be expected to comply with the law on equal opportunties and the association's Code of Conduct.

Accord is committed to providing the necessary training to enable management and staff to understand and implement their responsibilities under the policy.

The relevant statutory requirements are contained in the R.R.A. 1976, the S.D.A. 1986, the Disabled Persons Act 1986, the Rehabilitation of Offenders Act 1974, the Disabled Persons (Employment) Acts 1944 and 1958 and the E.P.A. 1970. It is also the intention of Accord, through the implementation of this policy, to fully comply with the Corporation's performance expectations on race equality and equal opportunities.

## 4. Responsibility for implementation

The management committee of Accord, having formally adopted the equal opportunities policy, accepts responsibility for its implementation and for monitoring its effectiveness. The committee will, when considering any changes in policy, look at the equal opportunities implications.

Day to day responsibility for implementation lies with the chief executive and the executive team. All staff have a responsibility to ensure the positive application of this policy, in addition to their statutory duties.

The policy applies in the areas mentioned under section 2 by:

(a) undertaking a review of current practices and identification of weaknesses in procedures;
(b) devising and implementing new procedures for monitoring equal opportunities in various functions;
(c) establishment of equality targets and regular performance reviews;
(d) devising and implementing positive action programmes where appropriate.

Breaches of the policy may be the subject of grievance and disciplinary procedures.

## 5. Monitoring the equal opportunities policy and implementation programme

The management committee has responsibility for monitoring progress. Regular reviews are undertaken to monitor:

(a) performance against targets;
(b) effectiveness of procedures;
(c) operation of the policy;
(d) progress of implementation programmes (including positive action) with respect to agreed timetables.

Where monitoring reveals that the policy and/or procedures are not effective, the management committee is responsible for ensuring that a review is undertaken and changes introduced.

## 6. Resources

Accord allocates appropriate resources, whether financial or staff, to ensure full and effective implementation of this policy.

This policy was agreed by the management committee of the association at its meeting on October 7, 1992.

# Appendix II

# Racial and Sexual Harassment Possible Remedies Checklist

## *Important reminder*

Because of the diversity of legal remedies available and the problems in pursuing them a victim needs expert help and advice. Housing agencies should therefore develop close links with solicitors, neighbourhood law centres, and similar agencies to make the process as straightforward as possible.

## 1. Criminal sanctions—the police

1.1 Offences Against the Person Act 1861—Physical attacks;
1.2 Public Order Act 1986—Racially abusive language;
1.3 Criminal Damage Act 1971—Damage to property and violent entry to premises;
1.4 Post Office Act 1969—Indecent or obscene mail and grossly offensive, obscene or menacing telephone calls.

## 2. Private prosecutions

2.1 All the above actions may be pursued by the victim where the police do not take action themselves.

## 3. Race Relations Act 1976 and Sex Discrimination Act 1975

3.1 Section 31 and Section 40—Pressure to discriminate;
3.2 Section 33 and Section 42—Aiding unlawful acts;
3.3 Section 2 and Section 4—Victimisation;
3.4 Section 20 and Section 29—Provision of goods, facilities and services;
3.5 Section 21(1) and Section 30—Disposal of premises;

3.6 Section 21(2) and Section 30(2)—Management of premises and in particular claim of "any other detriment".

## 4. Action by housing agencies and landlords

4.1 Informal action—Entering tenancy conditions, issuing warnings, getting support of police;

4.2 Grounds 1 & 2 of Schedule 2 Housing Act 1985 and equivalent grounds in Rent Act 1977 and Housing Act 1988—Eviction proceedings for contravention of tenancy clause against "sexual" and "racial harassment" if there is one, otherwise for nuisance;

4.3 Support for civil actions or private prosecutions—Financial support for victims plus advice and help.

## 5. Action by local authorities

5.1 Protection from Eviction Act 1977—Unlawful deprivation or attempted deprivation of residential occupation;

5.2 Section 222(a) Local Government Act 1972—Prosecution or defence or appearance in legal proceedings in the interests of the inhabitants of Local Authority area;

5.3 Control of Pollution Act 1977—Nuisance proceedings;

5.4 Section 137 Local Government Act 1972—Financial assistance for court hearings.

## 6. Action by C.R.E. and E.O.C.

6.1 Section 57 Race Relations Act 1976 and Section 75 Sex Discrimination Act 1975—General assistance for complainants;

6.2 Section 58L and Section 67—Service of Non-discrimination Notices;

6.3 Section 62L and 71—"Injunction" for persistent discrimination.

## 7. Civil action by victims

7.1 Generally the above remedies can be pursued by victims themselves where there is no support from an agency, by use of:

7.2 Injunctions—To restrain a perpetrator from committing further harassment;

7.3 Damages/Compensation—From perpetrator for mental or physical suffering or loss of trade;

7.4 Judicial Review—Compel "administrative agencies" to perform statutory duty.

# Appendix III

# Race Relations Code of Practice

## For the elimination of racial discrimination and the promotion of equal opportunity in the field of rented housing

## 1. INTRODUCTION

### Aims

**1.1** The aims of this Code are, first, to provide detailed guidance on the operation of the Race Relations Act 1976 in relation to the field of rented housing and the elimination of racial discrimination; and second, to give examples of good practice in the implementation and promotion of equal opportunities.

### Status of the code

**1.2** The Code does not impose any legal obligations itself, nor is it an authoritative statement of the law—this can only be provided by the courts and tribunals. If, however, its recommendations are not observed, this may result in breaches of the law where an act or omission falls within any of the specific prohibitions of the Act. Moreover, the Code's provisions are admissible in evidence in any proceedings under the Race Relations Act before the courts, and if any provision appears to be relevant to a question arising in the proceedings, it must be taken into account in determining that question.

### Applying the code

**1.3** The Race Relations Act applied to all housing organisations. The Code itself is not restricted to what is required by law, but contains recommendations as well. Some of its detailed provisions may need to be adapted to suit particular circumstances. Any adaptations that are made, however, should be fully consistent with the Code's general intentions.

## Discrimination in housing

**1.4** Research data and studies over recent years show that ethnic minorities have suffered severe discrimination in housing. This has operated in two ways. First, it has denied them access to housing; for example, accommodation bureaux have received and acted upon instructions from landladies and landlords not to let property to anyone who is black. Second, ethnic minorities have been discriminated against in the quality of accommodation they receive; for example, some local housing authorities have allocated poorer accommodation to ethnic minorities than to whites, even though their circumstances were similar.[1]

**1.5** Over recent years many organisations responsible for providing housing have begun to set up systems which should help to prevent discrimination. Apart from individual agencies a lead has been given by such national agencies as the local authority associations and the Housing Corporation, and policies have been developed which should, if they are implemented properly, prevent discrimination against ethnic minorities.

**1.6** This Code is based on what has already, in part, been developed in many areas, and aims to summarise the various aspects of a housing equality programme. It is concerned with the field of rented housing and covers the *social rented sector*, which includes local authorities, the voluntary sector (housing associations and cooperatives), Tenants' Choice Landlords and Housing Action Trusts; and the *private rented sector*, which includes private landlords, landladies and accommodation agencies, the functions of estate agents where they relate to the letting of accommodation, hotel and hostel accommodation, and services provided by the local authority. While the law is common to all these areas, and many of the recommendations on good practice are similar, there are differences of detail in some areas, particularly in relation to the roles of large and small landlords, and, where appropriate, these are indicated in the text.

# 2. THE RACE RELATIONS ACT

## Code of practice in employment

**2.1** Housing organisations, both public and private, are employers as well as service providers, and achieving equal opportunity in housing

[1] See Appendix I for examples of reports on racial discrimination and disadvantage in housing.

cannot be separated from equal opportunity in employment. This Code should therefore be read in conjunction with the Commission's Code of Practice in employment, which was approved by Parliament in 1983 and came into force in April 1984.

## Unlawful discrimination

**2.2 It is unlawful** under the Race Relations Act to discriminate on racial grounds, both directly and indirectly.

### *Section 3(1)*

*Racial grounds* are those of race, colour, nationality and ethnic or national origins, and groups defined by reference to these grounds are referred to as *racial groups*.

## Direct discrimination

### *Section 1(1)(a)*

**2.3** Direct discrimination is defined as treating a person less favourably than another on grounds of race and includes segregation of persons on racial grounds.

### *Examples*

**2.4** An accommodation agency does not give information about a particular letting to ethnic minority clients because the landlady has said that she does not want to let to them.
**2.5** A housing association allocates a poorer property to a black applicant than to a white applicant because of his racial origin.

## Indirect discrimination

### *Section 1(1)(b)*

**2.6** Indirect racial discrimination consists of applying, in the circumstances covered by the act, a requirement or condition which, although applied equally to persons of all racial groups, is such that a considerably smaller proportion of a particular racial group can comply with it than others, and it cannot be shown to be justifiable irrespective of the colour, race, nationality or ethnic and national origins of the person to whom it is applied. 'Justifiability' requires an objective balance between the discriminatory effect of the requirement or condition and the reasonable needs of the party applying the requirement or condition. The needs must be objectively justified and it is not sufficient for persons asserting that the needs exist simply to assert that they considered their reasons adequate.[2]

## *Examples*

**2.7** A housing cooperative fills its vacancies via friendship networks, ie by word of mouth, rather than by a more formal system of allocation. Where members of a housing cooperative are predominantly white, such a rule will disadvantage members of ethnic minorities.
**2.8** A landlord requires a lengthy period of local residence before an applicant can be considered for rehousing. In some areas such a rule will disproportionately affect members of ethnic minorities; for example, Bangladeshis who tend to have settled in this country very recently.

# Victimisation

## *Section 2(1)*

**2.9 It is unlawful** under the Act to discriminate by victimising a person.
**2.10** A person is victimised if he or she is given less favourable treatment than others in the same circumstances because it is suspected or known that he or she has brought proceedings under the Act, or given evidence or information relating to such proceedings, or alleged that discrimination has occurred.

# Pressure or instructions to discriminate

## *Section 30 & 31*

**2.11 It is unlawful** for a person to instruct or attempt to put pressure on another person to contravene the Race Relations Act. Such pressure need not be applied directly: it is unlawful if it is applied in such a way that the other perosn is likely to hear about it.

[2] See *Hampson* v. *Department of Education and Science*, Court of Appeal, December 1988.

*Example*

> **2.12** Tenants on an estate put pressure on their local authority landlord not to allocate a flat to a family because it is black.

**2.13 It is unlawful** to act on a discriminatory instruction or pressure.

*Example*

> **2.14** A landlady gives in to the discriminatory pressure put on her by tenants not to offer a property to a black tenant.

## Housing provisions of the act

### *Section 20*

**2.15 It is unlawful** for any person concerned with the provision of premises to discriminate by refusing on racial grounds to provide premises of like quality, or by providing premises of different quality or on different terms.

### *Section 21*

**2.16 It is unlawful** for any person with the power to dispose of premises to discriminate against another:

### *Section 21(1)*

- in the terms on which such premises are offered; or
- by refusing an application for such premises; or
- in the treatment of a person in relation to any list of people needing such premises.

### *Section 21(2)*

**2.17 It is unlawful** for a person who manages premises to discriminate against the occupiers of those premises:

- in the way access is afforded to any benefits or facilities, or by refusing or deliberately omitting to afford such access; or
- by evicting the occupiers or subjecting them to any other detriment.

## Small dwellings exemption

### *Section 22 and 23*

**2.18** Landlords and landladies in small premises who share their homes with other people are exempt under the Act. (See paras 4.15 and 4.16).

## Licences

### *Section 24*

**2.19 It is unlawful** for landlords, landladies or other persons to discriminate against another by withholding a licence or consent for disposal of premises.

### *Example*

> **2.20** If an existing tenant of a house wants to sublet to an Asian and needs her landlord's agreement, the landlord should not withhold that agreement on racial grounds.

**2.21** Other Sections of the Act which are particularly relevant to housing agencies include those relating to employers' liability and advertisements.

## The Liability of employers

### *Section 32*

**2.22** An employer is liable for any discriminatory act done by an employee in the course of his or her employment even if the act was done without the employer's knowledge or consent, unless the employer took all reasonably practicable steps to prevent such discrimination.

## Advertisements

### *Section 29*

**2.23 It is unlawful** to publish or cause to be published an advertisement which indicates, or might reasonably be understood as indicating, an intention to do an act of discrimination. (For exceptions see the Race Relations Act.).

# 3. EQUAL OPPORTUNITY POLICIES

## Basic principles

**3.1** Housing organisations should adopt an equal opportunity policy which states their commitment to equal opportunity and summarises the actions that will be taken in order to achieve it. The policy should include:

(i) A declaration that the organisation will abide by the Race Relations Act and implement the provisions of the race relations Code of Practice in housing as far as practicable.

(ii) An undertaking to notify tenants, members and prospective tenants or members of the adoption of the policy (translated where appropriate), and to make the race relations Code of Practice in housing available for inspection.

(iii) An undertaking to allocate responsibility to a specified person and/or groups of people for implementing the overall and component parts of the policy. Clear lines of accountability should be indentified so that progress can be propertly monitored and results reported at regular intervals to committee members and/or the management of the organisation as appropriate.

## Implementation of the policy

**3.2** In order to implement an equal opportunity policy effectively, all housing organisations should develop an action programme incorporating the following steps:

### *Reviews*

(i) The practices and procedures of the organisation should be regularly reviewed to ensure that they do not discriminate directly or indirectly, and changes should be made where it is found that they are or may be contravening the Act.

### *Code of practice in employment*

(ii) The race relations Code of Practice in employment produced by the Commission should be accepted by the organisation and progress on its implementation regularly monitored. Consideration should also be given to implementing the positive action provisions of the Act.

### *Training*

(iii) All staff should receive training and guidance on the equal opportunity policy to ensure that they clearly understand their position in law and the implications of the organisation's policy.

### *Racial harassment*

(iv) Effective action to combat racial harassment and to support victims of such harassment should be introduced.

### *Ethnic records and monitoring*

(v) The policy should be monitored. One way of doing this is to keep ethnic records and monitor them on a regular basis. We recommend that such records should be kept by large landlords in the social and private rented sector and by local authority services which have responsibility for work in the private sector. (See paras 6.1–6.3). In respect of accommodation agencies, while not recommending the setting up of ethnic record systems, we do reccommend a procedure for monitoring their practices to ensure that they do not discriminate. (See para 6.4).

### *Unmet needs*

(vi) Any unmet needs (*e.g.* those of the ethnic minority elderly) should be identified wherever practicable, and action taken to meet them.

Further details on some of these areas are set out in Chapter six.

# 4. RACIAL DISCRIMINATION AND DISADVANTAGE

## A. Access to housing

**4.1 It is unlawful** for housing organisations to discriminate directly or have policies and procedures that are indirectly discriminatory and operate in such a way that persons of one racial group are unable or find it disproportionately difficult to obtain access to housing.

# Examples of discrimination

## The social rented sector and large private landlords

### *Refusal to rehouse*

**4.2** A landlord refuses to rehouse a family because of its ethnic origin. This is an instance of direct discrimination.

### *Residence qualifications*

**4.3** A local authority imposes a lengthy residence qualification which persons of one racial group are less able to comply with than others. Such a rule is indirectly discriminatory, unless it can be justified (see para. 2.6).

### *Sons and daughters scheme*

**4.4** A housing department operates a rule whereby the sons and daughters of current tenants are given rehousing priority, although they do not have tenancy rights to such properties under the Rent Act, nor have they negotiated such rights under the terms of the tenancy agreement. Where the tenants are from one predominant racial group, other racial groups will be less able to comply with this rule. Such a rule is indirectly discriminatory, unless it can be justified.

### *Referral systems*

**4.5** A landlord operates a rehousing system which depends on word-of-mouth recommendations from existing tenants. Where tenancies are predominantly held by one racial group, such a system is likely to discriminste unlawfully against other racial groups, unless it can be justified.

### *Separated families*

**4.6** A local authority has a rule on the treatment of separated families which differentiates between families separated within and outside the United Kingdom; *i.e.*, it allows a head of household to register a family who are separated within the United Kingdom on the authority's waiting list, but disallows a head of household from doing so if the separated family is abroad. Such a rule is indirectly discriminatory, unless it can be justified.

### *Owner occupiers*

**4.7** A local authority imposes a rule whereby owner occupiers are refused access to social rented housing regardless of the condition of their property or the degree of overcrowding. Such rules have worked against ethnic minorities, in particular Asians, who are at present more likely to be owner occupiers than other groups. Such a rule may be indirectly discriminatory, unless it can be justified.

### *Passports*

**4.8** A local authority routinely asks ethnic minority housing applicants for their passports, even though the individuals concerned may have been born in the United Kingdom or have lived in this country for a number of years. Such requests are based solely on a person's appearance and raise doubts and uncertainties about the fairness of treatment they might receive and about delays in the processing of housing applications. They are directly discriminatory and therefore unlawful.

## The private rented sector[3]

**4.9** This sector includes accommodation agencies, including those dealing with student accommodation, small private landlords and landladies, hotels and hostels.

### *Refusing information*

**4.10** A landlady withholds information about available accommodation of the type being sought by a particular racial group.

### *Refusal to register*

**4.11** An accommodation agency refuses to register someone from a particular racial group because the agency has previously

[3] For further details on the law and recommendations on how to avoid discrimination, see *A Guide for Accommodation Agencies, Landladies and Landlords*, CRE, 1989.

experienced difficulty over payment with an individual or individuals from that racial group.

### *Separate lists*

**4.12** An accommodation agency keeps a separate list for UK and overseas and ethnic minority students in order to meet landlords' preferences.

### *Refusal to house*

**4.13** A landlady refuses to let a property to, or accept as a guest, someone from a particular racial group.

### *Refusal to sublet*

**4.14** A landlord withholds permission to sublet on racial grounds in a case where his consent is required.

## Small dwellings exemption

### *Section 22 & 23*

**4.15** While the examples given above are unlawful under the Race Relations Act, there is one area of property letting which is exempt under the Act. It is not unlawful for a landlord or landlady to discriminate on racial grounds in the provision or disposal of rented accommodation which is covered by the small premises exemption defined in Section 22 of the Act. In order to qualify for this exemption, which applies only to the letting of premises and not the *treatment of tenants*, **all** of the following conditions must be satisfied:

- the person or near relative (defined as wife or husband, parent or child, grandparent or grandchild, borther or sister) lives and intends to continue living on the premises; AND
- the person or near relative shares accommodation with the tenant other than storage space or means of access: for example, a bathroom or kitchen; AND
- there is, in addition to the accommodation occupied by the person or near relative, accommodation for no more than two other separate households under separate letting agreements or six individual boarders.

**4.16** This exemption applies only to landladies and landlords and not to accommodation agencies acting on their behalf. Accommodation agencies which carry out discriminatory instructions from landlords and landladies—even though the property itself may be exempt—will be contravening the Race Relations Act.

## Informal barriers

**4.17** Apart from the formal barriers to access to housing as outlined above, there are less formal barriers which can disproportionately affect ethnic minority households.

### *Examples*

#### *Communication*

**4.18** Communication difficulties, whether due to the inability of an applicant to speak and understand English or the unwillingness of a housing officer to try to understand or communicate, are often accompanied by lack of knowledge of the housing system and what it has to offer. Because of these difficulties ethnic minorities may fail to obtain the housing to which they are entitled.

#### *Large accommodation*

**4.19** There has generally been a failure to provide sufficient numbers of larger units of family accommodation in the public sector. This has had implications for ethnic minority households (particularly from the Indian subcontinent and Vietnam), whose family type at present tends to be larger than that of other groups. As a result, these families have not been rehoused or have had to wait considerably longer than other families for accommodation.

## Recommendations

**4.20** It is recommended that all housing organisations review systematically all their policies on a regular basis to ensure that they do not operate in ways that discriminate against or disadvantage any particular racial group.

**4.21** In addition, housing organisations should develop a policy for dealing with discriminatory instructions from landlords and landladies, hostels, and hotel owners or managers. This is particularly relevant to accommodation agencies and local authority housing advisory services. The Commission should be informed when there appears to be a contravention of the Act, and the use of the hostel, etc, should be discontinued and other agencies notified of what has happened.

## Action plans

**4.22** Housing organisations and, in particular, those responsible for large numbers of tenancies, should adopt the following course of action:

(i) Clear criteria should be laid down for allocating or granting access to housing which will not discriminate against or disadvantage particular racial groups. Generally, decisions about access to housing should be predicted on the *need* of the individual applicant or tenant.

(ii) Ethnic record-keeping systems should be set up (see paras. 6.1–6.3).

(iii) Specific measures directed at particular groups should be taken to help them overcome communication difficulties. Relevant leaflets should be translated into appropriate languages, especially, those giving information on the way the housing system actually works and on what housing is available. In addition, where necessary, intepreters should be used.

(iv) The particular needs of ethnic minorities in any given area—such as building programmes—should be indentifed. Appropriate strategies should then be devised to meet these needs, taking account of the resources available.

(v) Passports should not be asked for as a matter of routine when identification is required. The information needed to deal with housing applications should be precisely defined and examples of various possible identification documents listed (*e.g.* driving licence, medical card, etc).[4]

(vi) Despite the exemption clause of the Race Relations Act in respect of landlords and landladies (see para. 4.15), it is our view that any form of discrimination is undesirable, even though not, in these defined circumstances, unlawful. We recommend therefore that landlords and landladies do not

[4] The implications of immigration for public sector housing are addressed in the Commission's guide on *Immigration and Housing*, forthcoming, C.R.E., 1989.

rely on this exemption, and treat everyone equally regardless of colour or race.

## B. Quality of housing

**4.23 It is unlawful** for housing organisations to descriminate in the relative *quality* of housing that is given to individual applicants. This is particularly relevant for larger landlords who will often have a wide range of properties available of differing quality. This section of the Code is therefore predominantly aimed at them.

## Examples of discrimination

### *Priority systems*

**4.24** Housing organisations will usually have systems for determining priorities between different groups of housing applicants. In general, ethnic minorities have been over-represented in those categories tending to receive poorer properties, and underrepresented in those categories tending to receive better accommodation. For instance, homeless applicants receive poorer property than applicants who are being transferred from one public sector property to another.[5] The operation of such a rehousing system, which has the effect of one racial group receiving poorer accommodation than another racial group, is indirectly discriminatory and **is unlawful**, unless it can be justified.

### *Preferences*

**4.25** Housing applicants are generally given some choice about the type of property they require and the area in which they want to live. **It is unlawful** to discriminate in the way that information is given on the availability of properties or in the way in which this information is recorded and acted upon.

### *Offers and refusals*

**4.26** The way in which the offer and refusal system operates can have an important influence on the quality of properties given to

[5] See *Homelessness: Report of the local authority housing and racial equality working party*, June 1988, and a forthcoming C.R.E. report on homelessness for further information and advice on this issue.

applicants. For example, first offers of properties may often consist of poorer quality accomodation than subsequent offers. **It is unlawful** to discriminate in the quality of offers of accommodation made to the applicants and in the way in which such offers are made; for example, by putting pressure on applicants to accept such offers.

### *Subjective assessment*

**4.27** Some housing organisations continue to make subjective assessments of applicants in respect of their living standards or their supposed suitability for types or properties in particular areas or districts. **It is unlawful** to make any such subjective assessment, which is based on the racial origin of the individual applicant or tenant and which may lead to the allocation of poorer quality accommodation to the person concerned.

## Recommendations

**4.28** To avoid discriminating against or disadvantaging ethnic minorities, housing landlords should:[6]

(i) Review their allocation systems in detail to ensure that they do not discriminate against ethnic minorities in respect of the relative priorities given to different housing categories. A key part of this review should include setting up ethnic record-keeping and monitoring systems. (See 6.1–6.3 for further details.)

(ii) Ensure that the use of discretion is contained within the framework of an overall allocation policy that is non-discriminatory. The options available at various stages of the rehousing process should be clearly identified and communicated to all housing applicants.

(iii) Ensure that information on the operation of the housing system and what people are entitled to is readily available to the local communities and translated into the relevant languages.

(iv) Ensure that (subjective) assessments by housing staff are not based on the racial origin of the individual applicant or tenant. The main role of housing staff at the time of application should be one of giving advice, not assessment.

[6] For further detailed advice on good practice in this area and on equal access to housing, see *Allocations: Report of the local authority housing and racial equality working party*, 1988.

# C. Service delivery

**4.29** Apart from possible discrimination in the areas of access to housing and quality of accommodation, discrimination can also occur in the related areas of advice given to applicants and tenants and type of service provided to tenants once they have been allocated a property.

## Examples of discrimination

### *Higher rents*

**4.30** A landlady charges higher rents from a particular racial group.

### *Decorating*

**4.31** A landlord gives preferential treatment to white tenants by redecorating their flats and not those of ethnic minority tenants, where the properties are in a similar condition.

### *Repairs*

**4.32** A local authority responds more quickly and efficiently to requests for repairs from one racial group than another, when responsiveness to such requests should be determined by the condition of the properties only.

### *Advice*

**4.33** A housing aid service provides a lower standard of advisory work (*e.g.* on homelessness) for one racial group than another.

### *Legal advice*

**4.34** A tenant relations officer initiates proceedings in some cases but not others, on racial grounds.

## Recommendations

**4.35** To avoid possible discrimination in the areas of advice and service provision, all housing organisations, landlords and landladies should:

(i) Implement an equal opportunity policy (see chapter three) which includes local authority services such as rent officer services, tenant relations services and legal services.[7] Particular attention should be paid to training staff in their responsibilities and ensuring that the services provided are understood by clients. Documents should be translated and an interpretation service provided where appropriate.

(ii) Keep ethnic records and monitoring systems where practicable in respect of the clients who use the service. (See paras. 6.1–6.3.) Such records should include information on the nature of en enquiry or problem and its outcome and should serve as a source of information on the needs of the community, so that strategies can be developed to meet them. Analysis of the data should focus on the question of whether the organisation's services are being provided in an equitable way.

(iii) In the case of local authorities, review the policies and procedures of the various services provided to ensure that they both reflect the needs of ethnic minorities and do not discriminate against or disadvantage them.

# 5. RACIAL HARASSMENT

**5.1** Racial harassment at or near the home is a serious problem and occurs in the private as well as the public sector. It occurs not only in areas where there is a large ethnic minority population, but also in areas where their numbers are relatively small.

## Action plans

**5.2** Housing organisations can only play a part in countering such harassment and while larger landlords such as local authorities will have a major role in helping to counter such harassment generally, smaller landlords/landladies such as hostel owners and managers also have an important role to play if one of their tenants is being racially harassed. A number of steps can be taken:[8]

(i) An effective support system for victims should be set up by larger landlords, with efficient arrangements made to rehouse

[7] See *Anti-Racism for the Private Rented Sector*, London against Racism in Housing, 1988 for further guidance on these matters and on the private rented sector generally.

[8] See *Living in Terror*, C.R.E., 1987 for a detailed analysis of the issues involved in racial harassment at or near the home, and recommendations on ways in which to deal with it.

them should they so wish. Where the tenants wish to remain in their property, the landlord should continue to monitor the situation closely to ensure that the support option is working in practice, particularly with respect to the victims' own wishes. Smaller landlords and landladies should assist victims and contact the police, the local authority and the local community relations council or similar organisations which should be able to help.

(ii) Landlords and landladies should attempt to identify the perpetrators of any racial attacks and take appropriate action, including contacting the police and, where the perpetrator is a tenant of the same landlord and all the circumstances justify it, seeking a court order for possession. Racial harassment should be included in tenancy agreements as grounds for terminating the agreement.

(iii) Tenants and prospective tenants on waiting lists should be advised that racial harassment will not be tolerated and action taken when incidents occur. Targets should be set for the prompt removal of graffiti and making good damage, once the evidence has been documented, *e.g.*, by photograph. In addition, staff should also be made aware of the organisation's views and be informed of the action they should take in cases of racial harassment.

(iv) For larger landlords, an effective and regular system of liaison should be set up with other agencies such as community groups, the police and the local authority department, in addition to common strategies developed between various large landlords (*e.g.*, a local authority, housing associations and a Housing Action Trust). Landlords should also discuss their policies with tenants' associations or other representative groups to obtain their support and to agree a common front in tackling harassment. Landlords should consider whether estate-based management would be an appropriate way of tackling recurring problems on particular estates. In discussion with the police and ethnic minority groups, consideration should be given to improving the physical design and security of estates.

(v) The local authority should also take steps to assist racial harassment cases in the private sector. A strategy for the prevention of racial harassment, including information and publicity on such policies and detailed procedures should be made available to tenants and the local community.

(vi) Policies and procedures on racial harassment should include clear guidelines to staff on their responsibilities and on possible courses of action. Channels of communication and responsibility should be clearly identified and a reporting system should be introduced. Policies should be monitored to check that they are effective, and regular reports produced for relevant committee members and/or managers on the results.

# 6. STRATEGIES FOR GOOD PRACTICE

## Ethnic records and monitoring

**6.1** It is recommended that local authorities, housing associations and cooperatives, Housing Action Trusts, Tenants' Choice Landlords and private landlords and landladies keep ethnic records and monitor them on a regular basis. The main components of an effective monitoring system should include:[9]

(i) Consultation with local communities in order to explain why monitoring is being introduced and to obtain views on issues such as the ethnic classification system.

(ii) An understanding of the role of monitoring as one part of a general equal opportunity strategy that also includes employment matters, training programmes, reviews of policies and procedures, etc.

(iii) The confidentiality of individual records.

(iv) The designation of specific officers with responsibility for introducing and maintaining the system, to ensure that it is effective.

(v) Monitoring ethnic records on a regular basis with analytical reports produced at a minimum of every six months. The main areas that should be reviewed include:

- *Access*—who has received housing and by what process; this will include the length of time people wait for housing;
- *Quality—where and in what types of properties people are being rehoused; and*
- *Services delivery*—this may include such areas as the repairs services, approving improvement grants, etc.

Ethnic records can also be used to review the situation of particular groups—for example, ethnic minority elderly or women—to check that

[9] See also the forthcoming C.R.E. report on ethnic record-keeping and monitoring to be published in 1989. This includes an analysis of current progress in ethnic monitoring systems in housing, detailed advice on how to set up such systems, and advice on the concept of targetting.

equal opportunity is being achieved and to ensure that any particular needs are being met.

(vi) Making monitoring reports available to tenants and local people.
(vii) When a report reveals particular problems, such as differential allocations, a programme of action should be agreed, with a suitable timetable, in order to rectify matters.

## The use of ethnic records: measurement and targeting

**6.2** In order to assess whether different ethnic groups are being treated equally, a *measurement* or *target* needs to be agreed of the proportions of ethnic minorities that could be expected if equal opportunity was being achieved. The measurement or target will be based on the local ethnic minority population as well as other indicators of needs, such as numbers on a waiting list, etc. Deciding on a suitable target can be a complex task initially, as it involves taking account of differential patterns of housing, the housing preferences of ethnic minority applicants and the operating of the local housing market. Consultation with community relations councils, community groups and other housing organisations in the area may be helpful in identifying initial targets, and these will need to be kept under review.
**6.3** This measurement or target will be the yardstick by which the data are analysed to check whether ethnic minorities have received a fair share of the properties and services available. It is emphasised that targets or measurements should not be confused with predetermined quotas, which are unlawful under the Race Relations Act.

### *Accommodation agencies*

**6.4** In respect of accommodation agencies, including universities and housing advice centres, we do not recommend setting up a formal ethnic record-keeping system because of practical problems and because of the fairly limited scope of their operations. Instead, they should adopt the following monitoring procedure to safeguard against any discriminatory practices:

(i) Random checks should be carried out on the agency's records of vacant accommodation and landlords/landladies to ensure that there are no discriminatory instructions or odd comments or signs that might be a code for discriminatory instructions.

(ii) Occasional random checks should be carried out by the agency to ensure that applicants have been given details of *all* appropriate vacancies available. If not, it should be determined whether this is because of the applicant's race or ethnic group.

(iii) Where an accommodation bureau is responsible for large numbers of lettings for an institution (*e.g.* colleges and universities) it should prepare a report on a regular basis (at six monthly intervals) for the appropriate governing body on implementation of the equal opportunity policy and the results of such checks.

# Training

**6.5** Training plays a major part in the effective implementation of an equal opportunity policy.[10] Housing staff need to appreciate the importance which committees and management attach to such issues and to understand their personal responsibility in carrying out their particular jobs. Training on race equality policies needs to be part of an overall training strategy for the staff of housing organisations. It is recommended that a training programme should be set up for staff. Such a programme should:

(i) Ensure that employees are able to implement and monitor the organisation's equal opportunity policy.

(ii) Ensure that participants are fully aware of the Race Relations Act 1976 and of its implications for their work.

(iii) Assist the organisation in reviewing its current allocation policies and practices, identifying possible areas of discrimination and proposing ways of changing them.

(iv) Assist the organisation in adopting and implementing, where appropriate, an effective system of ethnic record-keeping and monitoring.

(v) Assist the organisation in adopting effective policies and practices to counter racial harassment.

# Positive action

**6.6** The Race Relations Act allows for positive action to be taken in some circumstances by organisations. We recommend that larger

[10] See *Training for Racial Equality in Housing*, C.R.E., 1989, which outlines an approach to training on race-related issues in local authority housing departments, and is relevant to other large landlords. It includes recommendations on the main components of such a programme. The Commission has also produced a guide on training in relation to employment issues: *Training: The implementation of equal opportunities at work,* Vols I & II, 1987.

housing organisations in particular take advantage of these provisions.[11] They include:

(i) *Sections 37 and 38*—Designated training bodies and employers may encourage applications from persons of a particular racial group or make training facilities available only to persons of a particular racial group, where it can be shown that members of that racial group are under-represented in the work in question. This does not, however, allow discrimination in favour of persons of that group in making appointments.

(ii) *Section 5(2)(d)*—Discrimination is permitted in certain limited circumstances at the point of selection.

(iii) *Section 35*—Action can be taken to meet the special needs of persons of a particular racial group with regard to their education, training or welfare or any ancillary benefits (*e.g.* the ethnic elderly).

[11] For further details see *Positive Action and Equal Opportunities in Employment*, C.R.E., 1985. In addition, an advisory document on positive action in housing will be published by the C.R.E. in 1989.

# Appendix IV

# Reports on Racial Discrimination and Disadvantage

## Commission publications

1980, *Report of two formal investigations into: (i) G. D. Midda and D. S. Services Limited; (ii) Allen's Accommodation Bureau.*

1981, *Report of four formal investigations: (i) Brymbo Community Council; (ii) Councillor K. Rogers; (iii) Mrs I. Stapely; and (iv) Mrs B. Greenaway.*

1982, *The Allocation of Council Housing with Particular Reference to Work Permit Holders: Report of a formal investigation.*

1983, *Collingwood Housing Association Limited: Report of a formal investigation.*

1984, *Race and Housing in Liverpool: a research report.*

1984, *Hackney Housing Investigated: Report of a formal investigation.*

1985, *Race and Mortgage Allocation in Rochdale: Report of a formal investigation.*

1985, *Walsall Metropolitan Borough Council: Practices and policies of housing allocation.*

1988, *Homelessness and Discrimination: Report of a formal investigation into the London Borough of Tower Hamlets.*

1988, *Racial Discrimination in a London Estate Agency: Report of a formal investigation into Richard Barclay and Co.*

## Other publications

Bonnerjea, Lucy and Jean Lawton, *Race and Housing in Brent,* PSI, 1986.

Brown, Colin, *Black and White Britain: The third PSI survey,* 1984.

*Ethnic Minorities in Public Housing in Islington*, PSI, 1985.

Henderson, Jess and Valerie Karn, *Race, Class and State Housing: Inequality and the allocation of public housing in Britain,* CURS, 1987.

*Housing Association Allocations: Achieving racial equality,* Runnymede Trust, 1985.

Parker, John and Keith Dugmore, *Colour and the Allocation of GLC Housing,* GLC Research Report 21, 1976.

Simpson, Alan, *Stacking the Decks*, Nottingham and District Community Relations Council, 1981.

Skellington, Richard, *The Housing of Ethnic Minorities in Bedford*, June 1980.

Smith, David and Anne Whalley, *Racial Minorities and Public Housing*, PEP, 1975.

Stevens, Karn, Davidson and Stanley, *Ethnic Minorities and Building Society Lending in Leeds*, Leeds Community Relations Council, 1989.

*What Price Equality? A report on the allocation of GLC housing in Tower Hamlets,* GLC Housing Research and Policy Report 9, 1986.

# Appendix V

# Equal Opportunities Commission: The Provision of Mortgages: Guidelines for Good Practice

## 1. Introduction

The Equal Opportunities Commission (E.O.C.) was established in 1975 under the terms of the Sex Discrimination Act (S.D.A.) to work towards the elimination of sex discrimination and to promote equality of opportunity between men and women generally. As part of this general duty, the Commission has looked at the provision of mortgages. The following guidelines are intended as an aid to all organisations who are concerned with providing mortgage facilities on a non-sex discriminatory basis.

These guidelines provide a basis for the re-examination of current lending policies to ensure that mortgage provision is within both the letter and the spirit of the legislation. Further information and assistance is available from the Commission.

## 2. General

The best foundation for the non-discriminatory provision of mortgages is a clear and up-to-date written statement of lending policy which is freely available to both staff and borrowers.

## 3. Lending

(a) Lending policy should be checked to ensure that the same criteria are applied to men and women both in theory and in practice, *e.g.*:

(i) A refusal to accept a woman's salary as the main basis for a mortgage solely because of her sex is unlawful;

(ii) Women should not be asked to provide guarantors in circumstances where men would not be required to do so;

(b) All forms used should cater for equal treatment of men and women, *e.g.*:

By providing sufficient space to carry full details of both joint applicants' employment and income.

(c) Conditions or requirements applied to mortgage applicants should be re-assessed from the stand-point of indirect sex discrimination, *e.g.*:

(i) Automatic refusal of a mortgage to all part-time workers is likely to discriminate against women because many more women than men work part-time.

(ii) A requirement that borrowers should be in their present employment for an unnecessarily long period could amount to unlawful indirect sex discrimination as many women spend time out of work because of family or domestic responsibilities.

(d) Staff should treat employment broken by maternity leave as continuous employment. (Employment Protection Act 1975).

## 4. Mortgage procedures

(a) Wherever possible, all parties to a joint mortgage should attend the mortgage interview/s.

(b) Staff should take sufficient time to fully explain the lending policy to borrowers.

## 5. Professional referrals

Professional contacts (*e.g.*, solicitors and insurance brokers) should:

(a) be fully informed about the lending policy and its interpretation.

and

(b) regularly receive up-dated instructions on the lending policy.

## 6. References

Employment reference enquiries should be precisely worded so that replies received are strictly objective and factual.

## 7. Arrears

(a) Every effort should be made to inform both partners to a joint mortgage of any arrears.
(b) Where, after marital breakdown, one spouse (often the wife) is left in the matrimonial home, assessment of capacity to continue with the mortgage should include all possible sources of income, *e.g.*, maintenance payments and social security payments.

## 8. Insurance

Wherever possible, lenders should arrange with insurers for joint insurance policies to be available to borrowers.

## 9. Training

(a) All staff should be made familiar with the relevant requirements of the S.D.A.
(b) A written statement of the requirements of the S.D.A. should be available to staff.
(c) Full training should take place before staff deal independently with mortgage business.
(d) Training literature should be free from terms commonly understood to refer to one sex only.
(e) Examples used in training literature should include situations where a woman's salary or part-time earnings provide the main basis of a mortgage.
(f) All staff should have easy access to senior staff and/or Head Office staff for assistance in unusual circumstances.
(g) All staff should be regularly re-trained.
(h) The effectiveness of staff training should be monitored.

## 10. Monitoring

Regular analysis of a sample of mortgages granted will provide confirmation that a non-discriminatory lending policy is being properly implemented.

Observance of these conditions by the lending body should ensure an effective non-discriminatory lending policy throughout the organisation.

# Index